Computer Assisted Learning

Selected Proceedings from the CAL 81 Symposium

Computer Assisted Learning

Selected Proceedings from the CAL 81 Symposium

held on 8-10 April 1981
at the University of Leeds

Edited by
P R SMITH

PERGAMON PRESS

OXFORD · NEW YORK · TORONTO · SYDNEY · PARIS · FRANKFURT

U.K.	Pergamon Press Ltd., Headington Hill Hall, Oxford OX3 0BW, England
U.S.A.	Pergamon Press Inc., Maxwell House, Fairview Park, Elmsford, New York 10523, U.S.A.
CANADA	Pergamon Press Canada Ltd., Suite 104, 150 Consumers Road, Willowdale, Ontario M2J 1P9, Canada
AUSTRALIA	Pergamon Press (Aust.) Pty. Ltd., P.O. Box 544, Potts Point, N.S.W. 2011, Australia
FRANCE	Pergamon Press SARL, 24 rue des Ecoles, 75240 Paris, Cedex 05, France
FEDERAL REPUBLIC OF GERMANY	Pergamon Press GmbH, Hammerweg 6, D-6242 Kronberg-Taunus, Federal Republic of Germany

First edition 1981

Reprinted 1982

Reprinted 1983

Library of Congress Cataloging in Publication Data
Symposium on Computer Assisted Learning (1981: University of Leeds)
Computer assisted learning.
"Published as volume 6, number 1 of the journal Computers & education"—T.p. verso.
1. Computer-assisted instruction—Congresses.
I. Smith, P. R. (Peter R.) II. Computers and education.
III. Title.
LB1028.5.S95   1981   371.3'9445   81-15413

British Library Cataloguing in Publication Data
CAL 81 Symposium (*University of Leeds*)
Computer assisted learning.
1. Computer-assisted instruction—Congresses
I. Title II. Smith, P. R.
371.3'9445   LB1028.5
ISBN 0-08-028111-7

Published as Volume 6 Number 1, of the journal
Computers & Education and supplied to subscribers
as part of their subscription. Also available to
non-subscribers.

Printed in Great Britain by A. Wheaton & Co. Ltd., Exeter.

CONTENTS

v

PREFACE

The 1981 Symposium on Computer Assisted Learning was held at the University of Leeds from 8th to 10th April and was hosted by the University's Computer Based Learning Unit; particular thanks are due to the Staff of the Unit for their devoted work in preparation for and during the Symposium, which ensured a well-organized and effective conference.

The increasing interest in computer applications in education was made evident to the CAL 81 Organizing Committee at an early stage when in the Spring of 1980, following the first announcement of the Symposium venue and date, a flood of applications for further details was received. This was followed by a good response to the call for papers and by a volume of applications for places at the Symposium, which resulted in the books being closed early in March when the delegate list exceeded 400. Delegates were drawn from some 15 countries of origin outside the United Kingdom, a total of over 70 delegates and 18 of the presented papers coming from abroad.

In addition to the presented papers the Symposium featured workshops, in which participants could explore a topic in depth, supported in many cases by practical examples of the relevant computer application. One session was set aside for 'round table' discussions, each devoted to a topic selected by the participants themselves, and this proved to be popular. Further opportunities for delegate participation were provided in discussion periods at the end of each main session.

A well-supported and well-attended exhibition ran in parallel with these activities, providing further evidence of the depth and variety of computer based learning techniques which are now available for use in education.

The paper sessions were arranged within four broad themes:

Hardware interaction with CAL: graphics developments, microcomputer applications, devices for special education.
Fundamental aspects of CAL: software design, learning and problem solving, intelligent teaching systems, remedial teaching.
Experimental studies with CAL: applications in education (including language learning), commerce and industry, simulations, data-base applications and computer managed instruction.
Current developments and future directions: Prestel, telesoftware, information/software exchange.

In addition to papers from each of these theme areas, the Selected Proceedings include two keynote addresses and three state-of-the-art papers. The keynote addresses are the opening presentation on 'A case for re-assessing the role of computers in learning' by Professor Alty of Liverpool University and the paper entitled 'Using microcomputer networks for multi-process simulations', which was given by Professor Dwyer of the University of Pittsburgh.

The state-of-the-art papers cover the topics of graphics in CAL (by Dr Skyrme of Digital Equipment Corporation), screen design and supporting software (by J. M. Jenkin of Mills and Allen Communications) and videotext and CAL (by J. W. Brahan of the National Research Council of Canada).

The Symposium was organized in conjunction with the Council for Educational Technology and Pergamon Press Ltd.

Queen Mary College   P R SMITH

CAL 81 ORGANIZING COMMITTEE

Symposium Chairman:
Geoffrey Hubbard   Director, Council for Education Technology in the UK

Symposium Secretaries:
Roger Hartley   University of Leeds
Keith Bostrom   University of Leeds

Papers Secretary:
Diana Laurillard   University of Surrey

Publications Editor:
Peter Smith   Queen Mary College, University of London

Exhibitions Director:
Andrew Cole   University of Leeds

Working Group Director:
Kenneth Tait   University of Leeds

Conference Office:
Patricia Greenwood   University of Leeds
Barbara Lewis   University of Leeds

Committee Members:
Barbara Barrett   Pergamon Press Ltd
Philip Boxer   London Graduate School of Business Studies
Sandra Crapper   Mills & Allen Communications Ltd
Brian Drinkall   HMS Nelson, Portsmouth
Rosemary Fraser   College of St Mark & St John, Plymouth
Anne Hawkins   State University of Utrecht
Mary Hope   Council for Education Technology
John Matthews   University of Exeter
Tim O'Shea   The Open University
Gordon Reece   University of Bristol
Charles Sweeten   MUSE
Suzanne Ward   Control Data Corporation

Comput. & Educ. Vol. 6, pp. 1 to 5, 1982
Printed in Great Britain

0360-1315/82/010001-05$03.00/0
Pergamon Press Ltd

THE IMPACT OF MICROTECHNOLOGY
A CASE FOR REASSESSING THE ROLES OF COMPUTERS IN LEARNING

J. L. ALTY

Computer Laboratory, University of Liverpool, Brownlow Hill and Crown Street, P.O. Box 147, Liverpool L69 38X, England

Abstract—Recent advances in microtechnology will have a significant impact on both Computer Aided Learning and Instruction. They will enable cheap systems to be configured for use in learning situations and will provide a sound basis for improved interface design. This paper first reviews the changes that have taken place and concludes that distributed systems based on standard network technology will become widespread and a new generation of users will emerge who are unskilled in computing and remote from professional advice. The system itself will have to provide guidance. Advances in Computer Aided Learning and Instruction and the work on Expert Systems in Artificial Intelligence will provide a basis for the design of guidance systems which the paper groups under the term Computer Aided Guidance. Such systems will have short-term goals and will be economically justifiable. The paper suggests that workers in Computer Aided Learning and Instruction should contribute to this new field of activity.

The introduction of microtechnology has resulted in dramatic changes in the various parameters associated with data Processing Systems. As well as the continuing improvement in value-for-money for processing and memory elements there has been a significant reduction in size, in power requirements, in heat output, in reliability, and in threshold costs[1,2]. The emergence of these new low threshold costs is particularly relevant. It means that for the first time really cheap data processing systems are now available to users who five years ago would not have contemplated using a computer at all. Value-for-money and threshold costs are separate and distinct parameters, and it is the latter one which will have the greatest effect. Between 1965 and 1975 the performance/price ratio improved at about 25% per annum but the actual cost of a system remained relatively stable. In the last 5 years however the actual money paid for a system has decreased. One can now buy a reasonable information processor for about £4000, and more rudimentary systems are available for under £1000. The effect of the new threshold costs on the market size will be highly significant. It has been suggested for example that the number of systems sold of a product depends upon the inverse square of the price[3]. If this is so, the small information processor will become very widespread in use and, by 1990, most individuals will be in contact with terminals for some aspect of their work.

Computer Aided Instruction (CAI) and Learning (CAL) are areas of research which are heavily dependent upon technological change. The initial reaction to recent changes in technology by the CAL community has been to view them as providing new economic incentives for the construction of systems and as opening up new possibilities for better interface design. A £6000 multimicroprocessor will obviously be more attractive to schools and colleges than a £70,000 minicomputer, and the really cheap processing power and memory available will enable advantage to be taken of adaptable user interfaces, colour graphics, touch sensitive screens, light pens, and even audio input/output.

This paper will first briefly review some of the technological changes which have taken place and their likely effect upon Computer Aided Learning and Instruction. It will then examine the wider effects of technological change on the computing environment generally. This examination leads to the conclusion that the very wide exploitation of computers will result in a geographical spread of users with little computing knowledge whose only source of guidance will be the computer system itself. A new opportunity therefore exists for utilising the results of Computer Aided Learning and Artificial Intelligence research to create adaptable guidance systems. The need for such systems can be justified economically and their successfulness can be readily measured. Thus this new proposed area of interest, Computer Aided Guidance, will provide the economic justification of CAI/CAL techniques which has so often eluded workers in the field previously.

That significant changes are taking place in the value of computing parameters is not in dispute. Table 1 lists some of the important parameters and some estimates of the percentage changes per year. In the table the changes are those seen by the users of a system rather than the manufacturer of the components.

Table 1. Computing parameter changes

Parameter	Mainframe or minicomputer	Microcomputer
CPU cost	Down 30% p.a.	Down 30% p.a.
Memory	Down 30% p.a.	Down 30% p.a.
Disks		
Present cost	£20 per Mbyte	£1000 per Mbyte
Trend	Down 40% p.a.	Down 50% p.a.
Cost per drive	£15K to £25K	£1K to £5K
On-line VDUs		
Full Interaction	£3K–£5K per VDU	£3K–£5K per VDU
Light interaction	£2K–£3K per VDU	£0.8K–£2K per VDU
Software costs	Up 20% per annum	Up 30% per annum
Reliability	Very high	Very high
Maintenance	5–8% of capital cost	10% of capital cost

In Table 1 a column has been included to show the changes taking place for minicomputers and mainframes. This has been included because people often overlook the fact that the improvements in technology affect computing at all levels, not just at the smaller end. The improvements in processing and memory costs for the large systems match closely the changes for the smaller systems. The table includes the effect on information costs as measured from two viewpoints:

(a) what does it cost to store information (per Mbyte)?
(b) what does it cost to buy one disk drive?

These two viewpoints are similar to the value-for-money and threshold costs mentioned earlier. In the disk calculations demountable disks have not been considered, so that the figures in the table refer to the costs associated with on-line storage only. Whilst floppy disks (at about £1000 per Mbyte) appear very expensive compared with the large mainframe disks (at about £20 per Mbyte) they do cost far less to install. Provided the user requirement is modest, the overall threshold cost is far less. Recently the development of the Winchester disk has closed the gap. A microsystem can now attach a larger drive (say 20 Mbytes) with a cost per Mbyte of about £100, though additional back-up storage devices are necessary.

From an information standpoint therefore the choice between a microcomputer, minicomputer or a mainframe approach is mainly dictated by the size and complexity of the information base which needs to be supported. The large mainframes certainly have an advantage if complex data bases are to be supported and if the information stored for an organisation is highly interlinked. Data processing professionals have spent the last twenty years trying to overcome the difficulties resulting from fragmented data and any organisation planning to install a discrete set of microcomputers will need to examine this point carefully. Furthermore it costs time and effort to maintain large quantities of data and this activity clearly is cheaper on a centralised system. On the other hand users have justifiably complained about the lack of responsiveness of centralised data processing departments in providing software or output reports for their needs. Perhaps the real answer lies somewhere between the two extremes; that is, centralised data with distributed processing.

The fourth parameter listed in Table 1 is the cost of on-line terminal interaction. Two figures are given in the table, one for full interaction (e.g. engineering design) and the other for light interaction (e.g. editing). The costs for the former are similar for both a central or microcomputer approach. For this type of work a sophisticated dedicated microprocessor system is required costing about £5000. Recent benchmarks have confirmed the view that this sort of cost also obtains for a minicomputer or mainframe approach. For light interaction on the other hand the PET or Apple with cassette input costs under £1000 and even with disks is less than £2000.

The last three parameters in the table are software, reliability and maintenance. Software costs are rising rapidly. Indeed with the advent of really cheap hardware the computer industry is becoming labour intensive. Software costs more on microsystems because of the peculiar tarrif structure. Good software always costs money and this will usually be true on microsystems as well. Mainframes have often been criticised for their poor reliability and in the past this criticism has been fully justified, mean time to failure often being less than 24 h. The new microsystems are very reliable but because the new mainframes and microcomputers are built on similar logic very high reliability figures are now being achieved on mainframes also. There will presumably be little to choose between either approach in the future. Maintenance costs have been relatively stable, but there are signs that the mainframe and minicomputer costs are reducing as the systems become more reliable. Some recent systems (e.g. the IBM 4300 series) have maintenance at the 7% level.

It may be concluded from the above remarks that the day of the mainframe is not over, and that the future environment will be mixed. The key to success will lie in communication, and more and more users will be interacting via terminals connected to microcomputers, minicomputers or a mixture of both. Communications has been problematic in the past with no real standards available. Fortunately this is changing rapidly. The X25 Data communication standards[4] are likely to be adopted internationally and, for local networks we have recently seen the emergence of the Cambridge Ring[5] and Ethernet[6]. The Cambridge Ring is illustrated in Fig. 1.

Information is carried round the ring in a packet or series of packets, one of which is depicted schematically at the base of the figure. Each packet has a source address, a destination address and a bit indicating whether it is full or empty. The packets rotate round the ring continuously. Any source wishing to transmit data places it in the next empty packet as it passes and this is then eventually picked up at the destination address which monitors the packets as they pass. If for any reason the destination address is busy, the packet simply carries on rotating and it is picked up on the next revolution. A variety of devices can be connected to the ring such as terminals, computers, filestores or user stations. A connection can be made to another ring. In the Ethernet philosophy a network is regarded as a hierarchy. A transmitter node sends out a broadcast to all nodes in the hierarchy and it is picked up by the destination node. The net can only be used for one transmission at one time, and a convention exists if two nodes try to send at the same time. The system is symmetrical because a hierarchy looks like a hierarchy from any terminal.

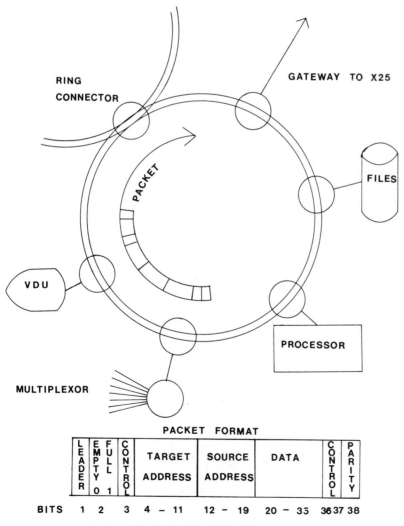

Fig. 1. The Cambridge Ring.

With the emergence of these cheap and (hopefully) mass produced networks, distributed computing will become a reality and it is the new technology which has enabled really cheap connections to the Ring or Ethernet possible. In the CAL or CAI fields of activity networking standards will enable multimicro systems to be produced cheaply. Already systems are becoming available which connect together sets of cheap microterminals, disks and special peripherals. For schools and colleges this will enable terminals to be provided for light interaction at less than £1000 per station with access to large disks and peripherals. At the larger end it will enable intelligent microsystems to cluster round powerful minicomputers or mainframes, with data spread across the network.

Technology has thus provided CAL and CAI with cheap hardware more flexibility and will encourage distributed computing. In computing in general it will cause a rapid expansion in the user base, with users in general accessing computing facilities on some form of network. It is important to consider the environment in which the new users will be working. Firstly they will often be remote from any computing expertise. If such a user gets into difficulties the only source of help will often be the computer terminal itself. Secondly, because of the cheapness of hardware, the traditional support which used to be provided by a manufacturer or software house will be on a much reduced scale. Thirdly because of the expansion of the user base such users will be truly naive in the computing sense and unable to help themselves by utilising some basic computing knowledge. Furthermore these users are performing tasks which will often be time critical in the sense that longer tasks will result in less productivity so that any difficulties with the user interface will be able to be measured in direct economic terms. Consequently organisations choosing software in the next decade will view the efficiency of the user interface as one of the most important of the criteria for software choice. There is already some evidence that the pressure for efficient user interfaces is being felt by manufacturers. The PRIME corporation for example has spent a considerable amount of money recently in improving the job control user interface on PRIMOS, and IBM is sponsoring major research programs into human-computer interface in its various laboratories.

Software designers are therefore going to need new techniques for helping and guiding users in trouble—a group of techniques which this paper calls Computer Aided Guidance. Providing such guidance or instruction is fundamentally no different than the traditional roles of CAI and CAL, and recent advances in Artificial Intelligences relating to Expert Systems[7] could considerably increase the potential of such guidance systems. The key point is that users requiring such guidance are highly motivated by cost considerations.

What are the characteristics of Computer Aided Guidance Systems? They are:

(a) an in-depth knowledge base of the application for which guidance is required;
(b) an ability to guide at different levels of user expertise or familiarity;
(c) an ability to isolate user misunderstandings;
(d) a capability for the provision of extended tutorials or examples when required.

The objective is to solve the users problem at the right level as quickly as possible. As a result one can immediately identify two software components—an expert system to provide (a) above, and a flexible interface language to converse with the user at the appropriate level. One such example is the SYNICS language of Edmonds[8].

Computer programmers are not skilled in the task of providing adequate guidance systems and the knowledge and expertise already gained in CAI/CAL could be invaluable in this respect. How does

Table 2. CAI, CAG and CAL comparison

	CAI	CAG	CAL
Objective	Instruction	Immediate problem solving (including instruction and education where necessary)	Education
Control	Computer control	Moderate user control	User control
Goals	Related hierarchy short term	Short term with some long term implications	Goals difficult to specify
User motivation	Often high	Very high	Difficult to evaluate

Computer Aided Guidance fit into the existing CAI/CAL area? Table 2 attempts to compare and contrast the aims and objectives of all three. The terms in the table are not meant to be precise but rather to provide an overall understanding of similarities and differences.

There is a fundamental difference between CAG and CAL. In the latter case one is trying to build up understanding and proficiency in a fairly wide area of knowledge. Whilst a user controls the pace of learning, the scenario is controlled by the system. In CAG the user specifies to the system a relatively short term goal—the solution of his problem on the interface. It may well instruct, teach by example, or provide a tutorial, but its activity area is reasonably well defined. Furthermore, since the objective is to improve user efficiency such a system need not solve all the problems of all users initially, but rather provide guidance in the most common and time wasting categories. Of course determining what is the real problem of the user will be difficult (rather like problems of understanding in a CAL system) and it is here where the work on expert systems may prove valuable. If the essential relationships in the knowledge base are stored in some form of semantic network, user entry will define an initial node and exploration of the difficulty will involve near nodes. This process could then be repeated recursively on particular near nodes. These are not simple problems but are worthy of study.

Guidance is required at three levels; for the unskilled operative, for the skilled user, and for senior management. The former will seek to tell the user "how" rather than "why". It is more akin to CAI than CAL. There will be little time here for examples or tutorials or extended reasoning (a typical example would be a clerk in an on-line airline reservation system). The middle level addresses the engineer, the manager, or the designer. The guidance required not only encompasses "how", but "why" as well, and "what can be done". The final level, that which will have the largest payoff is the most difficult of all—guidance to senior executives in modelling, simulation and projecting a company's activity. Here we are concerned with "how", "why", "what if" and "why not" categories of questions.

This paper has attempted to define a new area of activity—the provision of guidance to users of on-line systems. The objective is often short term and the user has high motivation to seek guidance. Computing systems in the future will require such guidance systems and the expertise for providing them exists in the CAI/CAL community. Since it is economically justifiable, Computer Aided Guidance will offer a cost effective way forward for CAI/CAL activity and enable workers to make a really valuable contribution to a problem which is recognised by computer professionals as a key area in the next decade. It provides skills and techniques which they lack.

REFERENCES

1. Alty J. L., Report of the Working Party on the Impact of Microtechnology on University Computing. Available from The Secretary, The Computer Board for Universities and Research Councils, Elizabeth House, York Road, London (1978).
2. Alty J. L., The impact of the new technology on computing. In *System Design with Microprocessors* (Edited by D. Zissos). Academic Press, London (1978).
3. Collins A., Micro system selection, micro systems in business seminar. On-Line Conferences Ltd, Manchester (1981).
4. Sloman M. S., X.25 explained. *Comput. Commun.* **6**, 310–326 (1978).
5. Corfield P., The missing link. *Systems* 47–48 (1981).
6. Whiteley J., Softnet. *Systems* 41–42 (1981).
7. Miche D., (Ed.) *Expert Systems in the Microelectronic Age*. Edinburgh University Press, Trowbridge (1979).
8. Edmonds E. A., Adaptable man-machine interfaces for complex dialogues. *Proc. European Computing Congress*, pp. 639–646. London (1978).

Comput. & Educ. Vol. 6, pp. 7 to 12, 1982
Printed in Great Britain

0360-1315/82/010007-06$03.00/0
Pergamon Press Ltd

MULTI-COMPUTER SYSTEMS FOR THE SUPPORT OF INVENTIVE LEARNING

THOMAS A. DWYER and MARGOT CRITCHFIELD

Department of Computer Science, University of Pittsburgh, Pittsburgh, PA 15260, U.S.A.

Abstract—One of the more intriguing challenges faced by educators is to help their students experience "inventive learning". This is learning in which the acquisition of factual knowledge is enhanced by creatively extending and/or synthesizing that knowledge. It is similar to the personal style of learning developed by intellectually curious adults, scholars, artists, and workers in research and development environments.

Two factors that can help cultivate the practive of inventive learning in students are supportive social environments and supportive physical environments. The Solo/NET/works project at the University of Pittsburgh is currently developing a microcomputer-based system that uses multi-process simulations to create such environments.

Students use personal-level microcomputers to design local processes that they then run within a larger global-process framework. It is hypothesized that learning to deal creatively with the unforseen interactions that characterize such multiprocess simulations will foster inventive learning as a natural extension of solo-mode program design. Our experience in developing a low-cost version of the Solo/NET/works system will be described, and examples of the variety of multi-process simulations that seem possible for the system will be given.

INTRODUCTION

There are many difficulties connected with the question of how to use computers in education wisely. One of the least appreciated of these is the problem of mismatches between computer technology and educational models. This can occur when the uses of interactive computing are determined by restricted pedagogies associated with mass education, particularly those derived from lecture-format teaching. Trying to use a computer to imitate even the best of lecturers is bound to lead to disappointment; it is as inappropriate as trying to use jet aircraft as replacements for the vehicles in a mass transportation system.

It would be an equally bad mistake to reject *all* the pedagogies developed over the past centuries when applying computers to education. One of the most intriguing of these is the activity required as the culmination of many programs of higher education where students are expected to produce and defend an original thesis or dissertation. The key pedagogical idea behind this requirement is to persuade students not only to acquire knowledge developed by others, but to consider it normal to adapt, reshape, enhance, and very possibly extend that knowledge. Let us call this activity *inventive learning*.

The purpose of this paper is to describe some preliminary work in developing a multi-microcomputer environment designed to support the practice of inventive learning on a much broader scale than has been possible in the past. The environment is also intended to support learning in areas that go beyond those accessible to students through conventional resources (books, papers, lectures, tutorials, etc.). The work goes under the name of the Solo/NET/works Project.

THE SOLO/NET/WORKS PROJECT—BACKGROUND

Solo/NET/works is the third of a series of projects that have been exploring the potential of interactive computing at the secondary school and college levels. Project Solo, which ran from 1969 to 1972 was concerned specifically with the use of interactive computing on a regular basis in a large high school. The assumption was that this kind of computing would require a variety of different kinds of support: courses for teachers, new curriculum materials, expert advice on technical matters, and the availability of a broad array of information about computers and learning. It was hypothesized that educators should, in addition, have a set of principles to guide them in making decisions about computing. Project Solo set out to discover and test such principles, and to make a start on providing the courses, materials, and relevant information needed to form a support system. The technology used at this time was based on timeshared use of a large central computer, with several terminals placed at each school.

The Soloworkers Laboratory Project which followed, running until 1977, focused on the use of interactive computers coupled to new kinds of input/output devices. The laboratory environment supported inventive learning in areas suggested by the unifying interdisciplinary ideas of algorithmic design, dynamics, synthesis, and modelling. The devices used included computer-controlled robots, lunar landers, a computer-controlled pipe organ, a flight simulator, plotters, and color graphics. At this point microcomputers began to be available and they were used for some of the labs. The appearance and phenomenal growth of personal computing magazines provided a medium for sharing some of the Soloworks* ideas. In addition, the Solo and Soloworks experience influenced several books†.

The Solo/NET/works Project, scheduled to run from 1980 to 1982 is a continuation of the Soloworks laboratory idea, but with an important difference: the collection of specific physical devices used to create the Soloworkers environment has been replaced by a low-cost microcomputer network. This network and its associated software will be designed primarily for use as an extensible environment for running role-playing simulations. The goal of the design is to enable users (instructors and their students) to write their own multi-process simulations. The reason for setting this goal is that we want the system to support inventive pedagogies as well as inventive learning. Before giving more details on this system, some further comments on inventive learning are thus in order.

INVENTIVE LEARNING AND MICROCOMPUTERS

Inventive learning occurs naturally in the intellectually curious adult, the scholar, the artist, and workers in research and development environments. It occurs much less often in schools for reasons that are complex and subject to much (sometimes emotionally laden) discussion. It suffices to say that one of the greatest challenges of teaching is to help students in school to experience inventive learning.

We have described inventive learning as that style of learning in which the acquisition of factual knowledge is enhanced by creatively extending that knowledge. Inventive learning can mobilize the cooperative, social instincts of students, and yet it can be highly individual. It can also incorporate elements of fantasy and humor. Our choice of a system to support role-playing simulations is based on our experience of the intellectual value of such social and imaginative exercises for both students *and* teachers. Such inventive learning is not involved in run-of-the-mill CAI lessons written by others. Teacher/student inventive learning requires a style of computer use which stands in sharp contrast to the notion of a pre-written sequence of tutorial programs, especially when the implied goal is to increase cost-effectiveness by eliminating the human tutor.

The advent of small, low-cost but powerful microcomputers has greatly opened up the possibility of extending the opportunity for true inventive learning in both homes and schools, for parents, teachers, and students alike. All ages are involved, and many different kinds of interests are accomodated by these machines: from the electronics hobbyist who can build computer circuits, to the business person who needs to manage information, to the science student who wants to explore complex models, to the teacher trying to create fresh curriculum. The microcomputer phenomenon makes it clear that the real problem of education is not only to import computers into the school setting, also but to generate the spirit of creativity they can trigger when used thoughtfully.

One way to set about doing this is to think of inventive learning as occurring near one end of a continuum of learning styles. Throughout the "Solo" projects we learned to look for the contrast between "dual mode" learning with computers and "solo mode". The terms "dual" and "solo" were borrowed from the experience of aircraft flight instruction where the course of study must start with two people in the aircraft—the instructor and the student—but must also include times (highly specified in this case) when the student flies alone. The requirement of taking full charge of the aircraft at some point in the course is educationally effective because it is analogous to the intellectual requirement of setting one's problem or topic for study, and carrying through with it creatively.

The flight training analogy also works well in another way: it emphasizes the *preparation* needed for solo flight or solo learning. For most people, inventive solo learning requires both a supportive social environment, and a supportive physical environment. This means the right kind of guidance, instruction, encouragement, criticism, written materials, time, space, and equipment. The nearer a teacher and school can come to meeting these requirements, the more likely it is that inventive learning will take place. We see the microcomputer and multi-process simulations as powerful components in such a supportive environment.

---

* Some of these in the United States are: *Byte, Popular Computing, Creative Computing, Dr Dobb's Journal, Personal Computing, Microcomputing*, and *Interface Age*.
† See for example, *BASIC and the Personal Computer*, Addison–Wesley, Reading, MA (1978); and *You Just Bought a Personal WHAT?*, Byte Books, Peterborough, NH (1980).

SOLO/NET/WORKS: SOLVING THE REPLICATION PROBLEM

The environments which were developed for the Soloworks laboratories were successful in promoting inventive learning. However there were problems associated with transferring these ideas and practices to less sheltered settings.

First, in some of the labs the personal tastes of the investigators were reflected. Although many students and teachers would be interested in a lunar lander simulation, a flight navigation simulation, or a musical composition system—not all would be. Second, the fact that these were mostly one-of-a-kind products meant that they were a long way from being mass produceable and easily maintained. Third, laboratories that involved special hardware would be difficult to modify once set up, leading to obsolescence. We began to think that the ideas present in the labs should be expressable in a more general way.

One laboratory in particular, the simulation laboratory, pointed to a solution to these problems. A student-originated project of this lab was a multi-player version of the familiar Star Trek adventure. In this "N-Trek" simulation game, as it was called, a number of players (N) took on roles as crew members of the space ship Enterprise: captain, navigator, weapons officer, etc. The players operated in a common "galaxy": a world of space, time, enemy ships, and starbases. Information on this environment was displayed on a color graphics screen, and dramatized with synthetic vocal warnings and flashing lights. To "win" the game the players had to coordinate their actions while fulfilling different functions. The fascination of this situation lead to a startlingly rapid assimilation of all the rules and skills of the game by new players. The learning of those who worked at designing (and redesigning) the game was even more impressive.

From this experience we decided that it would be possible to create a more general system to support other simulated "worlds" of the imagination. The content of these worlds could involve subject matter of many kinds. Further, the use of nonspecific technology (i.e., general purpose computers) implied that the system could be replicated in many schools.

The generalization we settled on was based on the idea of N *local processes* operating as part of a larger *global process*. The principal requirement on the system was that local processes to be able to influence the outcome of the global process. Learning activities on many levels of complexity could be built on such a supportive environment. Beginning students would be learning the content of the multi-process simulation, while experienced students would experiment with altering this simulation. This implied that it should be possible for both teachers and students to write the software for the simulation. This goal was achieved by developing a *template* approach to the software (described in the next section), and using extended BASIC as a language already familiar to many educators.

CURRENT IMPLEMENTATION OF THE SOLO/NET/WORKS SYSTEM

The current version of the system is based on the arrangement shown in Fig. 1. This is a general scheme which is independent of particular kinds of hardware, on the one hand, and particular simulations on the other. In this scheme the local processes are connected via a generalized communication channel (also called a communication bus). The scheme allows for a number of activities called *local processes*, and for a single *distinguished processes* that orchestrates all the activities of the system.

What the local processes and distinguished processes represent is up to the users' imaginations. For

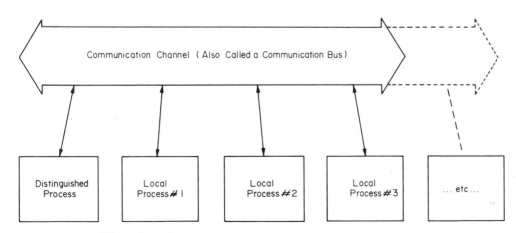

Fig. 1. General arrangement for a multi-process learning environment.

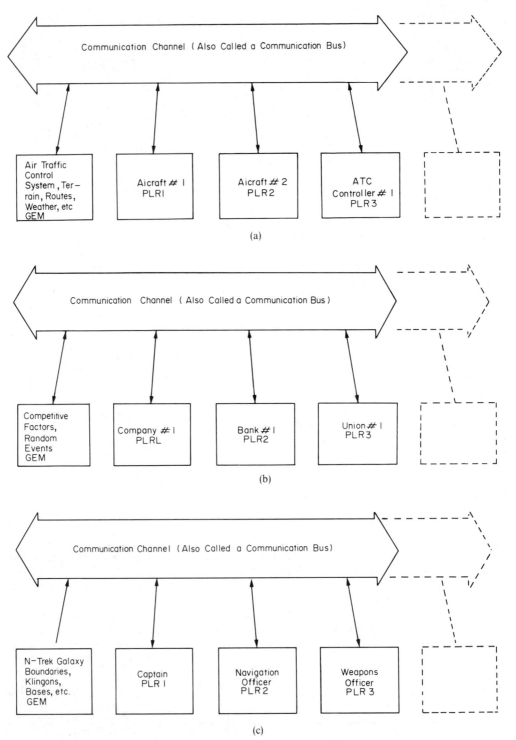

Fig. 2. (a) Air traffic control simulation. (b) Economics simulation. (c) N-Trek game.

example, the simulation might represent an air traffic control system. The student interacting with one local process would act as the pilot of a particular type of aircraft. The ground-based controllers assigned to guide these aircraft would be represented by still other local processes. The distinguished process would contain the rules and algorithms defining the air traffic control system within which pilots and controllers operate, along with environmental data (e.g., weather, terrain, and landing fields). The simulation might equally well represent a model of part of the economy, with the local processes representing companies, banks, unions, etc., and the distinguished process representing the structure of the market, along with randomly occurring events.

TRANSLATING THIS CONCEPT INTO LOW-COST HARDWARE

The general arrangement of our system is based on the concept of a "single bus" or "passive bus" type of network architecture. Each process is, in networking terminology, a "node" on the network. *Conceptually*, all processes or nodes communicate over the single bus on an equal basis. In practice, we are emulating the passive bus with a program segment (called COMPUS) that resides in the same computer that handles the distinguished node process (called GEM for Global Environment Master). Communication from local nodes is handled by program segments called LOCOM. These reside in the local nodes along with the local simulation program segments (called PLR1, PLR2, etc. meaning Process for Local Role No. 1, No. 2, etc.).

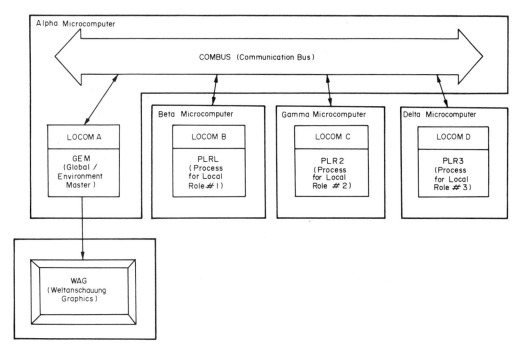

Fig. 3. General relation of software and current hardware.

The hardware chosen to implement this concept is relatively simple. A group of S-100 type micro-computers have been connected via three-wire cables connected to standard RS-232 interfaces. The microcomputers are alike in design, except for one which has the extra circuitry to handle the COMBUS communication functions. Our ultimate goal is that most of the nodes on the network will be implemented on very low cost personal microcomputers such as the Radio Shack, the Apple, the PET, or the Atari. The only requirement will be that they have RS-232 type circuitry.

The relation between the hardware we are currently using and the software segments described above is shown in Fig. 3. A program to provide a "world view" of the global environment has been added in this diagram. This program is called the WAG (WeltAnschauung Graphics). It drives a graphical display—either color or monochrome. As noted above, the program segments labeled LOCOM A, LOCOM B, etc. are routines which handle local communications for node A, B, and so on. In our current hardware configuration GEM, LOCOM A, COMBUS, and WAG happen to run on the Alpha microcomputer (the one with extra circuitry in the form of additional RS-232 ports).

Our plan is to provide the software for the system to users who want to write their own simulations in the form of a *template*. This is a fully functioning application, but the application segments (the parts labelled GEM, PLR1, PLR2, etc.) are replaceable. The idea is that when the user wants to develop a new simulation, he or she need only change these segments. The LOCOM, WAG, and COMBUS segments are meant to remain as the fixed parts of the template.

The present form of the template is a set of several rather large BASIC programs—one for each node. These contain carefully differentiated blocks of code for handling communication in the network (LOCOM m, COMBUS) and a window on the total environment (WAG), while other blocks of code contain a replaceable example simulation (GEM and PLRn blocks). A second version of the template programmed in the language "C" is under development.

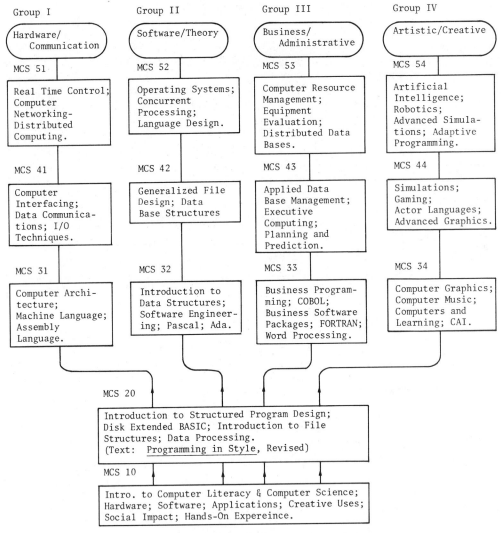

Fig. 4. An experimental microcomputer curriculum.

FUTURE PLANS FOR SOLO/NET/WORKS: POSSIBLE CURRICULAR INFLUENCE

In the immediate future we intend expanding the system by adding nodes to the network. We will also explore the possibility of using some of the low-cost local area networks that are starting to appear. The template program will be further refined and more complex example simulations will be provided.

As a parallel activity, we are looking at the implications of the availability of multi-process simulation networks for the undergraduate curriculum. A tentative scheme for such a curriculum is shown in Fig. 4. It is designed for the subject area we know best—computer science. The impact that such networks could have on other subject areas is a topic worthy of a good deal of study in the future.

Comput. & Educ. Vol. 6, pp. 13 to 24, 1982
Printed in Great Britain

0360-1315/82/010013-12$03.00/0
Pergamon Press Ltd

THE EVOLUTION OF GRAPHICS IN CAL

DAVID J. SKYRME

Digital Equipment Co. Ltd, Reading RG1 7QN, England

Abstract—From the early days of CAL, graphics has been regarded as a more natural form of student interaction with the computer than traditional methods. However, the relatively high costs of graphics terminals deterred their widespread exploitation in a CAL environment. Recent technology advances, in raster scan graphics and in personal microcomputers, has resulted in increased use of graphics in CAL applications.

This paper traces the evolution of graphics in a CAL environment. Different classes of graphics terminals are reviewed against the desirable requirements of a student terminal. The conclusion is that there will be a technology convergence between intelligent graphics terminals and personal microcomputers with graphics. Another conclusion is that in the future the cost of these students' workstations is not likely to be the major factor limiting their widespread acceptance. Other technical, social and political obstacles exist, but the author is optimistic that most of these will disappear during the next few years. The growth of graphics in CAL will then happen extremely rapidly.

THE USER'S VIEW OF CAL

The scope of Computer Assisted Learning

Computer assisted learning covers a broad spectrum of activities related to the computer in the learning process. "Drill and practice" CAI which for many years equated with the popular notion of CAL is but a small part of this spectrum; in fact, less than 10% according to a recent CONDUIT survey of the use of CAL in undergraduate teaching throughout the U.S.A.[1]. The predominant usage of the computer as a learning resource (rather than as the subject of learning) is for data retrieval, analysis and problem solving. Other uses include simulation, modelling and gaming.

This diversity of CAL applications could imply an equally diverse set of student-computer relationships. Even within a specific mode of operation, the interaction between learner and systems could vary enormously. For example, tutorial material may be presented in a fashion similar to a structured programmed learning text or it could be presented in a very flexible format highly oriented to student control. However, it is possible to isolate similarities and these will not be unlike those of many other interactive computer applications.

The student interface

The interface between the student and computer will generally be through an interactive terminal i.e. one in which the computer can present information to the student, and through which the student can make a response. Whereas the exact nature of the dialogue may vary enormously, the system-user transactions will follow a pattern similar to that of Fig. 1. Even this fairly basic diagram encompasses a very broad range of learning strategies. Fundamentally, CAL does not differ significantly from many other non-machine interactions and computer environments.

The key concepts in Fig. 1 are the presentation of information to the student and the systems ability to present *appropriate* additional or new information in response to the student's input. From the users point of view, there are several desirable attributes of such a system.

Presentation of Information—must be easy to see, visualize and comprehend.

Input to System—must be simple, unambiguous. It should be possible to correct mistakes as they are made.

System Response—should give immediate, positive feedback of acceptance of input with an "acceptable" response time for completion of the transaction and the generation of the next information display.

To these basic requirements should be added psychological, safety and ergonomic requirements. These include providing a noise-free and restful operating environment as well as providing motivation and variety.

The above requirements epitomize an individualized instructional "delivery system". Outside the world of CAL there are many different tools available for individual learning, ranging from self-study workbooks to audio-visual cassette courses. In non-individualized teaching environments, similar varity exists, with "chalk and talk" taking a place along side educational television programmes. In

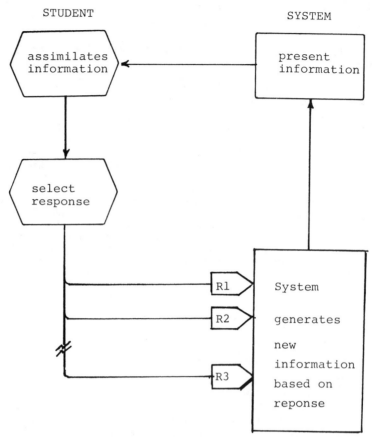

Fig. 1. A generalised schematic of student/system transaction profile.

every case, the material presented to the student encompasses many forms including text, numeric data, diagrams, graphics, charts and other images. Colour too, is playing an increasingly important role. Based on experience of these non-computer systems, when one translates the student's needs into a computer-based environment, the old adage of "one picture is worth a thousand words" appears appropriate. In other words, the most natural way for the student to interact with the computer is through a graphics display unit.

TERMINALS AND GRAPHICS DISPLAYS

In the late 1960s is used to be said that computer graphics was a solution looking for a problem. The reason was that the very expense of graphics precluded its general application in all but the very demanding problem areas of aerospace, electronics or military applications. A directed beam CRT (cathode ray tube) such as the IBM 2250 cost over £50,000 as a mainframe computer peripheral. Workstations which married the display with a minicomputer and local disc storage cost closer to £80,000. In comparison, an ASR-33 Teletype® cost only £750 at that time. It is, therefore, not surprising that most CAL applications dispensed with whatever benefits graphics could provide. Throughout the last 10 years probably more CAL work has been performed with low speed printing terminals than with any other device. Whole libraries of CAL software have been designed for alpha numeric input/output [2].

Psuedo graphics

Various devices are used to provide rudimentary graphic output on such terminals. The most popular methods employ "Is" and "—" to create boxes and graphic axes, and "X" to plot points on a graph. The precision of such graphs is limited to the basic character spacing, typically $\frac{1}{10}$". Examples of such usage are to be widely found in the Huntington simulation programs developed by the State University of New York at Stonybrook (Fig. 2).

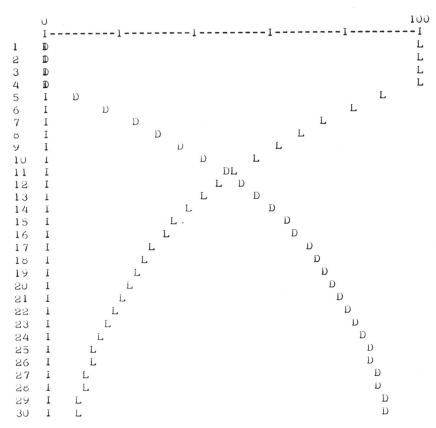

Fig. 2. "Graphical" output generated by a printing terminal.

A further drawback of the older printing terminals is that they are noisy, slow and mechanical. Slowness can be a severe detriment to the efficiency of CAL. James Johnson, the Director of CONDUIT, quotes

"the perfect of the terminal speed and response time of its support computer by comparing the times to complete a dialogue in two situations"[3]

Dialogue output: 100 frames of 10 words each, initiated by a student input to the computer
Environment No. 1:   10 char/s terminal on a system with a 5 s response
                        Time to print-out: 1100 s
Environment No. 2:   30 char/s terminal on a system with a 1 s response
                        Time to print-out: 300 s.

The difference between the two terminals on two different systems is over 13 min. This time is virtually lost since the average student can read at 6–8 words/s. Yet even in 1981 many students are using CAL daily in Environment No. 1.

Rather more appropriate for CAL output are visual display units (VDUs). Not only can they operate faster (up to 9600 baud or 960 characters/s in many instances) but their pseudo graphics is considerably better than the teleprinter's. Using reverse video facilities, spaces become solid squares, ideal for histograms. Many modern terminals also have optional "graphic" characters which provide a useful range of symbols. The only significant disadvantage of a VDU compared with a teleprinter is its inability to provide the student with hard-copy output. Today, many VDUs are comparable in price or even cheaper than hard-copy terminals.

The plasma panel display

It must not be presumed that computer graphics were not being used for CAL in 1970; by that time, developments in plasma panel displays which had started at the University of Illinois in 1964 had come to fruition. These displays constituted the student interface on the PLATO CAI system. A plasma panel consists of two coated glass plates separated by a space containing neon gas. A series of electrodes spaced at 25/cm are embedded in each plate. On one plate the electrodes are horizontal and on the other vertical, thus forming a matrix of intersections. If a voltage pulse is applied to both horizontal and vertical electrode an orange glow (a gas discharge) takes place at the point of intersection. The glow remains until a different voltage pulse cancels the discharge.

These terminals went into commercial production in 1971, and at a cost of about £6000 they provided fairly sophisticated facilities for the CAL user. The plasma panel display has a moderately high resolution (512 × 512), and does not require the continual drawing cycles required in refresh graphics displays. It therefore provides a steady good quality image. In the PLATO system, optional enhancements to the display terminal include a back-screen microfiche projector (for displaying non-computer generated images), a touch panel (to enable users to point at images or menu items) and connectors for attaching external devices such as random-access slide projectors. In conjunction with the PLATO system, the plasma display system has been used in a wide range of applications, most of them in the CAI drill and practice and tutorial modes. Many good examples are in evidence at the University of Delaware Plato Project, where over 50 terminals were reported in regular use by 28 faculties in their 1978 Report[4]. One of the most interesting applications is in the music department, where Hofstetter and Lynch developed a package for ear-training. In this application the PLATO terminal is used in conjunction with an audio digital synthesiser. The three-part process for student-terminal interaction follows closely the outline of Fig. 1. In the first phase PLATO displays a musical form on the screen; in the second phase a musical example is played. In the third phase, questions are asked about the student's perception. The response is initiated through the touch sensitive panel.

Despite some significant advantages, including the ability to handle dynamic images, manufacture of plasma panels is a difficult process and there have been few significant improvements or price reductions over the last 10 years.

The storage tube display

An important turning point in graphics technology came around 1970 with the development of terminals (ARDS, Computek) based on the Tektronix storage tube[5]. Similar to the plasma display, the storage tube does not require continual image refresh. A process of secondary electron emission takes place at a grid behind the screen and causes the image to be retained for a considerable time. To erase the image the screen must be "flooded" with electrons by changing the potential on the grid—this causes the familiar "green flash". No selective, erase of portions of the image is possible. When introduced the cost of a typical storage tube terminal, including an 8 × 6″ display screen, a keyboard, thumbwheels and a serial line interface to a multi-access computer was £4000. By 1972 the

	DIRECTED BEAM CRT	PLASMA	STORAGE
Brightness	30 ft-L	60 ft-L	10 ft-L
Contrast Ratio	10:1	20:1	5:1
Erase Speed	20 m.sec	20μ sec	700 m.sec
Vector drawing	150,000/sec	50,000/sec	400/sec
Dot Spacing	.2mm	.6mm	.2mm
Selective Erase	Yes	Yes	Only with 'Write through'
Other features or limitations		Flat panel allows back projection	Low tube life (≏ 2000 hrs)

Fig. 3. Comparison of major features of three graphics technologies.

Tektronix 4010 had reduced this price to £2500. One advantage of the storage tube is its ability to display a complex image without the penalty of flicker ever occurring, as could happen with certain refresh displays (Fig. 3). The storage tube terminal gave the CAL community a graphics terminal which could readily be supported by any terminal based computer system. This should be contrasted with the plasma display, which was exclusively associated with PLATO, a dedicated mainframe based system. In conjunction with simple FORTRAN, a reasonably extensive repertoire of CAL material has been prepared for use with storage tube displays.

A typical example of this type is illustrated by the work of Dr Smith at the Computer Assisted Teaching Unit at Queen Mary College[6]. Here, a PDP-11/40 supported six Teletypes and six storage tube terminals for the teaching of engineering design processes to undergraduates. Many engineering problems are multivariate with multiple inputs and outputs. The student can explore the effects of changing input parameters on different outputs. A typical session involves: (1) entering initial values; (2) selecting an input parameter and its incremental storage; (3) computing each output parameter for each increment; (4) displaying the output parameter over a range of increments. When such a learning session used slow teleprinters, significant time was consumed to output tabular data which needed careful inspection. With the graphics terminal the student could easily discern the effects of changing parameters, and select representative plots for hard-copy output. During the 1970s, Tektronix has produced a wide variety of different-sized terminals incorporating the storage tube principle. Several offer the feature of "write through" mode in which some portion of the image is refreshed conventionally prior to storing. This overcomes the former disadvantage of non-selective erase. Such a facility is particularly useful for entering student data when immediate corrections can be made and verified.

However, in recent years, the price of the lowest cost terminal has stabilized at between £2000–£2500 and no significant new breakthroughs in technology have occurred.

Directed beam displays

It is appropriate here to categorise the different displays to be discussed in this paper. Figure 4 shows one approach to categorisation. Variants of the cathode ray tube serve as a basic building block in most types of graphic display. In refresh displays the description of the screen image is stored in a local memory. Display generators, including vector (line) and character generators, convert this description to voltages which deflect the CRT electron beam (Fig. 5). To retain a steady image, this process must be repeated within the decay time of the CRT phosphor and the image refresh process typically takes place 30–60 times per s.

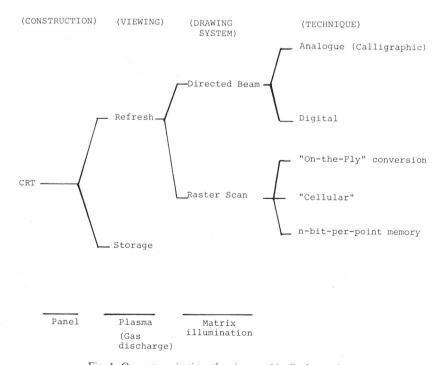

Fig. 4. One categorisation of major graphic display variant.

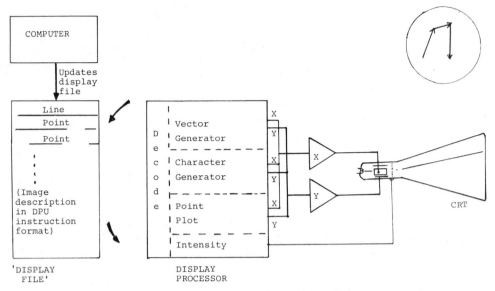

Fig. 5. Block diagram of a directed beam display.

Dynamically changing images can be constructed by changing the image description between refresh cycles. In the learning environment, this can be particularly useful for introducing difficult concepts such as wave motion theory. Compared to the storage tube, the relative expense of refresh directed beam displays in the 1970s restricted the range of CAL applications. However, some useful CAL applications using more affordable displays such as Digital £8000 VT11 have been described[7]. Most of these are in engineering disciplines where similar graphic displays are conventionally used for computer aided design.

Such applications are then transferred to the teaching environment. The dynamic features have been found particularly beneficial for teaching fluid dynamics, beam analysis and electrical filters. The light pen often used with such displays has proved a useful tool for identifying points of interest, selecting trial components and also for "sketching in" mechanical shapes.

RASTER SCAN GRAPHICS

For many years graphics users were looking for a terminal which combined the dynamic features of a refresh display with the price advantage of the storage tube. Since the late 1960s raster scan displays were seen as the potential way of fulfilling this promise. Their fundamental component, a robust cathode ray tube with a left-to-right, top-to-bottom beam scanning system, was already well proven in low cost domestic television sets. To handle computer generated images, there remained the complex problem of modulating the beam at precisely the right time during the scanning process to create lines and other graphic images. The natural way to achieve this is to represent every point of the screen with a binary digit (0 or 1) in a local memory to represent light or dark. The beam is then modulated by synchronising its scan to the read-out of the memory contents. Unfortunately, this approach requires a large amount of memory with a high read-out rate. For example, 262,144 bits (32 kilo bytes) are needed to store a 512 × 512 size image. Many attempts were made in the early 1970s to avoid this problem by using innovative techniques such as "run length encoding" or "on-the-fly scan conversion". None of these really caught on in commercial products. One of the earlier raster scan displays, the Data Disc, actually used a rotating magnetic disc to store the picture image. But the main upsurge in development of raster graphics displays awaited technology price/performance improvements in three areas.

First, the enormous investment in cathode ray tube technology has resulted in lower costs and improved products, particularly in the area of colour CRTs. Second, the steady evolution of microchip technology has resulted in price/performance improvements in microprocessing logic of a constant 40% per year. Third, there has been an even more dramatic decline in semiconductor memory prices by some 80% per year.

The fact that these improvements in semiconductor technology follow a predictable and well defined curve[8] allows realistic estimates to be made of the future prices and performance of graphics terminals and computer systems. These three converging developments have led to a fast

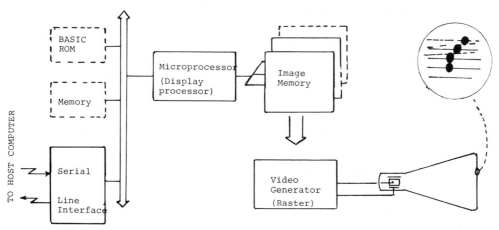

Fig. 6. Architecture of a raster scan graphics display.

growth in the number of available raster scan graphics displays during the last few years. Manufacturers such as Rantek, Tektronix, Hewlett–Packard and Digital have brought to market general imaging displays with colour and many additional features. Prices are declining steadily and several raster graphics terminals are now comparable in price to storage tube terminals.

The general architecture of such a display is shown in Fig. 6. Graphics commands from the computer are interpreted by a microprocessor based display processor. The appropriate bits in the single memory planes are set according to which entity—a line, circle, box etc.—is to be drawn. With multiple memory planes it is possible to define colours and other attributes. Erasure of an entity is possible simply by reversing the process, although this can give rise to leaving holes at points of intersection. Care, therefore, needs to be taken when attempting dynamic displays. The quality of lines displayed also exhibits a "staircase" effect. These are the only real disadvantages. On the other hand, raster displays offer many advantages for the CAL user. Colour becomes a relatively low cost addition limited more by memory costs than CRT tube costs. Other advantages accrue from the fact that standard video signals are generated. This permits inexpensive slave displays to be connected to more expensive large screen displays ($\simeq 2$ m diagonal) such as the Advent 1000 A. Both of these facilities are useful for classroom use. Video recording and playback is another possibility as is the mixing of external video signals with computer generated video output.

Standards

Some words of caution should be added at this stage, however, based on the fact that there is more than one video standard. The line scanning standard may be either 625-line (European) or 525-line (the U.S. based RS-170 standard) with 50 or 60 Hz refresh. However, many monitors and other equipment can be easily switched between standards. More crucial are differences in colour encoding standards. High quality raster displays adopt the RGB (red-green-blue) format and use a high bandwidth ($\geqslant 4$ MHz) monitor where each colour is transmitted on a separate cable. Colour televisions on the other hand use several different standards—NTSC in the USA, SECAM in France and PAL in the rest of Europe. The resultant image is lower in quality, limited to about 300 resolvable points across the screen or approximately 40 characters. However, the universality of TV and TV-related equipment (such as video recorders) has meant that the raster displays which come with personal microcomputers mostly conform to the local television encoding standard.

THE MICROPROCESSOR REVOLUTION

The steady decline in logic and memory costs has already been referred to. At the same time that this was influencing graphic display design, it was having an even greater impact in the field of small computers. The period 1975–1977 was one of rapid development culminating with the breakthrough of the £1000 barrier for a self-contained microcomputer system. This breakthrough came with the Commodore PET 2001 followed shortly after by the Tandy TRS-80.

Because of their low cost, less than that of many terminals, personal microcomputers have rapidly established themselves in the education community. A typica personal computer incorporates a microprocessor, a built in BASIC ROM, cassette storage, keyboard and a visual display unit which may offer some rudimentary graphics as standard. Some microcomputers provide a video output port for connecting a television monitor as the cheapest way of providing colour graphics. Now low cost graphics had arrived with a vengeance!

Graphics options on these micros take several forms, but all are of raster scan type. A typical low resolution graphics system subdivides the basic character cell into 6 elements which can be individually selected. This provides a resolution of 80 × 72. Medium resolution graphics would typically increase this to 150–200 horizontal points. "High resolution" graphics in the personal computer domain is exemplified by the latest "Apple" which, with the necessary plug-in boards, provides a resolution of 280 × 192 for 16 colours and an even finer 560 × 192 for monochrome.

The CAL applications of personal micros cover many disciplines. Many applications, particularly those in BASIC, have been converted from other computers. Even some of the graphics applications discussed earlier in this paper have been put on these micros. Statistics, biology, geography, economics—all have taken advantage of the limited graphics capability of even the cheapest micro.

Another factor appealing to the CAL user is the almost universal availability on micros of PILOT—a simple authoring language.

All of these factors have given CAL a tremendous boost in establishments from schools to university departments. They have also given a boost to microcomputer manufacturers who are reportedly selling tens of thousands of their systems to educational establishments every year. Graphics, in some form at least, is becoming universally available.

GRAPHICS—MATCHING THE NEED TO THE TERMINAL

It has been implicitly assumed in this paper, that a graphics terminal meets the need of the ideal student interface. Fortunately there is significant evidence that graphics presentation of information has definite advantages over non-graphic output[9].

Through a process called pre-attentive perception, the human brain can quickly assimilate an image more easily than it can decipher text. Particular visual effects improve the student's comprehension of a concept. Amongst these effects are *highlighting*—using blinking, colour, shading or intensity variations; *dynamics*—showing motion, or a rapid sequence of frames. The extent to which these different features are used in the CAL environment can have a marked influence on the effectiveness of the teaching material.

It is appropriate now to return to our earlier list of desirable characteristics for a CAL interface[10] and translate them into terminal features. This has been done in Fig. 7. The presentation features fall naturally out of the considerations discussed above. For the interaction process Foley and Wallace[11] have identified virtual devices known as "picks", "locators", "buttons" and "valuators". A "pick" points at an object; a "locator" creates a new object at a given position; a "button" is used to select a menu item and a "valuator" is for input of non-positional values. Hence a keyboard can very effectively provide the "valuator" function, and can with appropriate ↑ ↓ ← → function keys controlling a VDU cursor perform "picking" and "locating" functions. The latter, however, is probably more easily provided by a small joystick controlling cross-hairs, and the natural way to "pick" is to point a light-pen or a finger at the screen. Ergonomic factors however, would suggest that a workstation should not be cluttered with four input devices, one of which is ideal for each function. It is preferable to compromise with fewer easily controllable devices.

The other columns of Fig. 7 measure the characteristics of typical CAL terminals against the desired features. Specific models within a category may vary in detail but the table does give an indication of how well each type of terminal meets the student needs. The effectiveness of interaction, for example, will depend largely on which specific devices, e.g. joystick, light pen, touch panel, are available with a specific terminal. It will be noted that the raster scan display fulfils many of the attributes very well. The plasma panel provides a better quality image and in the PLATO environment provides additional features such as touch sensitive panels and general image presentation (through rear screen projection). If cost trends, as shown in Fig. 8, are also considered the raster screen seems to be the leading graphics technology for the next few years. If the impact of the video disc is factored in, its position seems unassailable.

Video-disc: the next revolution?

Currently creating a lot of excitement for CAL pioneers is a new device—the video disc[12].

A video disc, approximately the size of an LP record, stores audio and video information in microscopic pits on its surface. The most impressive characteristic of the video disc is its graphic information capacity. Information is extracted by video disc players which rotate the disc at 1800 rpm. A laser technique is used. Each disc stores 12,500 Mbytes of information—in other words 54,000 distinct colour images. When replayed at 30 frames/s this represents 30 min of motion material.

Video disc players for the home, which simply play picture frames in sequence have dropped in price to $700. In the learning environment an intelligent microprocessor based player is needed which has random access-capability, freeze frame and slow motion facilities. These currently cost around

| REQUIREMENT | TERMINALS | | GRAPHICS DISPLAYS | | | | |
| | | | Non-Refresh | | Refresh | | |
	Teleprinter	VDU	Storage	Plasma	Direct Beam	Raster	Personal Computer
1. PRESENTATION							
A. Types							
Alphanumeric	Yes	Yes	Yes	Yes	Yes	Yes	Yes
Graph	Poor	Poor	Yes	Yes	Yes	Yes	Fair
Histogram/ Bar Chart							
Diagrams			Yes	Yes	Yes	Yes	Fair
Images			Yes	Yes		Yes	Fair
B. Highlighting							
Intensity Levels		1–4			1–16 v.expensive	1–4	1–16
Colour		–			Yes	Yes	Yes
Blinking		Yes		Yes		Yes	Yes
Shading	Poor	Poor	Fair	Fair		Yes	Varies
C. Dynamics		Limited	No	Yes	Yes	Yes	Varies
D. Ergonomics							
Image Quality	Variable	Good	Good	Good	Good	Ave	Ave
Brightness/ Contrast	Good	Good	Poor	Good	Good	Good	Good
Limitations	Noise						Screen size TV resolution
Speed of Presentation	Slow	Fast	Medium	Medium	Fast	Med–Fast	Medium
2. INTERACTION							
Pick		{Cursor & keyboard}	{Cross-hairs & Joystick}	Touch (K/B)	Light Pen	{Cursor & Keyboard	{Cursor & Keyboard}
Locate				Touch	Joystick Light Pen	Joystick Keyboard}	
Buttons							
Valuators	Yes	Yes	K/B	K/B	K/B		Yes
3. GENERAL							
Hard-Copy	Yes	–	Addition	Addition		Addition (matrix printer)	Addition
Associated Features	–	–		Slide Projection		Video Output	Local storage + computation
4. TYPICAL COST/UNIT	£750	£750	£2500	£5000	£10K–£30K	£2500	£500–£2500

Fig. 7. Desirable features for a CAL terminal.

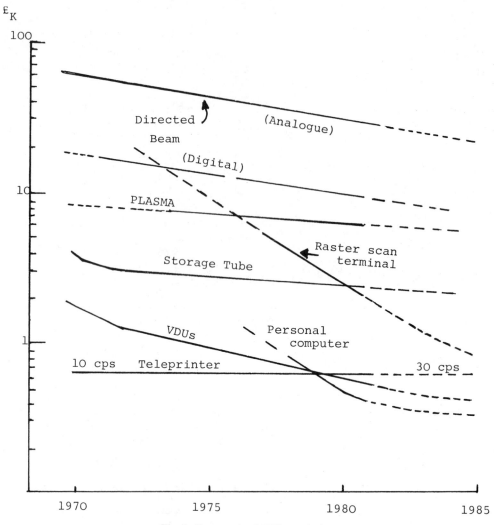

Fig. 8. Cost trends of CAL terminals.

$3000. The discs are read-only and a "pressing" currently has to be done at the manufacturers for a cost of about $2500. Individual copies cost only $20 in quantity. The output device for a video disc is a raster scan monitor or television. When incorporated as an adjunct to a computer driven CAL graphics terminal, a powerful student workstation is created. Small wonder that many believe that yet another revolution affecting individualised learning is underway.

Other influences on the CAL terminal

However important the student interface is regarded, there are several other influences which also determine the choice of CAL terminal. These include the teaching environment, the computer systems environment and financial constraints. The organisation of students in work groups, their backgrounds and the degree to which interaction is necessary with the teacher may dictate several system requirements. For example, the requirements of an individual student wanting to revise could be satisfied by a single terminal available at a convenient location and time, while the teaching of new concept to a whole class with a strict timetable may dictate a "teaching laboratory" environment.

When considering the total systems environment, it is instructive to note that only a small proportion of systems on which CAL is practiced are devoted exclusively to CAL. Even fewer, perhaps 1 in 100, are devoted to a specific type of CAL such as tutorials or drill and practice. CAL, therefore, generally coexists with other applications. Another factor to consider is whether CAL material "development" and "delivery" are to take place on the same system. The advantage of doing so is that material can be tested in the student environment as it is developed, and updates can be made without any transfer problems. On the other hand, separation of "development" and "delivery" can simplify systems organisation.

The cost factor

The main influence on the choice of CAL user interface is most likely to be systems consideration and costs. The very nature of CAL presupposes an interactive terminal based system. Today, the systems choice is either multi-user timesharing computer systems or multiple "personal" microcomputers.

The most evident cost is the capital cost of the terminal itself. There is an inherent tendency to plump for the lowest cost terminal commensurate with reasonable match to other requirements. However, to support these terminals needs a host computer system. To support 32 terminals would require a minicomputer costing from £40,000 to £120,000 depending on the facilities provided. At a minimum that equates to £1250 per terminal. To this must be added operating, maintenance and systems management costs. This would bring a typical system cost (using a 5-year life) to £750–£1500 per terminal/year (excluding the terminal costs). Fielden and Pearson in their book on costing CAL systems[13] reckoned that it was unreasonable to assume more than 500 h usage for each terminal in a year (i.e. 20 h per week over a 26 week student year). Hence, with a £750 terminal, the minimum cost/student hour works at about £3 per h, whereas a £2500 graphics terminal on a more sophisticated system would be about £4.50 per student per h. This should be compared with conventional teaching costs in higher education of £1–£3 per student hour depending on the mode of teaching (tutorial, lecture etc.). An even more dramatic way to represent the relation with teaching costs is to note that 1 months' salary of a teacher can purchase a microcomputer! Similar calculations show that the cost of a student terminal hour in 1972 were £10 for a graphics terminal (Tektronix 4010) and £5 for a teleprinter terminal, a ratio not as disparate as the capital costs of the terminals themselves. Calculations on a similar basis for PLATO terminals would show a decline from over £12–£15 per h to £8–£10 per h now. Such costs completely ignore development costs for CAL material! When these were added in Fielden and Pearson's calculations, they showed that typical costs in 1977–78 came to £6–£10 per terminal hour. In this league, the incremental cost of around £1.50 per h for full colour graphics seems a small price for its apparent many advantages. At first sight, the cost of multiple microcomputer systems seems significantly less, since each system in its entirety costs just the same as a terminal on a timesharing system. Such calculations, however, ignore many of the hidden costs and other penalties of personal microcomputers. Software coordination and distribution by itself is a logistics headache. Loading of programmes from cassettes can take a considerable amount of time. If, to improve this situation, each micro is provided with floppy discs, that is an extra price penalty. Experience of the keyboard reliability on many micros has shown it to lack the very high standards of those of specialist terminal manufacturers. Taken altogether, it is probable that the true cost when measured against functionality and throughput does not differ markedly from the centralized systems approach.

Systems convergence

Both approaches have their advantages. The personal micro approach has many attractions—portability, local control, local storage for student material. On the other hand, the centralized timesharing approach offers advantages of file sharing, more cost effective mass storage, easier software management and access to a much more extensive range of computer facilities.

There is already evidence that these two approaches are beginning to converge. Many microcomputer users have connected their systems into "micro-nets" with shared peripherals or are linking them to host systems for down line loading. In contrast, two suppliers of educational computer systems have recently announced microprocessor based student terminals which coexist with host computer systems. The first is CDC's "Micro PLATO" terminal which is a self-contained delivery system, complete with local mass storage. The other is Digital Equipment's "GIGI" terminal which can perform the multiple roles of a standard ASCII terminal, an APL or special symbol terminal, a colour graphics terminal and a BASIC-speaking terminal.

THE FUTURE OF GRAPHICS IN CAL

Cost, it would appear, should not be a significant obstacle to applying graphics more widely in CAL. The differential between graphics and non-graphics is not wide; in any case, today's graphics costs are considerably less than the costs of using alpha-numeric terminals in the past. Both costs are comparable to conventional teaching costs in higher education and the ratio is changing in favour of CAL. No, the obstacles to the use of graphics are precisely those which face the use of CAL in general.

A recent CONDUIT survey[1] gives us a clue as to what some of these factors are.

When questioned about the barriers to the wider use of instructional computing, department heads cited "lack of training, time, equipment, interest and funds" as major obstacles. Faculty members on the other hand, added "lack of software, support and absence of academic reward". "Lack of time" is an indication that CAL is seen as an addition and not a substitute for existing teaching. The NDPCAL survey conclusion that CAL is always an "extra" cost supports this argument. However, in certain establishments and in industry, CAL is regarded as a substitute *for certain parts of the course*. Convenience for the student also carries a bonus.

"Lack of software and support" may be true to some extent, but a lot of CAL material is now being developed. The obstacle is probably more the lack of being able to conveniently acquire and apply individuality to supplied material. Also important is the problem of transferability. No two BASIC dialects seem the same—CAL material is continually being converted from one to another. When the more efficient approach of using author languages is considered, there is also no standard. PILOT, TUTOR, COURSEWRITER and CAN all flourish. Addition of graphics only compounds the problem. Even where standards are emerging, such as the SIGGRAPH/ANSI standards in the U.S. and GINO-F in U.K. universities, they are far from being universally accepted. Technology also marches on, leaving these standards to cater for the lowest common demoninator across all classes of graphics equipment. In any emerging application of technology, the "spread of the gospel" takes place in phases. First there come the innovators—the small, select group of pioneers who show the potential of an application, even if the environment or the price is not right. For the use of graphics in CAL early PLATO users can be put into this category. The second phase is when the key followers could experiment and afford to join them. These were the CAL users of the Tektronix terminals and other vector graphics terminals of the 1970s. The third phase is the development of the mass market, when a technology becomes affordable by the majority in a given field. The 20th century has seen this pattern of development in telephones, automobiles and television, and hand-held calculators. The period over which the mass market develops varies according to the obstacles.

In the case of graphics in CAL, the price is now right, the motivating factors exist (at least for the student) and with the right will, the obstacles should be surmountable. There is an instructive parallel with the U.K.'s Open University which pioneered another unconventional approach to teaching. Quality material is developed centrally by experts and distributed or transmitted at low cost by radio and TV to students throughout the U.K. The role of their tutor is more of an advisor on learning strategies and an identifier and solver of their problem areas. There is nothing to suggest that Open University students are less well educated than their counterparts at traditional universities. Demand for places still outstrips supply. Yet the cost of their education to the community is considerably less. It would, therefore, appear that the major obstacles to CAL for the masses are more likely to be social and political. For during the next few years the momentum behind graphics and microcomputers is likely to intensify. They will be ubiquitous and affordable.

The computer manufacturers can meet the technology part of the challenge.

It seems difficult for anyone not to be impressed by the graphic demonstration of CAL material, particularly when it is dynamic and in colour. The stage, therefore, seems set to remove the remaining obstacles for widespread application of CAL and that is the part of the challenge which confronts the educational community.

REFERENCES

1. Computers in undergraduate teaching revisited. *PIPELINE* **5,** 5 (1980).
2. Examples include the Huntington Simulation Packages and CONDUIT Program Library in the U.S.A.; the Central Program Exchange (CPE) and the Geographic Association Package Exchange (GAPE) in the U.K.
3. Johnson J. W., The crucial link between the user and computing power. *PIPELINE* **3,** 2 (1978).
4. Hofstetter F. T., Third summative Report of the Delaware PLATO Project. University of Delaware (1978).
5. Stotz R., A new display terminal. *Comput. Design* (1968).
6. Smith P. R., Computer assisted learning in engineering. In *Computer Assisted Learning in the United Kingdom—Some Case Studies* (E. R. Hooper and I. Toye). Council for Educational Technology (1975).
7. Wood R. D., Interactive graphics techniques applied to teaching structural behaviour. In *Symposium on Computer Assisted Learning in Civil and Structural Engineering and Related Subjects*. Department of Civil Engineering, University College of Swansea (1978).
8. Bell C. G., Mudge J. C. and MacNamara J. E., In *Computer Engineering*. Chapter 2. Digital Press (1978).
9. Myers W., Computer graphics: a two-way street. *Computer* 49 (1980).
10. Cook V., The human factors aspect of the student terminal interface in CAL systems. Technical Report No. 7, Council for Educational Technology (1974).
11. Foley J. D. and Wallace V. L., The art of natural man-machine conversation. *Proc. IEEE* **62,** 462 (1974).
12. *PIPELINE*—Special Issue on Video-disc **5,** (1980).
13. Fielden J. and Pearson P. K.; The cost of learning with computers. Council for Educational Technology (1978).

Comput. & Educ. Vol. 6, pp. 25 to 31, 1982
Printed in Great Britain

0360-1315/82/010025-07$03.00/0
Pergamon Press Ltd

SOME PRINCIPLES OF SCREEN DESIGN AND SOFTWARE FOR THEIR SUPPORT

J. M. JENKIN

Mills & Allen Communications Ltd, 1–4 Langley Court, London WC2E 9JY, England

Abstract—The relatively unexciting issue of screen design has often been neglected in CAL or CAT. Changing technology and user requirements may make it more important. Authoring systems (languages, methodologies, software tools) need to satisfy certain requirements at different stages of the authoring process. Such requirements, relating to screen management, aesthetics, specification and documentation, implementation, maintenance and portability, are considered. Some can be met by adopting certain standards and techniques, and by the provision of software tools. Certain solutions are suggested, in particular, the software tools for screen design provided by a particular authoring system, COMBAT are described. These directly correspond to specification and documentation techniques, assist in implementation and maintenance, and help in the adoption of good design standards.

1. INTRODUCTION

There are many important issues to be considered by the CAL or CAT* author, and hence by the authoring system designer. These include answer matching, graphical output, educational techniques, strategy, and many others as well as subject matter. With so many aspects essential to pedagogic success and reliable man–machine interaction, it is hardly surprising that the relatively unimportant issue of output format or screen design has often been neglected.

In much the same way, text book authors have concentrated on the content and the diagrams and left layout and typesetting to the graphic designer and the printer. However, a skilfully organised and printed book is likely to contribute to better understanding and motivation than a typed or manuscript photocopy.

In CAL, two further factors have tended to reduce the need for the author to be concerned with the design of the output. The first concerns the technology: as long as the medium is a slow speed, hard copy device such as a Teletype Model 33 or 43 attached to a time-sharing system, the major consideration is how to minimise the time and hence the volume of output.

The second factor is the user requirement: as long as the student is interested in the subject matter and is sympathetic to the limitations of the medium, the author need not be too concerned with appearance.

However, both these factors are not always present. The technology has changed. The author now needs to cope with, and exploit, some or all of:

Single user, stand alone microcomputers
video terminals driven at high speed
paged rather than scrolled output
direct cursor addressing giving output anywhere on the screen
lower case characters
block (low resolution) graphics
user definable character sets
high resolution graphics
memory mapped displays giving instantaneous output or even animation
bit mapped displays
colour
highlighting, blinking, reverse video, underlining, half intensity etc.

User requirements may also be changing. In one area, Computer Assisted Training, users such as apprentices may be less academically inclined or less motivated, or alternatively in the case of senior management, have less time, be less tolerant and expect higher standards of presentation.

Experience in a related field, that of Prestel, gives an interesting comparison. Information retrieval systems have usually been concerned with the versatility of the search commands and with speed of

---

* Computer Assisted Training: Used here to refer to CAL in the vocational sector, i.e. industry, commerce, government, armed forces etc.

access. Prestel, on the other hand, has extremely simple search commands—many would say too simple—yet this is so that it can be used by anyone with very little training. After 2 years of public service, much of the competitive edge of successful information providers comes from the presentation of the end-pages. This use of the new medium has only come about through experience and has relied considerably on the influence of professional graphic designers[1].

Screen design affects the authoring process at a number of stages. Authoring systems (languages, methodologies, software tools etc.) need to satisfy certain requirements at each stage.

Requirements affecting the designer include:

Screen management:	the structure or organisation of information on the screen so that the student has access to, and a clear perception of the different functions: teaching material, instructions, errors etc.
Aesthetics:	attractive hence pleasant to read output.
Specification and documentation:	the specification of the design permitting reviews and communication between the designer, subject specialist and implementor etc.

Requirements affecting the implementor include:

Screen creation:	the means to implement the designer's specification without having to be concerned with tedious bookkeeping such as justification.
Maintenance:	the means to make changes in one area without affecting others.
Interaction:	the means of viewing and changing screens interactively. Such a system is suitable for non-programmers such as trainers or graphic designers.

In addition there is the following requirement:

Portability:	independence of design and implementation from a particular terminal, yet enabling advantage to be taken of modern terminal capabilities.

Some of these requirements can be met by adopting certain standards and techniques and by the provision of software tools. COMBAT, an authoring system for Computer Assisted Training, currently under development by Mills & Allen Communications, provides such software tools. These directly correspond to specification and documentation techniques, assist in implementation and maintenance and help in the adoption of good design standards.

The design of the software has been influenced by the Smalltalk Programming System of Xerox-Parc[2], and by the "Textport" System developed by Bork's group at Irvine[3].

Each of the above requirements is now considered both in terms of general principles and, by way of illustration, how the COMBAT supporting software is one solution to their realisation.

2. SCREEN MODEL

COMBAT screen design depends on an abstract model of input/output.

The central concept is the division of output and, to a lesser extent, input into distinct functional groups. For example, these might include "presentation", "location", "reinforcement", "dialogue" and so on. Each of these groups represents an abstraction defined by the author and corresponds physically to a rectangular area on the screen called a *window*. The screen may be divided into any number of, possibly nested, but non-overlapping windows, each of which may be programmed as if it were an independent screen in its own right, each maintaining, for example, the position of its "cursor", its size and its colour.

Text and, on suitable terminals, graphics may be *output* to windows. Text may be *input* from a keyboard and echoed within a window.

Each window has associated with it a set of *attributes*. These are summarised as Table 1. A fundamental principle of the design is that windows are attribute-invariant; i.e. attributes apply to the entire window and can only be set up when the window is created or initialised. This is to permit terminal independence as described later. Since a window can be any size from one character to the full screen no generality is lost, although there are storage implications.

Table 1. Window attributes

Individual window attributes	
Parent	The parent (surrounding) window
Position	A vector specifying position and size relative to the parent
Framed	Whether framed (boxed) or not
Cog	Characters or graphics
Background	Background colour
Justification	Left, right, full, centre justification or literal
Colour	Foreground colour
Style	Any combination of blink, bold, underscore
Char-size	Size of each character (single or double)
Char-set	Alternate character set e.g. block graphics
Cursor-position	Cursor position for this window
Screen attributes	
Screen-width	Width of screen in characters
Screen-depth	Depth of screen in characters
Screen-technology	Technology e.g. bit-map, viewdata
Screen-map	Characters currently on the screen

The functionality is of benefit to the designer, programmer and student. The discipline of the imposed functional abstraction will lead to easier development and maintenance. The designer and programmer have a convenient model for input/output without becoming concerned with unnecessary details. Perhaps more importantly, modifications are simplified since changes to one functional area will not affect independent ones. One point here is that all coordinates are relative to a specified window, not to the screen.

The student knows which regions of the screen to concentrate on for dialogue, which to study at length etc. He does not get bewildered by output appearing everywhere, seemingly at random. In certain situations he can browse through the tutorial text, say, without repeating the dialogue. All this does not imply that output layouts need to be stereotyped. A well written program will employ a variety of layouts, but for each layout there will be consistency.

3. SCREEN MANAGEMENT

Ensuring that the correct information is available, i.e. on the screen or recallable, and is suitably organised or structured is the task of the author. However, the COMBAT screen model and software assist in its management. Further, it may be desirable for particular pieces of "courseware" or courses to adopt certain house-styles or standards. These may depend on taste or the nature of the material or the user; some that have been found useful are described in this section.

A more detailed example is shown as Table 2 and, diagramatically as Fig. 1.

It will be seen, in the example given in the previous section, that the order in the table is in order of increasing transience, and of decreasing height on the screen, e.g. the location window will be the most static and at the top of the screen. Thus dynamic information occurs at the bottom of the screen, which is close to the keyboard; most students are not touch typists.

Ensuring the student actually reads what is displayed is another problem. Firstly, "transient" output may be overwritten before it can be read. Secondly, "permanent" output may take place in an unpleasing way e.g. too slowly or slightly too quickly. Thirdly, transient output may take place, and although not overwritten, may not be noticed.

Several strategies are available to overcome some or all of these:

Slow down: The output is slowed down (if necessary)
Delay: Output is normal speed, but a delay of a few seconds can take place afterwards

Table 2. Example of functional breakdown

Window	Function and attributes
Location	Title and location within course
Information	For teaching material: Usually top third of screen, full width, usually framed
Secondary information	For more particular information e.g. instructions: usually lower left
Input	For student input: can be anywhere but normally lower right, always (and exclusively) highlighted, black on white (reverse)
Error/comment	For errors, warnings, comments etc. normally lower right

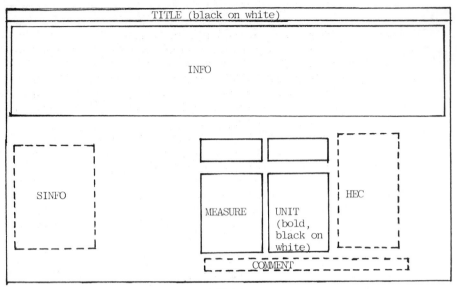

Fig. 1.

Emphasis: Important output can be emphasised e.g. by an audible tone, or by highlighting, or by
                 use of a bright colour
Suspension: A message can be output requiring the user to press a key when he is ready. (User
                 controlled suspension). This can be a symbolic message (——>) in preference to a
                 repetitious "press NEXT to continue", although this may be printed if no response is
                 received in say 30 s
Scrolling: The relevant window can be scrolled, but this may require special hardware

   One seemingly useful standard is to adopt suspension after all "textual units" of output except for
"trivial" error messages when delay may be used.
   Several other often apparently trivial considerations result in increased comfort to the user:

   For example, the suspension arrow is placed in the bottom right hand corner of the output window
if further output is due in that window, or at the bottom right hand corner of the screen if not.
   Error messages relating to invalid input are left on the screen until the repeated input has taken
place.
   On terminals where the cursor cannot be turned off and a delay is required, it is "rested" immediately outside the bottom left of the window if no further output is to take place within that
window, or at the next output position otherwise.
   Output should not normally jump from window to window except in the case of transient information such as error messages.

   COMBAT software takes much of the effort out of the above. For example the DELAY procedure
moves the cursor according to the standard before commencing the pause; there is software to handle
suspensions, error reporting, speed of output etc.

4. AESTHETICS

   Clearly, aesthetics is largely a matter of taste, so as such is left to the author. Software is provided
to allow him to select justification, filling, speed, foreground and background colour, position and size
of windows etc.
   Clearly the author has much scope to use the medium successfully or unsuccessfully. There is a
tendency to design screens as if they were paper; i.e. top to bottom, left justified etc. Less conventional
techniques such as "most interactive at bottom", use of right justified text on the right hand side of
the screen, grouping into functional windows, "split screens", proper use of colour and so on can all
have a pleasant effect.
   As with all such matters, experimentation is important; the screen design program, which is
described shortly, assists here.

5. SPECIFICATION AND DOCUMENTATION

In Computer Assisted Training, it is quite common for the "author" to be a team rather than an individual. Such a team might contain some or all of a subject specialist, a "courseware" designer, a graphic designer and a programmer. There may be more than one of each, and further individuals may review the design or implementation. In CAT, there may be fairly simple teaching strategies and techniques employed which rely on a fair amount of tutorial-type output that must be expressed in a particular or accurate way. All this means that the design of the material and in particular, the design of the screens, needs to be communicated by the designer to the other team members.

The COMBAT screen model provides a convenient abstraction for this, for example, as terminology, shorthand, and as a means of distinguishing functional components (Fig. 2). The programmer is then able to implement the design directly.

Many windows contain static or constant information. Those that do not can be specified by examples, informal algorithms, or some other means. At least they can be clearly isolated.

Software also exists both to print representations of the screen and the attributes of the windows from image files (described shortly) and to print snapshots of the screen at any time during program execution. This is useful in documentation.

6. SOFTWARE

The software itself may be used in two ways. The first is via a programming language interface: a UNIT from within UCSD Pascal. A UNIT is a form of package or module that provides the programmer with a set of constants, types, variables and procedures to implement the screen model including the operations on it. These operations are not listed here but are fairly obvious: windows may be dynamically created, setting up attributes, and broken; output can take place in a variety of ways; the screen map can be accessed etc.

In the second way, an interactive, command driven program, the screen design program or image editor may be used, possibly by non-programmers, to create or edit *images*. Each image corresponds to a window and is stored in an *image file* along with a key that may be used to access the image in order to restore it onto the screen of a running CAL program.

Each image may contain subimages. Attributes are stored along with the image, thus the exact picture may be saved and restored. Subsequent program generated output may take place to windows set up in this way. Thus the screen design program can be used to replace window creation as well as output. Also it is possible to store just the attributes; they can then act as a prototype for a screen or part of a screen to be filled in by an author. Both these are particularly useful in the system of "generators" that permits non-programmers to write certain standardised "courseware".

Interactive "editors" of this nature are much more effective in use than the writing and amending of programs, and of course are suitable for use by non-computer specialists. However, they cannot represent dynamic information.

Although the image editor has many characteristics of a text editor or word processor, it is specialised towards its particular task; e.g. the editing unit is usually a complete window, it is "mode-free" and it is easy to use.

In addition to their use within CAL programs, windows are used within the authoring system itself. For example, the command handler, a package derived from the Hertfordshire CAL standard[4], requires 6 windows to be specified by the author. These include windows for a menu, for help messages, for prompts etc. The image editor uses the command handler in an unusual way. The image to be edited is displayed in a window of the correct size, leaving an arbitrary sized region on the screen for use by the editor for command handling. This is allocated dynamically. In the extreme case a single line is sufficient for "prompt mode", but if space is available, windows are progressively created for menus, help messages etc.

7. PORTABILITY

As long as programs are dependent on the particular computer system (order code, compiler, operating system etc.), portability is difficult in any case, so restriction to a single type of terminal is probably realistic. However, with the advent of truly portable systems such as the UCSD p-system,[5] which enables the same program to run on the majority of disc-based microcomputers without change, effective use of the terminal can be the major limitation.

Many functions commonly found on terminals such as text output, erase to end of line, delete last character typed, move cursor to an arbitrary position etc. can be trivially mapped via a look up table or similar; indeed this is part of the UCSD p-system (the screen control unit).

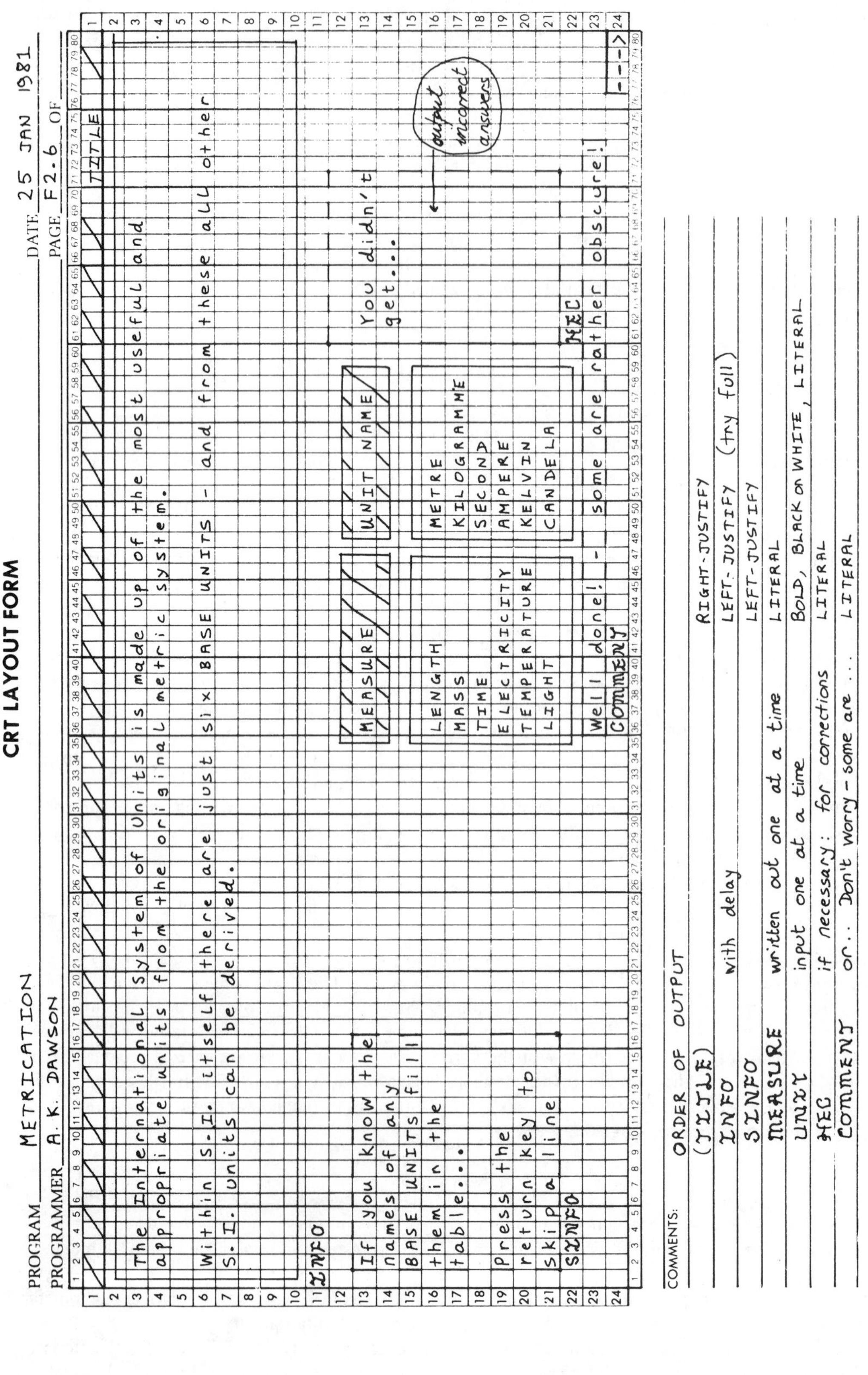

CRT LAYOUT FORM

PROGRAM METRICATION

PROGRAMMER A. K. DAWSON

DATE 25 JAN 1981

PAGE F2.6 OF

TITLE

The International System of Units is made up of the most useful and appropriate units from the original metric system.

Within S.I. itself there are just six BASE UNITS - and from these all other S.I. units can be derived.

INFO

If you know the names of any BASE UNITS fill them in the table... press the return key to skip a line

SINFO

MEASURE // UNIT NAME //

LENGTH	METRE
MASS	KILOGRAMME
TIME	SECOND
ELECTRICITY	AMPERE
TEMPERATURE	KELVIN
LIGHT	CANDELA

Well done! - some are rather obscure!

COMMENT

NEG   You didn't get....

output incorrect answers

COMMENTS:

ORDER OF OUTPUT

(TITLE)	
INFO	
SINFO	with delay
MEASURE	written out one at a time
UNIT	input one at a time
NEG	if necessary: for corrections
COMMENT	or .. Don't worry - some are ...

RIGHT-JUSTIFY

LEFT-JUSTIFY (try full)

LEFT-JUSTIFY

LITERAL

BOLD, BLACK or WHITE, LITERAL

LITERAL

LITERAL

Fig. 2.

However, more sophisticated functions such as colour, graphics, character set or size, and intensity cannot be catered for in this way. This is because terminals are frequently incompatible. With some, these attributes are stored with each pixel e.g. each character position; with others they are not stored but act only at the time of output. With yet others they are stored and affect a zone, typically the rest of the line. With still others, they are controlled by stored but non-printing characters that nevertheless require a position on the screen.

In COMBAT, these terminal dependencies are localised within the implementation. The incompatibility is resolved by insisting on attribute-invariance within a window, i.e. the entire window has the same attributes. However, since a window can be any size from one character to the full screen no generality is lost. COMBAT software generates the necessary control characters, escape sequences, etc; these can be quite complex. Thus the programmer only views the screen model, only one localised piece of code has to be rewritten for a different terminal and most of the modern functions are available to the programmer.

8. CONCLUSIONS

Good screen design plays an important part in Computer Assisted Training. The COMBAT software is able to assist in the design, creation and maintenance of screen layouts. Much of this may be carried out interactively by an image editor.

REFERENCES

1. Mills & Allen Communications Ltd. PRESTEL the editorial opportunity, London (1979).
2. Ingalls D. H. H., The Smalltalk-76 programming system design and implementation. *Proc. 5th Annual ACM Symposium on Principles of Programming Languages*, pp. 9–15. ACM, New York (1978).
3. Franklin S. D. and Shimsall T., Textport system reference guide. Educational Technology Center, University of California at Irvine (1980).
4. Tagg W., *A Standard for CAL Dialogue*, 2nd Edition. Advisory Unit for Computer Based Education, Hatfield (1979).
5. *Sof Tech Microsystems*. UCSD Pascal Users' Manual. SofTech Microsystems Inc., San Diego (1980).

Comput. & Educ. Vol. 6, pp. 33 to 38, 1982
Printed in Great Britain

0360-1315/82/010033-06$03.00/0
Pergamon Press Ltd

A MARRIAGE OF CONVENIENCE: VIDEOTEX AND COMPUTER ASSISTED LEARNING

J. W. BRAHAN[1] and DAVID GODFREY[2]

[1]Information Science Section, National Research Council of Canada, Division of Electrical Engineering, Ottawa, Ontario, Canada K1A OR8 and [2]University of Victoria, P.O. Box 1700, Victoria, British Columbia, Canada V8W 2Y2

Abstract—Videotex technology appears to offer Computer Assisted Learning (CAL) the potential for both effective distribution and enriched display possibilities. The limited degree of interaction which is permitted by the current approach to Videotex is, however, a major restriction. With the potential and the problems in mind, an experiment has been undertaken to link the Canadian Videotex development, Telidon, with the Canadian CAL system based on the course author/programming language NATAL. The original NATAL specification has been modified and augmented to incorporate a graphics facility consistent with the SIGGRAPH CORE language recommendation and support has been added to the NATAL system for the Telidon terminal. Thus, a system has been constructed which permits definition of course materials at a high level, with sufficient flexibility to respond to the wide range of CAL requirements with provision to link those materials to the Videotex environment. Initial examples of materials developed using the combined system indicate that it is possible to superimpose CAL on the Videotex system and achieve the benefits of both.

VIDEOTEX CHARACTERISTICS

The popular approach to Videotex since 1977 has been characterized by some of the same enthusiasms which CAL and CAI and CMI generated a decade earlier. The millenium, as reports and reporters rushed to inform us, was here. Or at least almost here. Unlike CAL, however, Videotex systems have become national properties and are seen, through the mists of our high technology future, as a major source of revenue in both the domestic and the export markets. The faith of governments, at least at the moment, is reflected in financial support for research, development and trials of various kinds. There are currently three major national systems: PRESTEL, ANTIOPE and TELIDON.

PRESTEL, the pioneering member of this group, is run by the British Post Office and has over 160,000 pages of information stored, according to current reports[1]. Earlier projections of 100,000 user terminals by 1980 have not been met; according to Segal, only 6000 terminals had been sold as of December, 1980[2]. Government support is approx. $60 million according to LINK[3].

In France, ANTIOPE is a similar system. Didon is the broadcast mode and Titan the interactive mode. The French government also has impressive plans to install approx. 250,000 interactive units in homes to serve as a telephone directory system. This will obviously create the necessary volume to bring the price of similar units down into the consumer market range. LINK estimates that the database at the moment is very small, however, and that the French government has to date invested only $12 million[4]. Even at $300 dollars each, the home terminals represent an investment of $75 million.

In Canada, the TELIDON system was developed by the Department of Communications, but is being marketed through private sector activities. Approximately $10 million of government expenditure to date has been matched by $30 million of private funding. An additional $27.5 million will be spent by the government during 1981 and 1982. 3000 terminals have been manufactured and 12 trials are underway. LINK asserts that 100,000 pages of information are in databases. This figure appears high, although the private sector (Bell Canada and Infomart) participation makes it more difficult to come up with an authoritative figure. We would estimate between ten and twenty thousand pages as a conservative figure. Richard Larratt of Infomart estimates that there will be 100,000 pages in the system by the end of 1981[5].

Unlike the other two systems, TELIDON is based on alpha-geometric rather than alpha-mosaic graphics. A stored picture can be displayed on screens of varying degrees of resolution. A microprocessor in each home unit provides the storage and intelligence to perform the translation from coded character transmission to picture display.

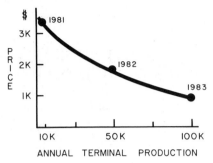

Fig. 1. Cost projections for terminal manufacture.

These Videotex systems, unlike CAL, have been designed from the beginning as a mass-market, low-cost item; an information retrieval system for news events, consumer goods, and sports, travel, government and entertainment information, with some games available. Although aided by current and projected reductions in hardware costs, the concept must, apparently, fail or flourish within this mass-market framework. Videotex is thus subject to a number of mass-market imperatives in a way that CAL is not. Success for Videotex will, however, have implications for CAL at all market-levels. The mass-market imperative can be seen in the hardware, transmission and software aspects of Videotex, most clearly in the hardware.

Figure 1 was derived from figures[6] supplied by Electrohome, a Canadian manufacturer of TELIDON terminals, but it is similar, of course, to other projections. Indeed, the original PLATO project predicted that the cost of the Plasma Display Terminal would fall to $1800[7] based upon very large quantity production which has not as yet been achieved. The top of this curve corresponds with prices both for PLATO terminals and for colour graphic terminals available from a number of different manufacturers. These prices should also be compared with costs for microcomputers such as the Apple, PET, TI, IBM, Sinclair and RCA units.

As far as transmission technology goes, all three major systems appear to be relying on existing technologies (telephone lines, cable TV, Broadcast TV) to satisfy their own mass-market imperative, with a boost expected from optic fibre and satellite transmission. The data transmission rates selected indicate that the intended flow of information is out to the user as there is often a slower rate for input from the terminal than for output from the central computer. In the hardware areas then, Videotex systems appear to be working in parallel with the existing technological momentum. The engineering involved is competent, slightly innovative, and glamorous enough in its possible applications to attract support.

In the area of database software, however, there is potential weakness. A mass-market prototype does not exist; none of the three major systems have yet revealed any degree of inventiveness, despite the crucial role of this factor; cost-cutting here appears to be based not on external inventions nor economies-of-scale benefits, but upon some plain and simple elimination of benefits. "Let your fingers do the walking," a popular North American telephone company jingle, sums up the approach. Rather than query by keyword or query by example, the existing Videotex systems count on the consumer to do almost all of the searching and indexing functions normally associated with information databases. The consumer can not, for example, say "Who's got the cheapest blue socks, size 10, all wool, within 5 miles of Picadilly Circus?" Standard database practice assumes a fairly complex relationship designed to simplify the system for the users and to prevent hardware constraints from crippling the conceptual system. Such an approach will be of increasing importance in the next generation of CAL systems.

User A1 might be an inventory clerk and User A2 might be the accountant. Obviously, with the exception of the database administrator, a full awareness of how the system operates is unnecessary. A user's view might be restricted to two or three standard relationships and thus information, from a limited portion of the database, can be extracted with great simplicity. Indeed, systems such as Query by Example[8] can create the necessary table for the user with an absolute minimum of input. If both CAL and Videotex are to be part of large-scale, mass-market national information and education systems, then obviously such complexity will have to be dealt with. A university might wish to have a Videotex database of 10,000–15,000 frames for its instruction in science. A certain sophistication at the database level becomes a necessity as soon as one begins to think of such sub-bases as merely components in a very large database[9]. In existing Videotex systems, with the exception of the French Teletel/Star experiments[10], this sophistication has been bypassed in favour of a method which offers little more than the traditional set of records in a file with access by known keys.

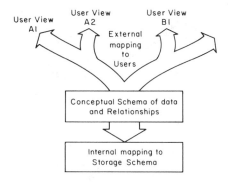

DATABASE FUNCTIONAL STRUCTURE

Fig. 2. Database organization.

The cost advantages of what is essentially a direct-key method are obvious. The fewer services the computer provides, the more users can be promptly taken care of. The mass-market imperatives of Videotex demand a large number of users per CPU and it seems unlikely that such friendly features as keyword searches, stored search lists, private menus and private pages (or branches within the tree of the database) will be implemented unless computer costs fall very drastically.

In CAL terms, the interactive responsiveness of the current generation of Videotex systems must be seen as somewhat restrictive.

CAL CHARACTERISTICS

Within CAL, a diversity of market-levels and of educational methods matches the diversity of languages and equipment being used. Standardization has not been very successful in practice. CAL includes tutorial and exerciser programs, simulators of varying degrees of complexity, simple and complex calculators, mediators, ways of managing both CAL and non-CAL activities, the structured and unstructured use of information sources, and some programs that combine a number of these functions within the same course or set of courses. Associated with these applications are a number of required characteristics in the supporting CAL delivery system. While specific requirements depend on the type of program, the subject matter and the student characteristics, the following requirements

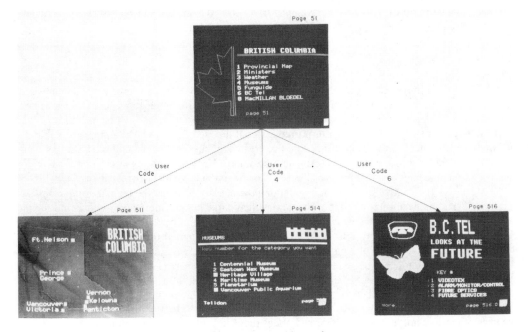

Fig. 3. User access to videotex frames.

are common to many applications:

CAL REQUIREMENT	VIDEOTEX RESPONSE
Fast response	Dependent on size of database and number of active users but in general adequate
Alpha-numeric display	Some limitations on special character sets but generally adequate
Graphics display	Resolution limited in some systems but adequate for most applications
Multiple choice input	Provided by all
Free form response	Accommodated by a few terminals with keyboards
Graphic response	No operational units
Response processing	Limited
Branching capability	Limited
Session-to-session continuity	Not provided.

CAL programs can be very small or very large, some large enough to equal existing Videotex programs. The larger ones require the maintenance of continuity from one student session to the next, the recording of user and program performance data, the recording of complaints, requests and suggestions, the use of external databases, and the registration of and reporting upon large numbers of student users grouped in various ways. Thus, in Videotex terms, all users become Information Providers. A single hour of instruction can easily utilize 300 or 400 "frames" of information. Responses must be interpreted and acted upon; a single course may have the equivalent of several thousand frames of data. The pathways through these data have to be selected in terms of student responses and of the algorithms written into the course by the author.

Given the wide range of software problems implicit in those requirements, CAL research has not been hardware-oriented. The larger systems have utilized a dedicated mainframe or mini-computer. To date, apart from a few relatively expensive systems, CAL terminals have been limited primarily to alpha-numeric display units. Graphics and colour, in particular, have seen limited use because of the added cost. With the development of the 8080 and 6502-based microcomputers, however, and the growth of the home-computer market, this barrier has been removed, at least potentially. The advertising of firms such as Apple (whose sales increased from $10 to $75 million dollars during 1979) has created an expectation of colour and graphic displays as part of the normal CAL experience. This trend can be expected to continue with increasing sophistication in the graphics display possibilities available to the user as the 16 and 32 bit microprocessors come onto the market.

Bearing all these factors in mind, some encouraging, some quite worrying, it still appears, on balance, that Videotex technology does appear to offer the potential for an effective distribution of CAL at a reasonable cost figure. With the potential, and the problems in mind, an experiment has been undertaken to link the Canadian Videotex system, TELIDON, with the Canadian CAL system based on the course authoring language NATAL[11].

THE NATAL SYSTEM

NATAL (the acronym stands for NATional Author Language) is a high level programming language designed to respond to the requirements of the course author. Of prime importance in the NATAL development were the goals of transportability and easy access to the facilities of the computer by the non-specialist. The transportability goal dictated that NATAL be implementable on a variety of computers so that courseware could be created independent of the hardware. At this time, NATAL implementations exist on a DECsystem-10, an IBM-MVS operating system, and a Honeywell Level-6 minicomputer. A subset is also operating on a microcomputer. The "high-level" nature of NATAL moves the control of the course programming activity towards the human, away from the machine. Thus, the resulting program incorporates the course design information in a human readable form, not hidden in a code which is intended for interpretation by the machine.

When comparing NATAL to other CAL systems, it should be noted that NATAL is based on an "open-systems" model, while the older and more commonly known systems such as PLATO and TICCIT are based on a "closed-systems" model in which every subscriber has the same terminal. In the NATAL system, content can be described in a manner detached from specific terminal details and adapted at the time of display to the particular terminal being used. Thus, while the functions provided by the terminal are of course important and necessary to run particular programs, the course author does not have to be concerned about the details of how the functions are implemented on a particular terminal.

This feature of NATAL is particularly important in the approach to the role of the terminal in graphics presentation. In many systems, graphics are prepared with the graphics space represented by the terminal screen. That is to say that the coordinate system (and the information contained therein) is restricted to the visible space of the particular terminal for which the materials are prepared. In the NATAL system, however, the user works in his own visual "world" and uses the terminal screen as a window to view a part of that world. NATAL also permits the definition of subscreens or boxes contained within the terminal display screen. Through the NATAL terminal handler, the user content is adapted automatically for display on the particular terminal used for course delivery.

THE TELIDON TERMINAL

The Telidon terminal[12] provides for the display of alpha-numeric and graphic information on a colour television receiver. Alpha-numerics are presented in a display field of 20 rows by 40 characters. Picture description Instructions[13] provide for a set of geometric drawing primitives such as point, line, polygon and arc. Attributes may be assigned to the primitives providing for control of colour, line style, area fill, etc. In its Videotex application, the terminal is primarily used with a keypad as the entry device. Provision has been made for keyboard input and this facility has been the main input device in the CAL applications of the terminal.

Connection of a new terminal to the NATAL system in general consists of the relatively simple process of defining the characteristics of the terminal for the system. Thus, it was possible to connect the Telidon terminal into the NATAL system very quickly. Even though the original definition of NATAL did not address colour graphics, nor some of the advanced functions found in the newer graphics terminals, it was possible to make these features of the Telidon terminal available through library functions which the user incorporated in his program.

This library-function approach, however, was not entirely in keeping with the NATAL emphasis on providing support for generality and transportability. The user was now required to address specific terminal characteristics at the detailed level and provide for these by adding modules to his program. Quite clearly a need existed to extend the NATAL graphics subsystem to bring it more in line with current and future technology. While the initial requirement was to provide full user support for the graphics in the Telidon terminal, it was important to provide a general rather than a specific solution so that the NATAL system would accommodate current and future graphics terminal technology made possible through advances in micro-electronics. Thus, as a guide to the enhancement of the NATAL system, the ACM Core language recommendation was used as the definition of commonly accepted graphics practice[14]. The resulting system provides the user with a general facility for designating geometric shapes and attributes and further provides for the adaptation of the user specification to terminal capabilities at run time. As an example, the user can specify any colour or shade of colour by assigning values to its hue, lightness and saturation. When a Telidon terminal is used for presentation, the colour displayed will be the one closest to the specified one but selected from the eight Telidon colours available on standard TV receivers.

With this basic facility embedded in the NATAL language, the next step was to consider application programs which would support the creation of graphics. As a first step in this direction, a graphics editor has been produced which allows a user to compose Telidon pictures using a graphics input tablet (a bit-pad) and a set of "high level" commands which relate to picture creation rather than computer programming. This editor program has been used by drafting room personnel with no computer expertise to create pictures which exploit the full capability of the Telidon terminal. The high level of productivity made possible by the NATAL language is demonstrated by the very short time (2 weeks) required to produce this editor program.

THE NATAL–TELIDON CONNECTION

The Telidon–NATAL link can take a variety of forms. To date, only the most obvious (Telidon terminal to NATAL computer) has actually been put into operation. Many more possibilities exist, however. Using the Videotex "front page" as an entry to third party services, it is possible to connect the user into the NATAL computer through the Videotex network. Adding a link between the NATAL computer and the Videotex database provides access to a large information resource for the CAL program and an alternate and more forgiving (albeit more expensive) access to the database by the Videotex customer. Further possibilities are offered by the micro-NATAL terminal. CAL courseware can be stored in Videotex frames and downloaded on demand for execution locally. Bandwidth is a consideration and in many situations, the downloading mode may only be possible over an extended period in non-prime time. A major advantage of this mode is that it is fully consistent with a broadcast mode of operation.

SUMMARY

In this marriage of convenience, what then are the contributions each partner makes to the union? The Videotex system provides a network for the widespread distribution of CAL materials as well as a large information resource in the form of a database of both reference and current (weather, financial, political, etc.) information. The NATAL–CAL system offers easier user access to the database as well as providing a new educational facility which will extend the Videotex service into new markets. In addition, the interactive nature of CAL provides the possibility of augmenting the Videotex database by permitting content to be derived from all user terminals. No longer is it necessary to consider the Videotex world as one divided into information providers and information users.

REFERENCES

1. Videotex: a worldwide evaluation. Research Report, Videotex Monitoring Service. VRR Vol. 3, (1981). LINK New York, NY 10003, p. 30 U.S.A.
2. Sigel E., Videotex: a new technology for the 1980's. The print publisher in an electronic world. A Conference sponsored by Knowledge Industry Publications Inc., 2–3 December (1980).
3. Videotex: a worldwide evaluation, p. 34.
4. Ibid. p. 34.
5. An Interview with Richard Larratt. Canadian Communication Reports. Maclean Hunter Ltd, Toronto, Canada M5W 1A7. p. 8, 31 December (1980).
6. Beam P., Cioni M. and Godfrey D. (Eds) Telidon and NATAL and Education. Proceedings and Supplemental Papers of a Conference held at the University of Waterloo, November (1980).
7. Kearsley G. P., The costs of CAI: a matter of assumptions. AEDS J. 10, 105 (1977).
8. Zloof M. M., Query by example. Proceedings NCC 44 (1975).
9. Rothnie J. B. et al., Introduction to a system for distributed databases (SDD-1). ACM Trans. Database Syst. 5, 1 (1980).
10. Tompa F., Gescei J. and Bochmann G., Data structuring facilities for interactive Videotex systems. CS-80-50. November, pp. 9–13. Computer Science Department, University of Waterloo, Ontario, Canada (1980).
11. Brahan J. W., Definition, implementation and assessment of NATAL-74: an authoring language for computer-aided learning. INFOR 18, 199 (1980).
12. Bown H. G. et al., A general description of Telidon: a Canadian proposal for Videotex systems. CRC Technical Note No. 697-E. Department of Communications, Ottawa, Canada (1978).
13. Bown H. G. et al., Picture description instructions PDI—for the Telidon Videotex system. CRC Technical Note 699-E. Department of Communications, Ottawa, Canada (1979).
14. Status report of the graphics standards planning committee. Comp. Graph. 13, (1979).

Comput. & Educ. Vol. 6, pp. 39 to 44, 1982
Printed in Great Britain

0360-1315/82/010039-06$03.00/0
Pergamon Press Ltd

A PORTABLE PROGRAM TO PRESENT COURSEWARE ON MICROCOMPUTERS

Charles van der Mast

Delft University of Technology, Julianalaan 132, 2628 BL Delft, The Netherlands

Abstract—In computer assisted instruction, certain main functions which have to be carried out by the computer can be distinguished. The performance of these functions will have different software and hardware requirements in different educational environments and both the requirements and the technology to implement them will change over time. It is therefore advantageous to make CAI systems as adaptable as possible. One approach to this is to divide the systems into independent modules each designed to achieve good portability both for software and for hardware. This paper describes such a module which is part of the Modular CAI System Delft. The program makes it possible to present on different types of microcomputers courseware designed using other modules of the system. The program is implemented in Pascal to yield maximum portability on modern microcomputers. Its future and portability are discussed.

INTRODUCTION

The use of computers to assist in learning and teaching is possible with many special CAI systems with different levels of complexity and quality. Although in the past a considerable amount of courseware has been written in general programming languages, we focus upon the use of special CAI systems because we think that they will be the main vehicle to disseminate the use of professional computer assisted instruction in the future.

Most well-known systems were implemented on large time-sharing computers (PLATO now marketed by CDC, IIS developed by IBM, ASET developed by Univac). Others work on time-sharing minicomputers (DECAL of DEC, SIMPLER of Modcomp and TICCIT), while recently, special CAI systems were developed for stand-alone microcomputers (Common Pilot[1] and VCAS of the University of Utah[2]). There has been a prolonged dispute between the proponents of large scale time-sharing systems and those of stand-alone microcomputers, but the opponents have now reached the consensus that a good solution would be an integration of large computers and microcomputers into the same CAI system in order to utilise the benefits of both and to eliminate their disadvantages[3].

The advantages of large time-sharing CAI systems are: the availability of computer power for complex calculations, fast accessibility to large amounts of data, easy and fast distribution of data to and from users, a variety of additional interactive educational services and a simple standardisation of software and courseware facilitated by the central character of these systems. Some disadvantages are: the need for large financial investments, high communication costs, relatively low system reliability caused by its complexity and the dependency of local units of users on central services.

Some advantages of stand-alone systems are: high system reliability, low costs per hour, ease of transport and an effectively linear relation between total costs and number of terminals. Some disadvantages are: lack of computer power (with present generation of microprocessors), standardisation of hard-, soft- and courseware is difficult to introduce and communication between users is only possible if stand-alone systems can be connected with a network. Moreover, authoring requires a lot more computer resources than student interaction does, so it will continue to be done on central and in most cases on large computers, although some small systems do offer good features for authoring[1,2].

During the coming years, however, the speed and the size of internal memory of microprocessors will increase so that some of these disadvantages will disappear. All in all, it seems a good policy to implement some of the functions of CAI on large computers and others on small stand-alone computers.

The main functions involved in any implementation of CAI are[4]:

authoring or developing and testing courseware;
report generating and evaluating student data;
distributing courseware and collecting data about its usage;

presenting courseware to students;

managing all data concerning the use of the system and the courseware.

While some of these main functions can be more conveniently implemented on large computers, others can be implemented very well on both large and microcomputers, depending on local needs[4,5]. For the application of CAI on a large scale, it seems reasonable to implement some of the main functions on different hardware in order to get an optimum mixture: the centrally oriented functions, authoring and report generating, on larger central computers; the distribution through a network and the individually oriented function, presentation, on minicomputers and on stand-alone microcomputers. The management could be done on the larger computer. This concept has been presented in [3,7] and the Control Data Micro PLATO station can also be regarded as a specimen of this concept[8].

Another important aspect of implementing CAI is the *adaptability* of hardware and software. A CAI system has to be changed and updated from time to time to meet new requirements caused by technological, economical and organisational developments. In other words, extensibility, modular organisation and a maximum ease of use are needed[5]. Adaptability is desired e.g. to extend the author language, to support new terminal devices and to make possible the use of the newest hardware inside the system.

The last important aspect in CAI which we will mention here is the *portability* of courseware. Between different CAI systems portability does not exist at all. The structures of author languages and general programming languages are so different that it is impractical to construct conversion programs. In spite of the development of portable author languages and delivery systems like NATAL-74[9] and PLANIT[10], no standard high level complex machine-independent CAI-language exists[11].

Adaptability and portability were important aspects during the implementation of the Modular CAI System Delft (MCSD)[4]. The presentation of lessons with the MCSD is effected by interpreting a machine-independent code on mini- and microcomputers. To make it possible to present the lessons on a wide family of microprocessors, a new lesson interpreter was built and written in Pascal, choosen because it is a widespread high level language for microcomputers.

THE MODULAR CAI SYSTEM DELFT

The MCSD has been designed as an experimental CAI system in order to achieve adaptability, flexibility and portability[4]. Its structure is based on a distributed implementation of the main functions; authoring, report generating and presenting. These functions are performed by separate modules of the system, which were built for various hardware and software environments. The most essential aspect of the MCSD is an intermediate CAI assembler code (CAIASCO) in which course-ware can be represented in a machine-independent way. In CAIASCO, all elementary actions necessary to do CAI are represented as a set of instructions which involve the minimum detail required to describe the features of different author languages. One compiler is needed for each author language and one CAIASCO interpreter for each type of computer on which courseware is to be presented to students.

The MCSD has been extended many times during the past and will continue to be changed. So far, the author language PLANIT has been used. Authoring and testing is done with the PLANIT system[10] which runs on IBM 370/158 computers. The PLANIT version of a lesson ready for presentation has to be translated into the CAIASCO code by a compiler developed as a part of the MCSD. After this conversion, the lesson can be presented by interpreters (CAIRSX, CAIMIC and CAIPAS) on different computers (see Fig. 1). CAIRSX runs in a time-sharing mode on DEC mini-computers[12]. CAIMIC has been built to present courseware on LSI-11-based microcomputers[13]. This interpreter takes the lessons from floppy disk and can also transfer new courseware onto the floppy disk from the minicomputer on which CAIRSX runs. The student data which have been stored on the floppy disk can be sent upwards to the minicomputer.

All interpreters store student performance data including course, student name and date in exactly the same format. After collection of these data, a program on the IBM/158 can generate reports on the progress of students. The data are currently transferred in both directions between the large system and the minicomputer on tape (see Fig. 2).

Recently a portable CAIASCO interpreter CAIPAS was completed to present courseware on other microcomputers. CAIPAS accepts exactly the same CAIASCO-code (distributed in ASCII) as the other interpreters and it produces student data in the same format.

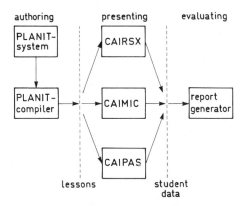

Fig. 1. Components of the modular CAI system Delft.

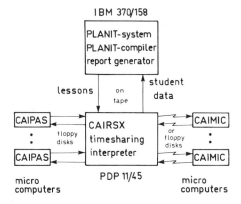

Fig. 2. The distributed implementation of the modular CAI system Delft.

THE PORTABLE LESSON INTERPRETER CAIPAS

CAIPAS is a program to present lessons and to keep performance records automatically for one student at a time. The program controls all processes needed to read parts of the lesson from floppy disk, to handle a dialogue on the terminal, to analyse student responses and to decide how the lesson should be continued.

CAIPAS uses 6 files with read (R) and write (W) access containing:

(A) a library of standard messages to the students (R).
(B) the lesson (R).
(C) the identification of an authorised user and some data concerning the point at which the lesson is to be continued for a new session or after a system breakdown (R, W).
(D) the student performance records (student data) according to the MCSD-format in ASCII code (W).
(E) mathematical functions defined in the courseware or by the student during a session (R, W).
(F) scratch-data for the page-back mechanism (R, W).

All these files have different but simple structures. To avoid complex file structures which decrease the portability of the program, the data have not been integrated into 1 or 2 files.

Because of its importance to author and teacher it makes sense to store the performance records on a separate floppy disk to which the student gets no physical access. The other files do not need to be protected in this way. So we use two floppies: a system floppy containing also performance records of many students and the "lesson floppy" which is unique to each student for the duration of his lesson.

The following are the most important features supported by CAIPAS:

no modifications are necessary to present any lesson which is presentable by other interpreters, if the same type of terminal is used;
the lessons have to be distributed to the students on personal floppy disks which are protected by a password;

the program will be started automatically after switching on the computer. Next the student has to enter date, time, name of the lesson and his password;

all responses of the student will be recorded together with data to identify student, lesson, date and time, position in the lesson, classification of the (un) anticipated response and the complete response. It is possible to list and edit the student data on the microcomputer, and a report generator is also available on a large computer;

the student can send messages to the teacher or author. The messages are marked and stored along with the student data and may be filtered out by the report generator;

the lessons may contain restart points which define entries at which a lesson may be continued at a subsequent session or after a system breakdown. An unfinished lesson will be continued at the immediately preceding restart point;

a software-controlled page-back mechanism is provided. All input and output appearing on the screen is stored in a circularly used scratch file from the beginning of each session. Simple commands are available making it possible to page back and forward through exact copies of the previous contents of the screen. The number of past screens accessible depends on the space allocated for the scratch file;

the student is able to work in a calculation mode where this is permitted. Single-line-expressions. can be calculated using constants, variables, functions, small matrices and strings. He can use all these elements if he is permitted to do so, for example the lesson involves a test of his skill in extracting square roots, then the use of the system function SQUAREROOT would be prohibited. The use of this mode is stored along with the student data;

time-excess is a possible anticipated answer;

the cursor on the screen can be controlled by the lesson;

a set of service programs is available to the manager of the system.

These and other features of CAIPAS are described in detail by Smit[14].

THE USE OF CAIPAS

Because CAIPAS was designed to present courseware a user should get a copy of the lessons he chooses to learn. In the current implementation the student needs a floppy disk which has been assigned to him for personal use. The manager or supervisor who controls the CAI service has to prepare a floppy containing the courseware by writing the name of the student and a password on it. Although it is possible to designate one floppy to several students at the same time, we advise giving every student his own copy. We use 8 in. floppy disks which can store 250 kbyte–1 Mbyte depending on the density and the number of sides. In our experience, one floppy with 250 kbyte can contain courseware to provide sessions of up to 10 h of dialogue. Because of the high compactness of the CAIASCO code, the size of the lesson files is mainly dependent on the amount of text written by the author.

The student has to insert the lesson floppy into the microcomputer. After switching on the microcomputer, CAIPAS will be started automatically and the name of the lesson, the password and the current date and time are requested. The student will then follow the lesson from the appropriate entry point. During the session he can go into calculation-mode and he can review the dialogue. He is always able to send messages to the teacher by entering a response starting with an exclamation mark and a colon. He can stop a lesson immediately whenever input is requested, but it is recommended to use the logical exits from a lesson.

Although it is possible to use a microcomputer with only one floppy disk unit, we think it is better to separate data about the system and the student's performance from the courseware itself. In order to provide sufficient space for the student data, but also to protect the contents of the floppy disks against damage and violation of privacy, the system floppy contains only software to present lessons and no system utility programs. Also, the system floppy cannot be physically removed by the student.

For the manager of computers on which CAIPAS is used, three service programs exist. The first one prepares the lessons which are distributed from the authoring computers in the machine-independent CAIASCO-code for presentation to the student. Referencing by labels inside a lesson has to be replaced by referencing by pointers relative to the beginning of the lesson file. This is necessary to yield low response-times because floppy disks are rather slow devices. Independently of the size of a lesson, only one access to the floppy disk is needed to fetch a new frame. Once more copies can be made with standard utility programs.

The second program is needed to assign a copy of a lesson to a particular student. This program requests the name of the student and a new password. It is also used to inspect or change some of these data and to allow or prohibit the use of the page-back and calculation features. With this program, the file with student data may be initialised and also listed. If this file is almost full, CAIPAS will send a message to the terminal to call the manager to insert a new system disk with free space for the student data. Depending on the free space, several thousands of student records (average length 35 bytes) can be stored on one floppy. The student data have to be collected from all system disks in use to make them available to the report generating program of the MCSD.

The last service program is used to create, inspect and modify the library with standard messages of CAIPAS. This makes it simple to create a library containing messages in another natural language.

DISCUSSION

Unlike the other interpreters of the MCSD, CAIPAS has been designed to be portable. It was completely written in UCSD Pascal with as little as possible use of the extensions of this implementation to Standard Pascal[14]. Only one routine has to be written in the assembly language of the specific microcomputer, because UCSD Pascal does not have a feature to cancel a READ statement after a certain time delay, and such cancellation is needed to handle the time-excess feature during input. If the microcomputer has no clock, or if one does not like to use the mechanism of time-excess, CAIPAS can be a 100% Pascal program. It is thus easily portable to microcomputers on which UCSD Pascal runs (including Apple-II, DEC LSI-11 and PDP-11, Intel 8080, Motorola 6800, North Star Horizon, Rockwell 6502, TI 9900, W D Microengine and Zilog Z-80, and soon on the 8086, MC 68000 and Z8000). The program should be run with at least 48 kbyte memory and one or two floppy disk units and about 50 kbyte for the CAIPAS system files (excluded the space for UCSD Pascal).

At least 200 kbyte is needed to store courseware. Although we have not yet transfered CAIPAS to any other complete Pascal implementations for microcomputers or for mini- and large computers, such transfer should be straightforward.

To support good portability, CAIPAS and the service programs have been designed and largely documented in a carefully structured way. Although the portability of CAIPAS will be good, it is anticipated that some slight modifications will have to be made for use with non-UCSD compilers and interpreters. For example, it is desirable to suppress certain error messages from the operating system since errors such as dividing by zero and some floating point errors should be handled directly by CAIPAS and this suppression will be system-dependent.

Another important item requiring mention is the response-time of CAIPAS, i.e. the time that elapses between transmission of the student's response and the first reaction of CAIPAS which the student sees on the display. It has been accepted that response-time in CAI dialogues has to be small (less than 2 s) with a small deviation.

Using stand-alone microcomputers, response-time depends only on the speed of the processor and the external memory and on the characteristics of the software. The current implementation under UCSD Pascal on LSI-11-type microcomputers with single density 8 in. floppy disk units (average access time 483 ms) guarantees mean response-time below 2 s for most lessons.

One should note that UCSD Pascal and CAIPAS are executed by a P-code interpreter which is rather slow compared to the execution of compiled Pascal programs. Moreover modern, floppy disk units support double density disks with half access times. So we may conclude that the response-time of CAIPAS will be sufficient on modern microcomputers.

In the near future we shall try out the portability and the performance of CAIPAS on different micro- and other computers on which good Pascal compilers and interpreters exist.

Acknowledgements—I am most grateful to the student R. J. M. Smit who played a major role in the development of the program. For their careful scrutiny of the English text I am indebted to D. McConalogue and P. J. van der Hoff. The technical assistance of B. Broere and of Ms J. W. Pesch, who did all the typing is also gladly acknowledged.

REFERENCES

1. Gerhold G. A., Teacher-produced CAI, In *Computer Assisted Learning* (Edited by R. Lewis and E. D. Tagg), Proc. of IFIP/TC 3 Working Conference, Roehampton, England, 3–7 September 1979. North Holland, Amsterdam (1980).
2. Brandt R. C. and Knapp B. H., *Video Computer Authoring System (version 1.1c): User's Guide*. University of Utah (1979).
3. Sugarman R. A., Second chance for computer assisted instruction. *IEEE Spectrum* 29–37 (1979).
4. Van der Mast C, A modular CAI system. In *Aspects of Educational Technology Volume XII* (Edited by R. Budgett). Kogan Page, London (1978).
5. Lower, S. K., IPS: a new authoring language for computer assisted in instruction. *J. Comput.-Based Instr.* 119–124 (1980).

6. Maybry F. J., Appel A. W. and Levy A. H., A microprocessor based CAI system with graphic capabilities. In *Proceedings/1978 Conference*, Dallas TX, ADCIS (1978).

7. Van der Mast C., The presentation of courseware by microcomputers using a modular CAI system. *ACM SIGCUE Bull.* 2–11 (1978).

8. Control Data Micro Station, product information Control Data Corporation, MN (1980).

9. Brahan J. W. and Wesbaum M. L., NATAL-74: first results. In *Proceedings/1978 Conference*, Dallas, TX, ADCIS (1978).

10. Frye C. H. *et al.*, *PLANIT author's guide and PLANIT language reference manual*. System Development Corporation, Santa Monica (1970).

11. Chambers J. A. and Sprecher J. W., Computer Assisted Instruction: Current trends and critical issues. *Commun. ACM* 332–342 (1980).

12. de Haas H., Design and implementation of a CAIASCO interpreter under RSX-11M. Internal report, Department of Informatics, Delft University of Technology (1980) (in Dutch).

13. Kwekel F., A CAI presentation system on a PDP 11/03 micro-computer. Internal report, Department of Informatics, Delft University of Technology (1980).

14. Smit R. J. M., A system to present lessons on microcomputers written in UCSD Pascal. Report INF80-03, Department of Informatics, Delft University of Technology (1980) (in Dutch).

15. Jensen K. and Wirth N., *Pascal User Manual and Report*, 2nd Edition. Springer-Verlag, New York (1978).

Comput. & Educ. Vol. 6, pp. 45 to 50, 1982
Printed in Great Britain

0360-1315/82/010045-06$03.00/0
Pergamon Press Ltd

AN INVESTIGATION OF THE MICROCOMPUTER AS A MATHEMATICS TEACHING AID

RICHARD J. PHILLIPS

Shell Centre for Mathematical Education, University of Nottingham, Nottingham NG7 2RD, England

Abstract—Three short computer programs are being developed to aid the teaching of elementary graph interpretation in the first years of the secondary school. They run on a microcomputer which is used as a teaching aid and which supplements rather than replaces existing teaching methods. The programs exploit a variety of effective graphics including animation. A long term aim is to prepare the pupil more adequately for graphs in the real world by shifting the teaching emphasis from graph plotting to graph interpretation, and by greater use of graphs which depict data rather than mathematical functions. Classroom trials suggest that the programs are useful for class teaching and with small remedial groups. However, it is argued that the success of computer-based teaching material can only be accurately assessed when it is available to a substantial number of schools.

INTRODUCTION

Like books and television, the microcomputer is a medium of communication, and like other media there are some ideas it will communicate well, while others are best expressed in a different way. In education we are beginning to appreciate the variety of uses for microcomputers, but we are a long way from discovering what they do best.

It is an area where prediction is very difficult. Consider what are arguably the two most successful computer games: *Space Invaders* and the rather more cerebral *Adventure*. It would be impossible to predict the success of these games from a written specification of what they do. And it is no easier to predict what will be the best uses for microcomputers in secondary education in 5 or 10 years time.

At present, schools are receiving a lot of suggestions about how to use their microcomputers and there is also some systematic research to evaluate applications. Although these activities are extremely important they face a serious limitation: it is sometimes apparent that material which works well in the hands of the group who developed it, fails to get taken up by others. For "survival outside captivity", computer-based teaching material must cope with a long series of practical obstacles, it must also fulfil a need, and it must appeal to the imagination of the teacher who is using it. No one can accurately predict such a complex process, and therefore it is important that the process should be set moving as speedily as possible. Only by giving teachers a wide choice of good materials and ideas which can be implemented on the computers they have, will we begin to learn what really works; and without this knowledge we cannot know whether the considerable effort put into writing any particular kind of computer-based learning material is justified. Material, ostensibly for secondary schools, is often developed to run on machines which very few schools possess, and which they are unlikely to be able to afford. While such projects are often exciting and innovative, they ultimately delay one of the most important ways of advancing the art: the need to get material out into many schools and see what really works.

This is not an argument for sacrificing quality at the expense of speed. Unless material is good it won't be used for long, but on the other hand, excellent material will also not be used if there are no schools that can run it, and more important, we will have missed the chance to prove its excellence.

TEACHING AIDS FOR MATHEMATICS

This paper is a progress report on the development of some computer programs which are teaching aids for mathematics [1]. They are being developed with Burkhardt and Swan at the Shell Centre for Mathematical Education, University of Nottingham, and we are working closely with the ITMA* team in Plymouth.

Our aim is to produce challenging and well-tested microcomputer teaching aids which can be used with the resources which many British schools possess. The "teaching aid" style requires the use of a single microcomputer in the classroom which is under the teacher's control. The machine can be called upon to do many things including simulation, graphics display and data logging, as well as more anthropomorphic tasks such as playing games or providing humour [2].

* Investigations on Teaching with Microcomputers as an Aid, College of St Mark & St John, Plymouth.

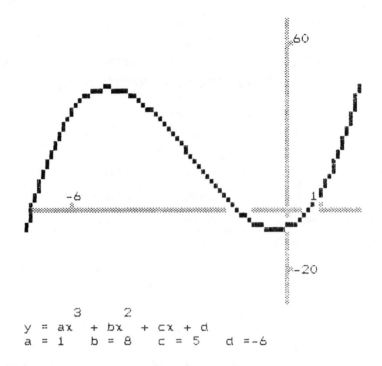

Fig. 1. Graphs of functions are taught extensively but they are rarely encountered after a pupil leaves school. The illustration is from the author's Menu Graph Plotter.

Part of this work has been directed at the problems of teaching graph interpretation in the first years of the secondary school. Quite a number of educational computer programs have been concerned with plotting mathematical functions on Cartesian graphs, but our interest has been mostly in graphs which depict data. Graphs are an especially useful part of the mathematics curriculum: whatever one's job, hobbies or interests it is difficult to avoid encountering them. However a number of studies point to the fact that school leavers and adults frequently misinterpret graphs. These are not just minor errors in reading values from a graph, but often a complete failure to understand what a particular graph is about; a common error is to interpret a graph as if it were a picture [3].

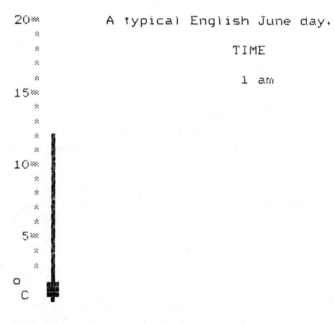

Fig. 2(a).

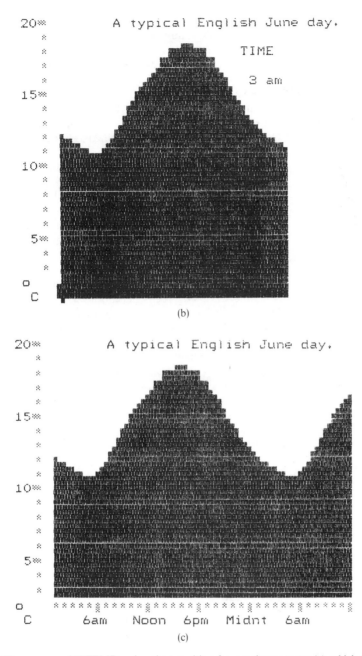

Fig. 2. The program AIRTEMP makes the transition from a thermometer (a), which is moved across the screen (b), and becomes a graph (c).

The approach described here draws from the work of Janvier [4], Burkhardt *et al.* [5] and Swan [6], and aims to prepare the pupil more adequately for graphs in the real world. It is hoped to broaden the experience of using graphs, by introducing a greater variety of graphs than is usually used in the classroom, and to shift the emphasis away from plotting graphs: in the outside world we are more likely to be reading graphs than plotting them.

One approach to first understanding graphs is to make the transition from representing quantities along a single dimension to representing them on two dimensions as on a Cartesian graph. This kind of presentation should help to dispel the idea that graphs are the same as pictures. The one dimensional representation is already very familiar from a number of experiences such as measuring things with a ruler, reading the time from the hands of a clock, and reading a speedometer on a car.

The program AIRTEMP uses the task of reading a thermometer to make the transition from one to two dimensions. When the program is first loaded the screen shows a thermometer and the time of day. It is one o'clock in the morning on a typical English day in June. The mercury in the thermometer starts to move showing how the air temperature changes throughout an average day. The next step is to consider what would happen if the thermometer is moved a small distance to the right every half an hour, while marking its reading in each position. As the program does this, it slowly builds up a graph of air temperature vs time on the screen. When it has finished, it is only necessary to put a scale along the time axis to complete the transition to a two dimensional graph. This transition can be repeated a number of times to make it quite clear. It is then up to the teacher to show that the graph is useful. It can be used to answer questions such as: When is it warmest? When does the sun rise? When is the temperature 17°? These could be answered by watching the thermometer move but it is faster and more accurate to read them from the graph.

AIRTEMP makes use of the microcomputer's power to produce animated graphics. It does something which could not be done easily on a blackboard, and even with a film or video, the teacher would not have the moment-to moment control which the computer offers. But animation is not the only reason for using a micro to teach graphs. Its power of computation allows new and complicated situations to be graphed rapidly, making it possible for children to check their intuitions about what shape a graph will be. These aspects of teaching with a microcomputer are illustrated in two further programs: the first is about the water level in a bath, and the second is concerned with the rate at which a forest fire spreads.

The bath program, which is called EUREKA, illustrates what happens to the water level when a bath is filled, when a man gets in, and when the plug is pulled out. These operations are shown pictorially in the upper half of the screen, while in the lower half a graph is plotted of water level against time. The idea of gradients can be discussed by considering the different gradients which result from filling the bath, from emptying it, or from emptying it with the taps left on. Step functions are illustrated by the man entering and leaving the bath. The man can also be made to "sing" to suggest the passing of time with no change in the water level.

There are a number of ways to use this program. One possibility is to start by showing the class the most usual sequence of events when someone has a bath, watching both the animation and the graph being drawn. Then the microcomputer is turned off and the class are asked to think of a different sequence of events; for example, the man has to get out to answer the telephone, or he forgets to turn the taps off and the bath overflows. Each pupil is asked to write his sequence down in words and then to sketch a graph of water level vs time. Pupils can then be asked to exchange graphs and try to discover the sequence of events that they describe. A number of graphs can be discussed by the whole class, finishing with some pupils typing the events into the microcomputer to check whether the computer's graph agrees with the predicted one.

The forest fire program, ISLAND, was developed from teaching materials devised by Malcolm Swan. It illustrates what happens to a forest fire as it spreads across an island which is uniformly

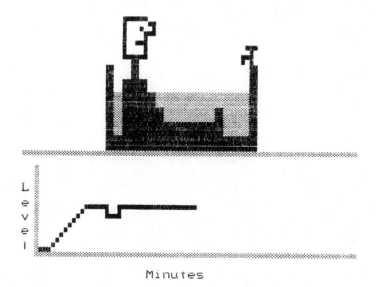

Fig. 3. What events does the graph describe? The picture shows what was happening when the last point was plotted. The illustration is from EUREKA.

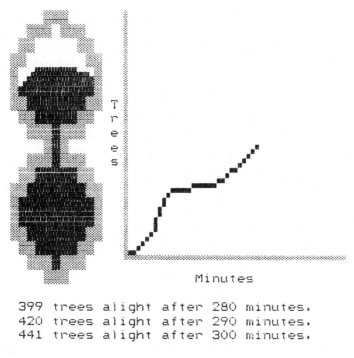

```
399 trees alight after 280 minutes.
420 trees alight after 290 minutes.
441 trees alight after 300 minutes.
```

Fig. 4. A forest fire has started on an island, and the graph plots the number of trees alight vs time. The illustration is from ISLAND.

covered with dry trees and where there is no wind. The program show the fire spreading and simultaneously plots a graph of the number of trees destroyed vs time. The shape of the graph depends on the shape of the island and where the fire starts. The user can choose between two standard shapes of island, or draw a new shape, and has complete control over where the fire starts.

One way to use this program in the classroom is to start by thinking about what would happen when the fire starts in the centre of a roughly circular island. Before the computer is switched on, children can simulate this on paper and draw the corresponding graph. Then they might consider what happens when the fire starts on the edge of the same island. How would this change the graph? At this point the computer could be switched on to check the shape of the graphs. The discussion could then lead into predicting the shape of the graphs from more irregular islands, and predictions could be tested on the computer.

The microcomputer shares a number of features with other classroom teaching aids such as a blackboard, a film strip projector or a working model, but in some ways it is unique. Like the blackboard it is a flexible device which can be adapted in a matter of seconds to whatever is being discussed in the classroom, but unlike the blackboard it can calculate rapidly and produce graphical displays which move. This gives scope for activities which were previously impossible. In the ISLAND program, a child may draw an island with a complicated shape and want to know what kind of graph it will produce. The chances are that this particular problem has never been tackled before so it won't appear in any textbook, nor is it feasible to solve it by hand calculation as this would take too long. But the program can both calculate the answer rapidly and illustrate it with graphics which may help to teach an appreciation of why a graph should take a particular shape.

THE DEVELOPMENT OF TEACHING UNITS

Many obstacles lie between the development of materials for the microcomputer and their actual use in the classroom. The ITMA group has given a lot of consideration to the practical difficulties of using computer materials in a lesson. For example, it is important that programs should never crash even if they are being misused. If a program crashes when it is being used with a class, it may not only discourage the teacher from using that program again, but discourage any use of computer-based material.

The graph programs AIRTEMP, EUREKA and ISLAND have been tested in a number of schools, and observation of their use is still continuing. Many small practical problems have emerged which have been rectified by making changes to the programs or their manual. One special difficulty has been the poor quality of graphs in low resolution graphics: when the line of a graph is built up by plotting small squares the effect is crude but often quite satisfactory for teaching purposes. However, occasionally things go wrong, for example, when small differences between one graph and another are not shown clearly. Teachers will tend to blame limitations of this kind on the programs. The difficulty is easily overcome by drawing the graphs using high resolution graphics (for example, on a Research Machines 380Z Computer), but at present few schools have facilities for high resolution graphics. It is tempting to release only high resolution versions of the programs, but this limits the availability of the materials and makes it harder to assess the value of the programs for general classroom use.

Although the programs are intended as teaching aids this does not rule out their use by individual children. There appears to be some value in allowing individuals to explore the different shapes of graph produced by ISLAND, using islands which they have drawn themselves. EUREKA may be valuable for the remedial teaching of mathematics. One child with a very poor understanding of graphs played with the options offered by the program for several minutes, and so built up a complicated graph on the screen. He then had little difficulty in interpreting the graph in terms of his actions. EUREKA and similar programs could provide a gentle introduction to graph interpretation without the need to introduce algebraic concepts.

CONCLUSIONS

Three experimental programs for a microcomputer have been described which help to teach elementary graph interpretation in the first years of the secondary school. The microcomputer is used as a teaching aid under the teacher's control and supplements rather than replaces existing teaching methods. The programs exploit the microcomputer's power to produce a variety of effective graphics, including simple animation. They also use its power of computation which makes it easy to check guesses about the shape of graphs. There is considerable scope for more programs of this kind, although the success of this kind of material can only be accurately assessed when it is available to a substantial number of schools.

REFERENCES

1. Phillips R. J., Swan M. and Burkhardt H., Airtemp, Eureka and Island. ITMA, Plymouth (1980).
2. Burkhardt H. and Fraser R., Teaching style and program design. ITMA, Plymouth (1980).
3. Hart K., Children's understanding of mathematics 11–16. Murray (1981).
4. Janvier C., The interpretation of complex Cartesian graphs representing situations—studies and teaching experiments. Ph.D. Thesis, Shell Centre for Mathematical Education, University of Nottingham (1978).
5. Burkhardt H., Treilibs V., Stacey K. and Swan M., Beginning to tackle real problems. Shell Centre for Mathematical Education, Nottingham (1980).
6. Swan M., The language of graphs: a collection of teaching materials. Shell Centre for Mathematical Education, Nottingham (1980).

Comput. & Educ. Vol. 6, pp. 51 to 54, 1982
Printed in Great Britain

0360-1315/82/010051-04$03.00/0
Pergamon Press Ltd

SOME BENEFITS OF MICRO-COMPUTERS IN TEACHING STATISTICS

W. J. EMOND

Department of Mathematics and Computer Studies, Dundee College of Technology, Bell Street,
Dundee DD1 1HG, Scotland

Abstract—Using computer programs written in BASIC and the graphics facilities of micro-computers, students can be made aware of the assumptions of statistical models. The paper deals with the author's approach to two topics—linear regression and the design of experiments which are usually taught in appreciation courses for students not specialising in Statistics.

INTRODUCTION

For many years calculating machines and computers have been used to aid students in the arithmetical computation required for the statistical analysis of data. Almost every computer has an associated "statistical package" which may, or may not, be efficient in its technique or in its presentation of results.

The idea behind this paper however, is not to produce yet another package, but to demonstrate the use made of a micro-computer as an *aid to teaching and understanding* topics in statistics rather than assist with arithmetical computation.

Very many courses in statistics at the elementary level are taught from a purely arithmetical view point, and give little opportunity for students to gain an understanding of the assumptions and models involved in the "theory" of the subject. This is especially true of statistics courses given to social science, life science and business studies students. It is regrettable that little effort is made to develop a "feel" for the true art of the statistician.

The approach taken by the author in teaching statistics to such students has been to attempt to get away from the purely computational emphasis and to move towards a development of a knowledge of some statistical models and associated assumptions, and above all, an intuitive understanding of statistical processes.

MICRO-COMPUTERS IN THE TEACHING OF STATISTICS

As well as carrying out routine statistical calculations the relatively cheap graphics facilities which are now available make it possible for the models and assumptions involved in statistical models to be presented in graphical form rather than the usual lists of numbers.

The equipment used in the development of the programs was an Apple II micro-computer which had 64 K of store, a single disc drive and a colour T.V. monitor.

Programs have been written to aid the teaching of linear regression and the elementary design of experiments and the associated analysis of the results. (Copies of the programs which are written in BASIC, are available from the author.)

LINEAR REGRESSION

The approach to the topic of linear regression is firstly to consider the situations in which two dimensional scatter diagrams can arise, examples being drawn from the appropriate discipline. Having drawn a scatter diagram the problem of drawing a line of "best fit" by eye and by least squares is discussed and the computational aspects mastered by the use of simple data and by use of a computer program.

Having mastered the arithmetical aspects students can now be exposed to the linear regression model and its assumptions, viz:

Ass. I   Model: $\eta = \alpha + \beta x$
where η is the true regression line

Ass. II   Observation: $y_i = \alpha + \beta x_i + z_i, i = 1, 2, \ldots, n,$
where z_i are independent $N(0, \sigma^2)$ variables.

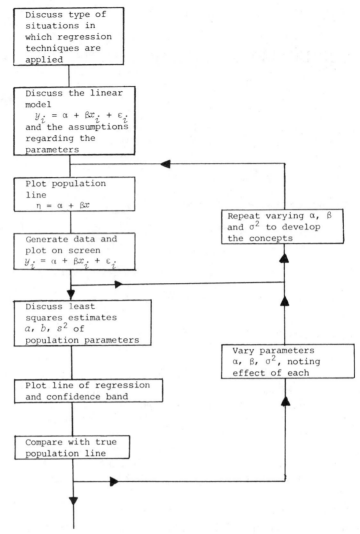

Fig. 1

To use the program REGSIM.WJE the student inputs values for the parameters α, β and σ^2 and the number of observations required. The program displays the random generated data points. By varying α, β and σ^2 students quickly develop an awareness of the significance of each parameter.

After a suitable prompt the program then goes to find the least squares estimates of α, β and σ^2 and draws the least squares line on the scatter diagram. At this stage students can observe the "fit" of the line to the data points. Repetition of the "experiment" so far with the same α, β and σ^2, gives students an opportunity to observe the changes in the estimates and in the least squares line of regression and measure of "fit". This reinforces the ideas of sampling.

The program next plots a confidence band for the true regression line, $\eta = \alpha + \beta x$. Students at this stage are made aware of the fact that some of the observations may be outwith the confidence band. This then leads to discussion of the problems of prediction and extrapolation via least squares. (These are usually the areas of application which are of interest to such students.)

It is important that the program is not treated as yet another game on a micro-computer and that the values of the parameters input to the program are recorded and compared with their estimates. For this important purpose it is recommended that *pro forma* sheets are issue to students.

The approach to developing an understanding and feel for linear regression can be summarised by the flow chart in Fig. 1.

THE DESIGN AND ANALYSIS OF EXPERIMENTS

The most common problem in teaching the elementary aspects of the statistical design of experiments is to develop in students an intuitive idea of what happens before the results are presented in the usually rectangular table for analysis of variance. The program DESSIM.WJE is based on a completely randomised design with three levels for the factor, viz.

$$x_{ij} = \mu + T_i + z_{ij}, \qquad i = 1, 2, 3,$$
$$\Sigma T_i = 0$$
$$j = 1, 2, \ldots$$

where x_{ij} is the observation from the jth plot which has had treatment i, μ is an overall mean, T_i is the effect of treatment i and z_{ij} is an independent $N(0, \sigma^2)$ variable.

Having input the values of the parameters μ, T_i and σ^2 the student is presented with a picture of an L-shaped field which is divided into 14 plots (assumed to be homogeneous). The student is then invited to allocate randomly the treatments A, B and C to the 14 plots. This leads to a discussion of how this might be achieved and of the problem of unequal numbers of observations per treatment.

The program then generates the yield for each plot and presents the yields on the associated plot in the L-shaped field. Only after this is the student given the yield in the normal rectangular form. The program finally carries out an analysis of variance of the data and gives the results in the usual ANOVA table.

By varying the parameter σ^2 with constant values of μ and T_i enables students to develop a feel for the sensitivity of the Mean Square Ratio and for the estimate of the variance σ^2. The approach to using this program is given in Fig. 2.

SUMMARY

It is not intended that the programs are in any way self-contained. The author is a firm believer in the concept of the *teacher* using all the teaching aids possible to develop in his students a fundamental

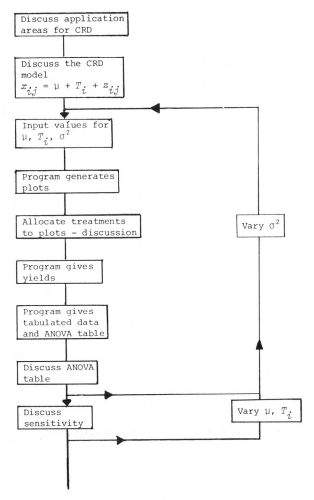

Fig. 2

understanding of statistics. The programs, however, have been used to enable students gain an insight into the way statistical models are applied.

The advent of micro-computers with relatively cheap colour graphics facilities has enabled these programs to be developed.

Acknowledgement—I would like to thank Mr S. L. Gardner of the Computer Centre at Dundee College of Technology for his keen interest in the design and his help with the program DESSIM.WJE.

REFERENCES

1. Johnson N. L. and Leone F. C., *Statistics and Experimental Design in Engineering and Physical Sciences*, 2nd Edition. Wiley, New York (1977).
2. Moonen J., The teaching of Statistics and CAL. In *Computer Assisted Learning* (Edited by R. Lewis and E. D. Tagg). IFIP/North Holland, Amsterdam (1980).

Comput. & Educ. Vol. 6, pp. 55 to 60, 1982
Printed in Great Britain

0360-1315/82/010055-06$03.00/0
Pergamon Press Ltd

COMPUTER ASSISTED SUPPORT FOR BLIND STUDENTS

THE USE OF A MICROCOMPUTER LINKED VOICE SYNTHESIZER

T. Vincent

Manchester Regional Office, The Open University, 70 Manchester Road, Chorlton-cum-Hardy, Manchester M21 1PQ, England

Abstract—The generation of computer programs (in BASIC) for a limited configuration microcomputer with synthetic speech as the only output medium is described. This has involved the development of a dictionary/conversion program that replaces PRINT, INPUT, DATA and string statements in a program written for VDU output, provides the phonetic commands for a Voice Synthesizer, and incorporates subroutines that will assist a blind student to use the programs.

Developments in microcomputer technology have created new opportunities for the application of computers in teaching. This is particularly true where cost has previously been an inhibiting factor; a significant feature in providing computer assisted support to blind students. This paper describes a project that commenced in 1980 with the objective of producing computer programs (written in BASIC) that could be used by blind students using a low-cost microcomputer system with synthetic speech as the only output medium.

BLIND STUDENTS IN THE OPEN UNIVERSITY

Since 1970, the Open University has made extensive use of computers to support the distance teaching of undergraduate and associate students[1]. Currently, over 30,000 students each year are advised or required to make use of a computer facility either in a local Study Centre or at Summer School. Generally, this involves access via a teletype to one of three main-frame computers. Various microcomputers are also used at Summer Schools. The computers are used for a variety of activities which include programming, data-handling, simulation and tutorials.

For the blind student, there are two methods which can be adopted to make use of the Student Computer Service facilities offered by the Open University. Firstly, a normal sighted person can be present at the terminal to relay details of computer generated questions and responses to the student. This arrangement can be satisfactory; however, it does require the presence of a second person for long periods, and it excludes independent use. The second method allows independent access by using the commercially available Optacon[2]. This device transduces information that appears under a lens into a character representation on a pad of vibrating pins. Hence, computer output on a screen or teletype can be scanned and read. At present, the cost of this device has resulted in only a small number of students using this method of access. Generally, blind students avoid courses where there is a significant amount of computer use involved. The number of students taking programming courses is very small.

SYNTHETIC SPEECH

Direct synthetic speech output from a computer terminal would help to overcome the problems experienced by blind students using a VDU or teletype. Some progress has been made in the U.S.A. with the development of commercially available talking terminals[3]; however, the wider application of these new peripherals has probably been inhibited by their cost.

Good quality synthetic speech is difficult to achieve because of the dynamic properties of the human-speech mechanism that have to be simulated. It is well known that essential components are required to generate human speech[4]; research continues into the development of hardware and software to exploit this knowledge. Synthetic speech, however, is still not acceptable to critical ears but may well be acceptable if this means of communication creates opportunities that would not otherwise exist.

Three techniques can be identified with the generation of synthetic speech: speech-by-rule, look-up tables, and compressed digital speech.

Speech-by-rule

Computer-generated speech from unrestricted text take place in two discrete steps. Firstly, the text is converted into a series of commands that are associated with a voice generation unit. Secondly, the commands are interpreted by the voice synthesizer to produce audible output. Commonly, this is achieved by using a speech-by-rule computer program which translates text into its phonetic equivalents using a restricted set of commands that are available to the voice synthesizer which, in turn, creates synthetic speech from the phonetic commands.

A comprehensive speech-by-rule algorithm has been reported[5] which uses less than 1000 pronunciation rules to produce generally acceptable speech quality. The algorithm was originally written for a PDP11/45—the rules occupying approx. 11 K of memory, pronunciation code and tables 5 K, and a further 2 K for the interactive display and maintenance of tables. The algorithm has been implemented subsequently on a microcomputer system (Intel 8080A-based) at the U.S. National Institute of Health[6].

Speech-by-rule synthesis has a particular advantage in that it has an unlimited vocabulary.

Look-up tables

This technique differs from speech-by-rule in step 1; in this case the phonetic equivalent of words are derived from a table of information rather than by synthesis. This requires alternative methods for generating the phonetic equivalents and storing the information in memory prior to extraction and transmission to the voice synthesizer when a word or phrase is output.

The vocabulary is limited by the size of the look-up table which, in turn, is directly dependent on the amount of memory available. Typically, 100 words and their phonetic equivalents can be stored in a table occupying 2 K of memory. An additional amount of memory is required to store, retrieve and transmit the phonetic commands to the voice synthesizer.

Compressed digital speech

At the simplest level, speech can be recorded in an analogue form on magnetic tape. The addition of addressing and timing information on a second track allows the recorded audio to be replayed under computer control. The serious disadvantage of this system is the slow serial access that a magnetic tape provides.

The access time can be considerably improved by using a random-access audio disk; this has been successfully implemented for the Plato computer-based education system. Twenty minutes of high quality speech can be pre-recorded with the advantage of random access and minimal data transfer for message selection. However, a sophisticated disk drive is required to manage the disk.

OPEN UNIVERSITY PROJECT

The prime objectives of the project described in this paper are (a) to provide synthetic speech output for blind students using computer programs (BASIC) on a microcomputer, and (b) to use a low-cost commerically available speech synthesis system that could eventually lead to it being made widely available to students.

The first objective excludes the need to consider the support for computer programming. This simplifies the project as, on the whole, an individual computer program has a limited text output requirement which can be met by a restricted vocabulary that incorporates individual alpha-numeric and other keyboard characters.

The second objective proved to be very restrictive—the system finally selected was a Tandy TRS-80 microcomputer and Voice Synthesizer.

Hardware

Two configurations were chosen: one for program development; the other for use by blind students to run programs.

Development system	Student system
Keyboard/VDU	Keyboard
48K CPU	16K CPU
2 Disk drives	Cassette recorder
Cassette recorder	Voice synthesizer
Line printer	
Voice synthesizer	

It was decided not to include a VDU with the student system during the development stage as experience could be gained of program requirements by a wide range of users (not necessarily blind students) when visual output was not available. In practice, a monitor or TV output can be provided readily which will be useful if a blind student is assisted by, for example, a tutor.

Voice synthesizer

The TRS-80 Voice Synthesizer is capable of producing 62 phonemes; the commands to produce these speech units are generated from the microcomputer software.

As the Voice Synthesizer is driven by phonetic commands, it can be used as the second stage for both synthesis-by-rule and look-up table techniques. The choice between these techniques was determined by the nature of the computer programs that would be used by students. Synthesis-by-rule was eliminated because (a) an individual program has a restricted output requirement that can be met by an appropriate vocabulary and (b) considerable time would have been needed to develop a software package for this technique.

The interface of the Voice Synthesizer has been designed so that a BASIC PRINT can be used as an output command. This has been achieved by address mapping the interface into the last 32 locations (992–1023) of the video display. Any method of PRINTing, POKEing or loading into these locations, combined with a "device select" character (a"?"), causes the Voice Synthesizer to produce the specified sounds. A second "?" closes the device.

The following BASIC program illustrates one method of inputting any combination of the Voice Synthesizer's 62 phonetic commands and producing the equivalent sound:

```
10 INPUT "ENTER PHONEME(S)"; A$
20 PRINT @ 992, "?"; A$; "?";
```

which can be compared with the input/output statements of text for a VDU:

```
10 INPUT "ENTER WORD"; A$
20 PRINT @ 992, A$
```

This relatively easy adaptation of a program to provide synthetic speech output is an important feature in relation to the development of programs to use this facility.

Use of phonemes

Virtually any word in the English language can be produced using the 62 phonemes provided in the TRS-80 Voice Synthesizer. In the absence of a translator, a dictionary of words and equivalent phonetic commands is created within a look-up table. As an aid to this, the sound units are assigned special symbols. For example, the vowel sound in "beg" is represented by EH1; the shorter version of this sound is EH3 and is used in a word like "jacket". The number at the end of the symbol indicating the duration of the sound (an inverse relationship).
An example of this construction is:

word			—	seven					
phoneme symbols									
(for notation and reference)	—	S	EH3	EH2	V	EH2	N	N	
ASCII symbols									
(to be PRINTed)	—	S	5	4	V	4	N	N	

The BASIC statement which would result in the Voice Synthesizer "speaking" the word "seven" would be:

```
10 PRINT @ 992, "? S54V4NN ?"
```

Programs incorporating synthetic speech output

Initially, trial programs were written for the TRS-80 microcomputer that incorporated output to the Voice Synthesizer with phonetic commands extracted from a dictionary, developed manually outside of the microcomputer, to assist in the production of the appropriate PRINT statements. This method did not prove to be entirely satisfactory, and the need for a dictionary resident within the microcomputer soon became apparent. In addition, facilities to experiment with phonetic constructions, and to provide updating, printing and sorting for the dictionary were also identified.

The development of a memory resident, interactive dictionary proved to be a valuable aid to the programmer; however, there still remained a time-consuming step when programs were being revised or debugged. Running a program where all the output is via the Voice Synthesizer cannot be accelerated in the same way as with video display where PRINT statement output can be presented at a rate that is only limited by the output rate to the VDU. Normal speech rate is much slower than this, and cannot be speeded-up as it would then become undistinguishable.

To overcome this difficulty, it has proved helpful to have two versions of any program—one with video output and the other with synthetic speech output. This has resulted in a major revision of the dictionary support software to include the automatic conversion of a source program (video output) to an object program (synthetic speech output) with the provision to (a) convert all text in strings to phonetic commands extracted from the dictionary, (b) rewrite all PRINT, INPUT, DATA and string statements, and (c) add subroutines to aid the subsequent use of the object program.

The method adopted is illustrated in Figure 1. The dictionary/conversion program is first loaded from disk into the development microcomputer system where, after initialisation, the facility exists to update or extend the dictionary using the following menu:

System Command ⟨ ⟩	Action
⟨ · ⟩	ENDS THE PROGRAM
⟨ / ⟩	UPDATES THE DICTIONARY DISK FILE
⟨ ; ⟩	LISTS PART OF THE DICTIONARY ON THE VDU
⟨ # ⟩	PRINTS DICTIONARY ON LINE PRINTER
⟨WORD⟩	REQUESTS PHONETIC COMMANDS IF WORD IS NOT IN DICTIONARY; OTHERWISE, RETURNS COMMANDS TO VDU AND VOICE SYNTHESIZER
⟨WORD⟩ ⟨@⟩	CHANGES PHONETIC COMMANDS FOR SPECIFIED WORD
⟨$⟩	OBJECT/SOURCE PROGRAM CONVERSION.

The final system command initiates the conversion of a pre-defined source program held on disk. The program is input line-by-line. Lines are separated into individual statements (where necessary) before the PRINT, INPUT, DATA and string statements are converted to synthetic speech program formats. If strings within these statements are found to have words that have not already been recorded in the dictionary, this facility is re-called to allow experimentation with phonetic command combinations until a satisfactory sound is obtained. The phonetic combination is then entered into the dictionary before returning to the object program to continue the conversion.

A typical line conversion is:

source line:

$$\text{10 PRINT ``COMPUTER SCIENCE''}$$

object line:

$$\text{10 VZ\$ = ``K7MPY(UQ/SA; * \# NTS'': GOSUB 50000}$$

In addition to the word/phonetic command conversion of the string, the line is restructured to meet the needs of a synthetic speech output subroutine [see (a) below] that is added to the object program. After all of the source program lines have been converted, several subroutines are added to facilitate the final use of the program by a blind student on the limited configuration microcomputer previously described. To date the following subroutines have been identified as essential.

(a) *Synthetic speech output*. An alternative method to that using PRINT @992,"? phonetic commands?" has been developed to accommodate lengthy strings. The PRINT method is restricted to a maximum consecutive output of 32 characters by the capacity of the Voice Synthesizer buffer. The speech output subroutine handles strings longer than 32 characters by the introduction of short delay loops at regular intervals, e.g. after every word. This has no effect on the rate of speech output but does allow the buffer time to clear.

(b) *Repetition of speech output*. This subroutine allows a student to request a repeat of the last output from the Voice Synthesizer. It is activated by pressing the "space-bar" (as an alternative to the "enter" key for continuing) at appropriate times.

(c) *Validation and chainging of input data*. It is essential that during the entry of data to an INPUT statement that the student responses can be echoed via the Voice Synthesizer, and the opportunity given to change the data. This subroutine is designed for this function. If data is satisfactory the "enter" key is pressed, if not, new data is typed. The first character received indicates that a change is being made—this method limits the number of keyboard entries, i.e. a "change data" command is not necessary.

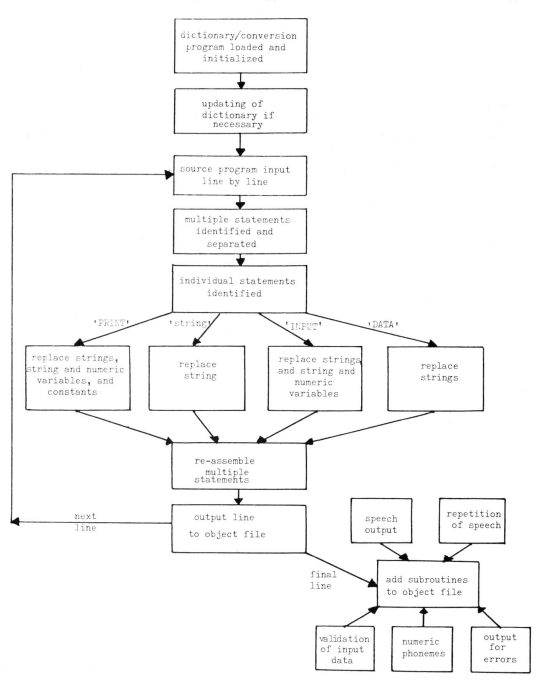

Fig. 1. Conversion of source (video output) to object program (speech output).

(d) *Numeric phonemes* (0–9). This subroutine is provided to allow numeric values to be output via the Voice Synthesizer. Numbers are "spoken" character-by-character including "+", "–", "." and the exponent.

(e) *Output of errors*. If a system error arises during the course of running the object program, this subroutine provides for a suitable error message to be output via the Voice Synthesizer.

After the addition of the subroutines, the object program is stored on disk ready to use. It can be accessed by the programmer for testing—if it is not satisfactory, it is possible to return to the source program for debugging or revision, followed by a further pass through the dictionary/conversion program to produce a revised object program. Small changes to the object program can be made directly by the normal editing facilities available on the TRS-80.

The final version of the object program is copied to cassette magnetic tape for use by a student on the limited configuration microcomputer.

Initial trials

During the first phase of the project described in this paper, two existing programs for video display output have been used for the developmental testing of the dictionary/conversion program. In addition, a special program has been written for use by a student to gain familiarity with the microcomputer keyboard. These programs are:

(a) *keyboard awareness*—designed to allow a blind student to "explore" the keyboard by (i) typing any key, (ii) responding to random requests to type particular keys, and (iii) responding to requests to type selected words. In each case the microcomputer responds through the Voice Synthesizer with characters, words or messages.

(b) *statistical analysis*—data-handling is an important application in the project. This particular program inputs and validates data, fits the function $y = mx + c$, calculates standard deviations, and outputs the results to the Voice Synthesizer. An important feature of the program is the validation of the data which would be common to many data-handling routines.

(c) *conditional registration*—an interactive program that assists with the completion of a Conditional Registration (course selection) form. Questions are asked relative to the various sections on the form and responses checked—finally, the responses are output to the cassette magnetic tape for the subsequent re-creation of a hardcopy of the completed form.

PRELIMINARY FINDINGS

The first phase of the project described in this paper has concentrated on (a) the production of a programmer support system to facilitate the incorporation of synthetic speech output into computer programs, and (b) the identification of supplementary subroutines that will assist a blind student to use a computer program.

The programmer support system has been provided by the dictionary/conversion software already described; this has proved to be an essential facility. The availability of a source program that has VDU output and a matching object program with synthetic speech output (provided by the dictionary/conversion program) is a key factor at the program development stage.

Seven subroutines have so far been identified as being necessary to incorporate into the final version of a program to be used on a limited configuration microcomputer with only synthetic speech output. The subroutines can readily be added using the dictionary/conversion program. If further subroutines are found to be necessary during future trials, it would only require a modification of the dictionary/conversion program followed by the re-conversion of the source programs.

The speech quality of the Voice Synthesizer used for the project is limited by the lack of pitch or speed control. This is evident in the monotone nature of the speech; however, this has not proved to be a problem. The programs developed so far are interactive with only short periods of synthetic speech at any one time. Any lack of quality is compensated for by the ease of use and relatively low cost of the Voice Synthesizer.

With recent announcements of new higher quality/lower cost synthetic speech chips, the prospects for blind students gaining wider access to computers is very encouraging.

Acknowledgements—The assistance of G. Stephenson in the development of the dictionary software, and P. Stableford in the phonetic translations is gratefully acknowledged.

REFERENCES

1. Bramer M. A., CAL Research Group Technical Report, No. 1, The Open University, Milton Keynes, England (1980).
2. Optacon®, Telesensory Systems, Inc., Palo Alto, CA, U.S.A.
3. Maryland Computer Services, Inc., Maryland, U.S.A. Kurzweil R., *The Kurzweil Report*, Kurzweil Computer Products, Cambridge, MA (1979).
4. Flanagan J. L., Coker C. H., Rabiner L. R., Schafer R. W. and Umeda N., *IEEE Spectrum* **7**, (1970).
5. McIlroy M. D., Computer Science Technical Report, No. 14, Bell Telephone Laboratories, Murray Hill, NY (1974).
6. Songo D. C., Allen S. I., Plexico P. S. and Morford R. A., *IEEE Spectrum* **17**, (1980).

Comput. & Educ. Vol. 6, pp. 61 to 66, 1982
Printed in Great Britain

0360-1315/82/010061-06$03.00/0
Pergamon Press Ltd

REPRESENTATION OF KNOWLEDGE IN CAL COURSEWARE

P. David Mitchell

Graduate Programme in Educational Technology, Concordia University, Montreal,
Quebec, Canada H3G 1M8

Abstract—Conceptual systems analysis analyzes the organizing principle binding related concepts, procedures, relations, etc. together. It permits the construction of visual representations of a subject matter so that the scope of this conceptual system and its subordinate and superordinate systems can be seen readily. Any teacher or instructional designer must have and use a model or representation of the subject matter, no matter how inchoate. Equally the instructional system (e.g. computer program) must incorporate a knowledge representation of the subject matter. But it must also have a representation of the student's knowledge and representation of his capability for carrying out required operations though this feature is difficult to implement today. Ideally the instructional system will have a knowledge representation of the teaching process or learning opportunities so that it or the student can select an optimal route through the knowledge structure. In the absence of such intelligent software, the use of knowledge representations as teaching aids is a valuable addition to the theory and practice of educational technology.

INTRODUCTION

Most computer based systems involve pre-stored presentations of knowledge (which seldom are tailored to the individual's personal background or learning style) and pre-stored teaching strategies (which either are fixed or essentially non-individualized with respect to learning style). Adaptive systems can be prepared but these are very costly if we seek truly individualized instruction. Yet adaptive systems can make hypotheses about the student's knowledge state, based on sample testing of his capability, and can record and use his learning rate, learning style, cognitive skills, etc. to select a new lesson. The most that we can anticipate without fundamental *theoretical* change is de-synchronized instruction where the student works at his own pace through essentially the same material as his fellows. How can we find an effective compromise solution that avoids the assumption of uniformity amongst users of CAL and permits an inexpensive way to cater to individual differences?

ADAPTIVE INSTRUCTION

Most instructional tasks and decisions described in standard texts limit the scope of instructional design to the production of lessons which can then be used on a wide scale. Yet face-to-face tutorial dialogue, which usually is assumed to be best, is an adaptive decision process in which the tutor reacts to the student's statements and actions, forming inferences about the latter's capability and testing hypotheses about what might best be presented to him. Many instructional design texts fail to communicate the utility of feedback controlled instruction. This is perfectly reasonable in so far as they are concerned with such static products as workbooks, TV programmes or other non-adaptive materials. Yet at its best, instruction involves an adaptive exchange between the student and an instructional system which generates or selects knowledge, communicates knowables (or demonstrates skills), monitors the learner's developing capability (e.g. understanding of the topic), and repeats this cycle, adapting to each student's needs. Thus lesson planning and the decision about what to present next should draw upon feedback derived from interplay between a student and the current lesson (and perhaps the student's prior capability and the rate or style of learning with earlier lessons). To do so requires human intervention. It is unlikely that any single sequence of lessons, no matter how well prepared, will prove to be optimal for everyone.

Successful teachers are flexible and able to respond with a variety of strategies. As an adaptive controller the human teacher monitors the effects of instruction on students and attempts to modify the content of his presentation, organization of topics, provision of opportunities for students to respond, discuss, etc. in order to improve the goal-directed process of enhancing student capability[9]. This process relies on dialogue both between teacher and students, and between students, to undo errors or obsolescence in knowledge, skills and attitudes. Indeed more advanced or experienced students can share their information and ideas with other students and instructors as well as learning from them.

Such a responsive educational system appears at first to be inconsistent with the notion of a self-instructional system that relies on carefully prepared and validated lessons. Yet instruction need not imply a total absence of contact with either a human monitor and controller or a set of learning resources.

Ideally it should be possible for the computer to engage in a kind of conversation with the student who will identify a topic or objective which he wishes to pursue, indicate what he already knows about the subject and would then receive a prescription suggesting a recommended sequence of learning activities that permits him to link up his present with his intended capability. This is not yet feasible at a reasonable cost. However there is a reasonable alternative that has the advantage of shifting some of the responsibility for his education from the instructional system to the student. It is rooted in a systems analytic approach to knowledge as a system. And it recognizes that what a person has learned already will affect both the knowledge that can be acquired easily and the manner of acquisition.

THE PARADOX OF INSTRUCTIONAL PLANNING

To design a lesson suitable for one student may increase difficulties for others. Let me first illustrate the instructional planner's dilemma. Suppose I were to be a guest lecturer presenting the case for a daily supplement of Vitamin E to reduce the probability of cardiovascular disease. The kinds of topics or points I might wish to make include: medical and nutritional research, experience of Vitamin E with race horses and athletes, differential effects of natural and synthetic Vitamin E, explanation of difference due to stereoisomers rather than to other nutrients etc. I would organize my lecture very differently if I knew that all of my audience were: (a) medical students; (b) nutrition students; (c) chemistry students; (d) people with a propensity to develop cardiovascular problems; (e) a mixed audience. Clearly for some people the concept of stereoisomerism and optical isomerism will be completely novel whereas others will be thoroughly familiar with it and others may know a little about optical activity but not stereoisomerism. For some the structure of d- and l-α-tocopheryl will be important in coming to understand the mechanisms involved whereas others could not cope with heterocyclic compounds. Similarly people will be differentially familiar with relevant and conflicting research and opinions. In short, the key points of this mini-curriculum are straightforward but the path to follow in leading the learners must build upon what the learner already knows. And this will be idiosyncratic or, at best, will consist of several incompatible paths (unless we begin with basics and risk boring some). Is there any way to represent this curriculum so that it may be presented via CAL but through different sequences of topics depending upon the learner's initial knowledge?

Individualized instruction requires a new approach to curriculum analysis, one similar to task analysis but stressing the structure of the subject matter. Such conceptual analysis clarifies important ideas as well as skills and, most importantly, shows their inter-relationships. It is thus a manifestation of systems analysis (dealing with knowledge as a system).

CONCEPTUAL SYSTEMIC ANALYSIS

A key idea of system theory is that a model of a system consists not only of the entities perceived as important (e.g. objects, attributes, concepts) but also their inter-relationships. The latter reflect the organizing principle perceived as binding the system together. Relationships characterize the system.

One of the core realizations of the systems analysis and research movement is that systems are organizations of entities (or ideas) that lose their essential properties when reduced to their components. Systems thinking therefore considers a system not as consisting of subsystems but rather it is expansionistic. The system is conceptualized as part of one or more larger systems which cannot properly be decomposed into components. Thus the system under consideration becomes explained in terms of its function in the *larger* system of which it is a part. (In addition systems analysis may consider component subsystems to discover how it works.) Systemic analysis is macroscopic rather than microscopic.

KNOWLEDGE AS A SYSTEM

Despite the fact that we can analyze a course and select content for lessons using the means-ends analysis of the now classical instructional design model, it is possible to approach the problem differently. Knowledge in a given discipline can be analyzed as a system of concepts, procedures, relations, criteria, etc.; these may be thought of as subsystems. Meaningful relationships exist between many of these subsystems and their relations. The subject matter representation may take a variety of forms (e.g. relational network, entailment structure; *cf.* Pask[6]). A curriculum can be constructed and content selected to exemplify the structure of knowledge and to help the student create his own understanding of the topics and their relationships.

The basic idea is simple; construct a conceptual systemic model of what may be known (or a problem to be solved) and determine whether the model contains component subsystems that are already within the person's repertoire. If so, he may begin to study any lesson which is linked to a topic that he has mastered. If not, it is necessary to subdivide each component topic into related subtopics and/or link it to other topics that are expected to bridge the gap between the target system and the individual's current capability state. Ideally the instructional designer would then consider clarifying and elaborating the various topics and linking them to other knowledge systems further removed from those that are immediate prerequisites. Naturally in some instances there will be insufficient prior knowledge and it must be instated or obviated by means of an algorithm or other job aid.

This systemic orientation to knowledge identifies topics that could include not only concepts, principles, etc. but also the cognitive processes, structures, and clusters of procedures that underly competent performance. Thus a topic label for a cognitive system can function as a label for a performance as well. By using a systemic representation of knowledge we stress the coherence amongst ideas whereby components are organized to form a meaningful whole and avoid the dilemma of the behavioral objectives movement whereby lists of objectives are created which are devoid of epistemological foundations and which destroy the sense of structure that a learner might have developed.

The interconnectedness of ideas is immediately obvious if we stop to think about any subject or topic with which we are familiar. In order to understand that topic we must understand other topics which in turn entail our understanding of further topics.

NETWORK REPRESENTATIONS

It is convenient and pedagogically useful to construct a visual representation of an area of subject matter (or, equally, a skill or value system) so that the scope of this conceptual system and each topic, or subsystem— and the relationships between topics—can be seen readily. Such a model represents the structure of knowledge for the purpose at hand. Such interconnectedness is not the familiar hierarchy. Rather the image may be that of a fish net where the knots represent the topics; grab any node and shake the net to produce the appearance of a hierarchy but note that another node could have been selected as the target topic.

Whether such a model is presented to, or created by, the student it permits understanding of topics at a variety of levels. Thus one might begin to understand a selected topic in one module but not develop further understanding without understanding related topics. Eventually one may come to understand the inter-relatedness of the subject matter as he creates his understanding of the *system* of concepts represented. This integration, in which principles, operations and groups of facts coalesce into a higher order of knowledge, involves *creation* rather than appropriation of knowledge (e.g. insight rather than recall). It is characterized by the absence of predetermined objectives (though predictions may be made of the outcome if a coalescent transformation occurs).

MULTIPLE ROUTES THROUGH KNOWLEDGE

Returning to the Vitamin E illustration, if we were to identify several different starting points through that mini-curriculum and prepare a possible perspective on the subject matter from each viewpoint we would expect to find several quite different views about the subject and its arrangement. For instance, the chemistry student might arrange it to build upon his knowledge of stereoisomerism and heterocyclic compounds and then move through biochemistry, including antioxidants, etc. before dealing with cardiovascular aspects of the problem. He might never get to foods that may provide a source of Vitamin E much less a consideration of how food processing may reduce it. A nutrition student on the other hand might begin with foods and questions of health and move toward medical research but would not necessarily get to the point of considering racemic mixtures.

What I am trying to say is this. There are many different ways of organizing or representing knowledge for individualized instruction. One of the most important problems of educational systems research is the integration of diverse perspectives of a problem or a system of knowledge into a unified representation of the system that allows us to teach and learn more effectively. A teacher-imposed organization of topics will not be equally useful for all students. It may be that the student should learn to take different perspectives but even so he might do so more efficiently if he masters one first. Such systemic understanding, especially if it is characterized by procedures, principles, theoretical hypotheses and other speculative areas, is seldom the focus of mastery-based instruction and may be ignored if the **instructional** designer follows the interventionist approach which reflects input-output systems in contradistinction to self-organizing cybernetic systems. And it is critical if we wish to personalize instruction by *building upon the learner's existing knowledge*. Today's and especially tomorrow's students should be able to build complex cognitive associations with new academic information and learn faster than their counterparts of a few decades ago.

REPRESENTATION OF KNOWLEDGE FOR PERSONALIZED TEACHING AND LEARNING

Any teacher or instructional designer who plans to individualize instruction must have and use a model or representation of the subject matter. The structure of knowledge includes facts and concepts as well as the various operations and processes which are required to understand the subject. Equally important but often neglected is the need for the instructional system (e.g. computer) to incorporate a *knowledge representation of* the *subject matter*. This may be trivial (e.g. a network of topics) or represent organic structure; it may be as complex as Pask is[6] conceptual entailment structures for conversational teaching systems. Despite the popularity of behavioral objectives, a representation of *knowledge* is more important for curriculum development than a list of behaviors. Knowledge cannot be represented best by a list structure but by a complex network of related topics (cf. research on human memory).

Similarly for personalized instruction the instructional system must have a *representation of each student's inferred knowledge state* and representations of his capability for carrying out the required operations to acquire new knowledge or skills. At its simplest this may entail only a network of topics with an indication of which have been mastered[1,4] but more complex probabilistic representations can be made which indicate the likelihood that the student will acquire (or has already mastered) a new topic. The traditional notion of prerequisites is too narrow; with a conceptual mesh there are different "prerequisites" depending upon what the learner wants to understand and where he comes from.

There are many different ways to approach a subject and therefore there exist many different possible paths through a reticulated curriculum. Individualized instruction would permit a learner to follow virtually any path of his choosing and not simply allow him to proceed through a standard sequence at his own rate.

Finally the teaching system must have a knowledge *representation of* the *teaching process*. This makes possible the selection, organization and implementation of teaching strategies and tactics matched to the learning style and capability of each student. Teaching algorithms form the basis of this knowledge representation. Chip-based devices and micro-computers are well suited to this. Indeed advances in micro-electronics make possible many opportunities but we need much basic research first.

CURRICULUM PLANNING

Here we wish to consider the macro-structure of knowledge which we intend to present to students. It becomes a curriculum if the topics can be expressed in terms of intended learning outcomes, e.g. the student will be expected to understand the knowledge system represented by this curriculum mesh. We can consider major groupings of intended learning outcomes as an objective (e.g. the student will understand the role of d-α-tocopherol in preventing heart attacks) without articulating all the component concepts and procedures. And we certainaly do not need to deal with unwieldly lists of specific "behavioural objectives" which would be more accurately termed behavioral measurements from which we may infer understanding (except for a few very specific skills) (cf. Mitchell[8]).

It will be noted that some groupings of topics have a close affinity to one another. These topics can be grouped in much the same fashion as the overall topic so we could reduce the complexity of the mesh as an initial representation and present it in more detail as an elaboration in a manner analogous to using a zoom lens to see something in more detail. We could just as easily zoom back and portray this particular conceptual system as one topic in a larger system (e.g. the Vitamin E mini-curriculum could be part of a course in nutrition or chemistry or preventive medicine). At some point the educational engineer will want to make clear the cross-reference between different curricula so that major clusters of topics might be shared with different courses. This can be done if we take a conceptual systems approach to instructional planning and use a reticulated curriculum mesh but is almost impossible if students enter the *same* lesson sequence with different aims and backgrounds.

IMPLEMENTATION OF CONCEPTUAL SYSTEMS ANALYSIS

It will be noted that both the tone and the spirit of this paper are explicitly philosophical even though CAL implementations are the intended end-point. The reason is simple: the problems associated with adequately defining and implementing individualized instruction are fundamentally philosophical, not technical. To be sure, computer terminals are notably deficient in their ability to portray complex graphics such as that shown. Currently we use a printed display but a random access slide projector controlled by the computer would be possible.

Has conceptual systems analysis led to an operational CAL system? Not quite. We are attempting to implement it in my course Ed. Tech. 653: Educational Systems Analysis which is a mixture of systems theory and operational research applied to the problems of lifelong learning within or without schools. This course introduces operational research to graduate students whose background in quantitative methods may range from virtually none to considerable. One module is a multi-media multi-computer system to teach Linear Programming[7]. Another being developed is Queueing Theory.

Queueing Theory and its application consists of a network of inter-connected topics. Depending on one's intentions it is possible to begin studying any of a wide variety of component topics and move toward mastery of queueing theory. And one may enter the system at any level of complexity depending upon one's initial capability and one's intentions. Thus if one merely wishes to develop capability in applying the queueing theory model to educational problems it is not necessary to know a great deal about probability theory, differential calculus or computer programming. On the other hand, if one wishes to tackle very complex problems or to develop new approaches, computer simulation and in-depth understanding of probability distributions is essential. The key point here is that such a system of knowledge cannot be represented best by a list structure but by a two (or multi-) dimensional network representation. In practice students of queueing theory do not yet have CAL lessons other than some computer simulations. (Print remains cheap and easy to develop and cost-benefit analysis is not needed to demonstrate that CAL cannot be justified for a small group of students who learn readily without it.)

Following such a **representation** of knowledge—where each topic may represent one or more CAL lessons—permits understanding of topics at a variety of levels regardless of the learner's background. Thus one might begin to understand a topic in one module but not develop further understanding without understanding related topics. This may entail returning to the original topic later for an additional lesson. Eventually the student may come to understand the inter-relatedness of the subject matter as he creates his own understanding of the system of concepts involved. This integration of new principles, operations and groups of facts with the learner's existing knowledge allows a coalescence to a new level of awareness, something which seldom happens with a straightforward presentation of a sequence of lessons. Because it is idiosyncratic, it makes possible individualized instruction once materials become available.

CONCLUSION

Representation of knowledge is a central theme in artificial intelligence but not yet so in education. This graphic representation of a reticulated conceptual system need not be used solely for individualized instruction. The network can serve as a conceptual model of the structure of knowledge in the subject. Preparation of such a model can be valuable to any teacher or instructional designer because it clarifies his thinking about the subject and suggests patterns for educational communication that may integrate the subject for the learner. Presented to the student, this representation of a subject can provide an overview which may guide the learner, serve as an *aide-memoire* or facilitate recall of associated knowledge.

In addition, it is possible for an instructor to teach two or more sections of a class in a non-individualized mode and—by following different paths through the curriculum mesh for each class—appear to be offering quite different courses. In this way the teacher can avoid tiresome repetition if he offers several parallel courses.

The research reported represents an attempt to establish an analytic and theoretical framework for understanding the systems structure of knowledge and the dynamics of individualized instruction without regard to specific course content or instructional activities. Scientific and technological investigation in the manner outlined can make a significant contribution to the theory and practice of educational technology for personalized learning, the implications of which extend for beyond the classroom or even the institution.

REFERENCES

1. Mitchell P. D., A curriculum mapping technique for individualized instruction. Presented to the Canadian Association for Curriculum Studies, Fredericton, N.B. (1977).
2. Mitchell P. D., Feedback controlled instructional design. In *Advances in Cybernetics and Systems* (Edited by F. Pechler). Hemisphere, Washington (1974).
3. Mitchell P. D., The concept of individualized instruction in the microelectronics era: educational technology comes of age. In *Aspects of Educational Technology XIV* (Edited by L. Evans). Kogan Page, London (1980).
4. Mitchell P. D., *Systems Analysis in Planning Self-Instructional Systems*. Croom Helm, London. (Accepted).
5. Mitchell P. D., *Conceptual Systems Analysis*. Cybersystems, Montreal. Accepted for publication.
6. Pask G., *Conversion Theory*. Elsevier, Amsterdam (1976).
7. Vazquez J., Winer L. and Mitchell P. D., A multi-media package for teaching linear programming to educational technology students. Unpublished manuscript.
8. Mitchell P. D., The sacremental nature of behavioural objects. In *Aspects of Educational Technology* (Edited by K. Austwick and N. D. C. Harris). Pitman, London (1972).
9. Mitchell P. D., Needed: student-centred self-instructional systems for adult learners. In *Trends in Educational Publishing*. PIRA, Leatherhead (1979).

Comput. & Educ. Vol. 6, pp. 67 to 76, 1982
Printed in Great Britain

0360-1315/82/010067-10$03.00/0
Pergamon Press Ltd

SPECIFYING CONTROL AND DATA IN THE DESIGN OF EDUCATIONAL SOFTWARE*

STURE HÄGGLUND[1], JOHAN ELFSTRÖM[2], HANS HOLMGREN[1],
OLLE ROSIN[3] and OVE WIGERTZ[3]

[1] Software Systems Research Center, [2]Department of Surgery and [3]Department of Medical Informatics, Linköping University, S-581 83 Linköping, Sweden

Abstract—When using the computer as a tool for learning, it is useful to distinguish between the *contents* and the *realization* aspects of an interactive session. We describe an approach which makes this distinction explicit to the author by viewing the programming process as one of giving independent specifications of:

(a) data, i.e. what is to be learned, and
(b) control, i.e. the particulars of the dialogue.

A system, MEDICS, for training medical students in clinical decision making is presented as an illustration of the approach. We stress the importance of providing an interactive environment supporting powerful *editing* operations as the primary tool for the author. The paper specifically describes the MEDICS environment for construction of medical simulations and how control of execution is specified.

INTRODUCTION

Computer Assisted Learning has traditionally been an area where a strong emphasis is assigned to the task of providing easy-to-use dialogue interfaces to computer programs. This is true both for interactions with the exercising student and for the author of educational software. Numerous author languages, such as Tutor[1], Coursewriter etc., have been designed in order to simplify the creation of dialogue intensive programs, which is a task poorly supported by ordinary programming languages.

Still it seems that further improving the author support is a key area to be attacked in order to release the full potential of CAL. We think that time now is ripe to de-emphasize the role of the author language *per se*, and instead concentrate on facilities in an interactive *programming environment* including management of author dialogues. This paper presents an approach where such a support is realized and discusses some principles for software organization, which should facilitate the creation of educational programs to a considerable degree.

Our discussion will be carried out in terms of an application concerning the creation of simulation programs, patient management problems (PMPs), to be used for training of decision making, specifically for medical education. Such simulations provide for the student to gather selected information and act according to his/her perception of the situation in order to attain a desired result, in our case the proper management of acute surgery cases. We have implemented a system, called MEDICS[2,3], which supports interactive development and maintenance of such simulations, with a minimum of computer proficiency required. The system is implemented in Lisp[4] and runs on a DECsystem-10 computer. It allows a physician to create simulation programs, almost without programmer assistance, and it is used by surgery students (often working in groups) during free hours. The presentation below will refer to this implementation.

There is a *data* aspect in the design of such simulations, which is similar to an ordinary database design problem. Thus we have to define a model of the simulation situation including specifications of all entity types concerned and their relationships, and then store instances of these entities for a specific simulation. It is customary that such design problems are treated by creating an abstract data model and retaining an independence of its physical realization as far as possible. Our approach to specification of educational simulation programs conforms to this model.

On the other hand there is also a *control* aspect of a simulation. Especially since we emphasize a high degree of interactions between the student and the simulation program, we have to handle both the dynamic aspects of the simulated case and the monitoring of the end-user dialogue. We claim that the specification of control for program execution should be treated in analogy with that of the data for a simulation, i.e. we will strive for control independence, in the sense that the particulars of the

* This work was supported by the Swedish Board for Technical Development under contracts 77-7535, 78-4167, 78-5269, 79-3921, 79-4958.

end-user dialogue may be charged without affecting the contents of the simulation. This is usually not well supported in conventional computer programs.

Though we will not present a conclusive conceptual framework in this paper, but rather discuss the MEDICS application as a pragmatic example, we think that this kind of program organization is generally applicable to educational (and some other kinds of applications) software. We feel that there is a fundamental *contents* aspect of a CAL program, which is concerned with object data and some fundamental executional structures. Further there is also a *realization* aspect, concerned with data representation and the dynamic appearance of a terminal session. This view should be justified on grounds of portability to new language environments, as well as adaptability to different educational needs.

RATIONALE FOR THE DESIGN METHODOLOGY

Using a conventional programming language for the implementation of patient management problems (PMPs) may require the writing of a procedural program which expresses the algorithm for the simulation with the students terminal input as parameters for the execution. In practice such a program would often be written as an *interpreter*, or a *driver*, which uses an exchangeable database containing the data which defines the current simulation. The definition of this interpreter expresses how control is to be executed, with PMP data acting as a parameter structure for the current case.

In this way we may create a new simulation program by specifying new data. The approach used in the MEDICS project, as described below, in addition treats the *control flow* aspect of the simulation in an analogous manner. Thus the appearance of a specific simulation, e.g. the definition of the end-user dialogue, may be changed by assigning a new control specification, i.e. by substituting (part of) the interpreter/driver. It should be emphasized that it is to be expected that a major part of the programs needed will be devoted to dialog management (of the order of 60% for typical interactive applications according to a study cited in [3]).

The basic model used for PMP simulations is one of a number of *activity sections*, each defining a context for some specific type of information gathering and/or treatment actions. Some actions invoke an explicit or implicit change of section context. (Fig. 1.). Each action or piece of information is represented as an *item* entity, having an associated response among its attibutes. Items corresponding to an explicit choice to leave the current context and start a new activity are called *decision items*. Notice however that such a transition of control may be forced by any item, as defined by the simulation author. Sections may be thought of as (not necessarily disjunct) clusters of items.

It should be pointed out that this model of an interactive session as consisting of current contexts (or *sites* in the terminology of [5]) and occasional transitions to new contexts is a fairly general one. It corresponds to a frame selection system for database queries as described by LeBeux and Gremy [6], to a time-sharing operating system viewed as number of subsystems with local command sets and also directly to the organization of computer games of the so called *Adventure* type [7].

We believe that the proper way to create such a simulation is first to specify the general characteristics of the simulation, such as the parameters of the simulation model and the specific data of a simulation problem, and then supply a specification of the control as it is to be executed when a simulation is run with a student at the terminal. Given that a default control structure is always defined, this makes it possible to work out and test the contents of a simulation before any details of end-user interactions are provided. As we will show, definition of control (in addition to the one implicitly given in the simulation model) is far from trivial and to a large extent independent of the actual simulation data.

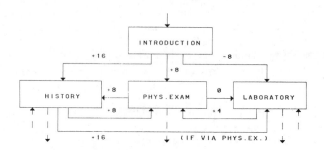

Fig. 1. Example of the overall structure of a PMP simulation.

Section D. Physical examination.

Choose as many items as you think are indicated.

1. Abdomen.
2. Blood pressure.
3. General appearance.
4.   . . .

    . . .

After collecting this information, select from the
list below what further action you wish to take.

Choose only one!

1. Take detailed history.
2. Order chemical investigations.
3. Order X-ray examination.
4. Give emergency treatment.
5. Admit the patient to the ward.

Fig. 2. Example of activities within a section.

The ambition in our system is that the amount of work performed during an interactive session for creation of a simulation program should be comparable with the level of detail needed to direct a knowledgeable programmer, who knows what are reasonable defaults for most aspects of a simulation.

We try to reach this goal by organizing a simulation program with control and data modularized and separated. This means that a new simulation may be constructed by putting standardized, albeit adjustable, building blocks together. It is also important to supply powerful strategies for generation of default data under control of high-level problem-oriented parameter specifications.

For execution of a simulation, a very simple top level monitor is invoked. This monitor starts interpretation of the simulation activity sections and is further responsible for dialogue supervision, i.e. every interaction between the terminal user and the program is controlled by this monitor, guaranteeing a uniform treatment of help request and other types of exception handling[8,9].

Not only one, but a number of interpreters are available for carrying out the simulation within each activity section, with control transferred from the top level monitor. The specification of which interpreter to invoke is considered part of the data structure representing the section. Since we are primarily concerned with simulating decision making, dialogue control is an important part of the simulation. Different modes of interactions may be judged appropriate depending on the purpose and contents of the simulation, which means that a choice of the degree of user initiative in the dialogue can be made by assigning a suitable interpreter to each activity section. The first interpreters implemented in the MEDICS system supported primarily menu selection techniques (see Fig. 2). Subsequently interpreters for dialogues with less guidance have been introduced and successfully applied also to previously constructed simulation problems.

It is important that this inverted view of a program as a data structure containing simulation data together with references to the procedures to be invoked for carrying out the simulation allows the author to have a very simplistic model of a simulation program to be designed. Thus the whole specification is done by using a data editor to assign values (which may have the form of executable program statements) to attributes for sections or items. This editing process is integrated with trial execution of a stimulation, which means that effects of an edit operation may be immediately inspected and that the problem of providing a key for the item to be edited is eliminated. At the same time it is easy to extend the simulation model by defining new execution monitors, which interpret the existing or suitably extended section data structures.

SIMULATION MONITORING IN THE MEDICS SYSTEM

A prime objective in our development of software tools to implement patient management simulations is the design of an application oriented computer representation that elucidates rather than obscures the process of simulation as carried out inside a program. The intended users of the system were already familiar with PMP simulations as they were performed using the booklet method of McGuire *et al.*[10]. This model of a simulation seemed to be easily comprehended and thus constituted a suitable basis for a conceptual framework to be supported by the MEDICS system.

Before we proceed to a presentation of the facilities for execution of a simulation we need a brief introduction to the data structures used for representation of PMPs. These matters are further discussed later in this paper.

Discussion on data structures

As was mentioned in the previous section, the description of a PMP simulation is modularized into activity sections, which are contexts for information gathering and decision making. A second important concept for modelling of PMPs is the one of a selectable *item*. Items are used to represent pieces of information about the simulated case and the action options available to the student during a simulation.

Each item is defined by a set of attribute values. A randomly generated identifier is used as a key and other attributes may be:

TEXT: a describing text string identifying the item, which is used, for example, when the item is presented in a menu for selection.
RESPONSE: a value or an answer that is returned in response to a selection of this item.
SCORE: an associated score.
TIME: simulated time delay associated with the selection of this item.
NEXT: a forced transfer of control to another activity section.
ISA: a generic reference if the current item is an instance of a more general concept, which may be searched for missing attribute values.

These attributes may have literal values, i.e. explicitly stored values which are normally not changed during a simulation. (This means, for example, that if the patient's temperature is lowered due to a treatment action, this may be represented by different items with the same TEXT attribute, which are valid in different contexts.) But we may also store a procedural module as the value for any attribute, which is then executed when the attribute value is retrived in order to produce the response to the student. Thus, a score may be defined by an expression, which is then evaluated in the current context when the score is retrieved, instead of having a constant value.

The data retrieval operation available in the MEDICS system is further parameterized with respect to how a specific attribute is stored[9]. This may be used not only to allow a change of internal representation, but also to specify that values for a certain attribute is not stored in item records, but are to be retrieved from a dynamic simulation model.

Sections and items are the basic structuring concepts for specification of PMP simulations. However there is also a need to cluster items available within a section. This need has been expressed both on semantic grounds and for reasons of dialogue control. There are basically three types of items to be considered.

information items (retrieval of data values)
action items (procedure invocation, side-effects)
decision items (change of context).

Although an item cannot always be uniquely classified as belonging to one or the other of these types, it is often practical to manage the decision items as a special group within a section. For instance, the booklet versions of PMP simulations usually present decision items separately. However, such additional structure may also be called for by the dialogue monitor. When menu selection techniques[11] are used, which is one important dialogue mode within the MEDICS system, we need to partion the set of items depending on screen size limitations. A subset or a power set of the items in a section, which is managed as a unit for some purpose will be termed an *item group* in the following.

Thus we need data structures for representation of simulation sections, items and sets of items within a section. Part of the structure is needed to support the internal specification of a simulation, while still other parts may be needed for dialogue control.

Execution of control

The execution of control is performed at three distinct levels in the MEDICS system. The top level concerns the overall control, i.e. the invocation of subsystems, where the simulation execution is but one activity available in the PMP development system. In fact there is a number of utilities available, which interpret the stored descriptions of PMPs in more or less specific fashions.

The following facilities in the MEDICS system are all driven by the current structure and contents of a stored PMP:

1. *The execution monitor* performs a simulation with the student at the terminal or simulates a student run for the author.

2. *The construction system* starts from type declarations of the simulation sections to be included and then monitors the detailed specification of section contents in a way which resembles a simulation execution. This is further described in the next section of this paper.

3. *The structure editor* supports navigating in the PMP structure. Editing operations are however usually performed while executing a test simulation or within the construction system.

4. *The student feedback system* allows the student to rerun a simulation in a slightly different mode, providing feedback and possibilities to examine alternative choices of actions.

5. *The booklet formatter* interprets the same structure and prints out the pages of a booklet to be used for paper-and-pencil simulations (where responses have to be developed with a special pen).

6. *The booklet scoring aid* simulates a student run with input data from paper-and-pencil simulations in order to simplify the computation of scores.

7. *The documentation aid* is of course also guided by the stored structures, when a complete formatted listing of one PMP in the simulation database is requested.

The excution of any of these services imposes a specific mode of control on the database representation of a PMP. It should in principle be possible to isolate the procedural definition of these programs from minor changes in the schema describing the structure of a specific PMP, i.e. these programs should be driven by the current structure as chosen by the simulation author. The present prototype implementation of MEDICS does not exhibit this property in every respect, but a further development in this direction seems promising. Only the first three of the services presented above are further discussed in this paper.

The intermediate level of control concerns the program execution within any of the subsystems mentioned above. The grain size chosen as a basis for control specification within a PMP simulation is the activity section. Thus each section has an associated interpreter, which may be chosen either among a set of standard modes for execution or else is written exclusively for a specific simulation. Although a new interpreter for an existing section may require additional structure or data associated with the section, this approach provides a basis for modularization of the control aspect of a simulation.

The lowest level for specification of control is associated with retrieval of responses to end-user interactions. This retrieval is not limited to explicit data values, but may as well invoke execution of a program in order to produce a response. In the MEDICS system this may be achieved either by storing program statements instead of literal data values in attributes, or alternatively by defining special retrieval procedures associated with a specific attribute. In this way we may change a static simulation, where all possible responses are stored beforehand, to one based on a dynamic simulation model.

The rest of this section will be devoted to a discussion of the intermediate level of control within a PMP simulation. Programs executing the simulations are defined as small delimited drivers, which interpret this data structure. These interpreters are modifiable and exchangeable and stored as integrated parts of the data base containing the simulation problems.

Execution within a simulation section

The control aspect of an activity section is expressed as its *execution type*. Each execution type has an associated interpreter, which is a program that executes a simulation in a specific way according to the data and structures defined for the section. As will be further explained below, it is possible to understand the execution type both as a description of the particulars of dialogue monitoring and as a specification of a user view of the stored structure. The latter is important, since it has turned out practical to allow excution of a section assuming different execution types for different users. For instance, when working in the construction sybsystem (or in edit mode), displayed menus of items may be preferred, even if they are not used for students interactions. This requires the stored structure to contain all information needed by any of these user views.

As was explained above, a database representation of a PMP may be viewed as a number of sections, each containing a number of item groups consisting of selectable items or other item groups. Figure 3 shows this kind of structure, assuming that *management* and *decision* are names of item groups and that the *management* group consists of a number of item groups in its turn. Thus we have a hierarchic structure with items in the leaves of this structure.

We may view the execution of a simulation as a process of selecting a number of items in a specific

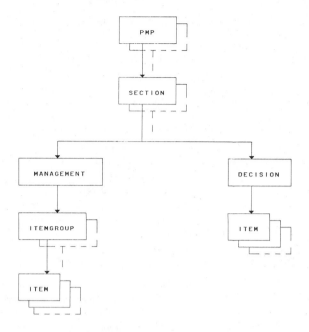

Fig. 3. Example of PMP structure.

order. In this case the data structures define access paths for the item selection. For instance, the student selects a section, then traverses the item groups in some order and retrieves data values when reaching groups which have items as leaves. The use of a frame selection system for a database query, as described in [6] corresponds directly to this view of a PMP simulation.

On the other hand, we may also view the stored structures as an internal representation of a program. Given that we supply an additional specification of the transfer of control, i.e. how the item groups of a tree-structured section are to be interpreted as *compound* statements, *case* statements or *for*-sequences, a section may be directly interpreted as a program with items corresponding to executable statements. (Data and program structures will be discussed in the terminology of [12].) Notice that this control information is normally not explicit in the stored structure, but implicitly defined by the assigned execution type. The generality of this view of the section description as a program structure, is further elucidated by the fact that item responses may be specified as program text, which is interpretatively executed when retrieved as described above.

The purpose of the MEDICS system is to supply a simulation specification mechanism, which is in principle as powerful as a general-purpose programming language, while observing the simplifications which are possible due to the fact that in practice only a few program variations are actually needed. Obviously our data structure view of a PMP with simple associated interpreters meets this criterion.

If we look at which intra-section control structures have been called for within the MEDICS project (where about 20 simulation cases have been worked out so far, each containing typically 5–10 sections), it turns out that a few simple structures are generally preferred, but also that some variations of these are soon needed. The physicians often want to divide a section into a *management part* and a *decision part*. Sometimes only one of these parts is needed, i.e. if control is to be automatically transferred to a new section when activities within a section are completed, or if a section is simply defined as a context for a number of decision alternatives.

A section may thus be defined as a cartesian product of one or more parts, which implies the execution as a compound statement (one part after the other). This is the only control structure used in booklet PMPs. When a computerized menu selection technique is used, we are however forced to divide large item groups into smaller ones. This may call for a refinement of a section part into a cartesian product of its constituent item groups (to be traversed one after the other at execution time) or as a sequence of a discriminated union (where the student may repeatedly select any one of the partioned item groups).

The user perceives the execution of control as the exhibition of a sequence of *screens* (or the equivalent if a typewriter terminal is used; other terms for the same concept are *frames* and *pages*), where each screen usually defines a context of selectable items. Each item group which is visible according to the user view implied by the current execution type for a section has a corresponding screen realization. But there may also be screens which do not correspond to any items, for instance, screens presenting a text or a picture to be viewed before proceeding.

This discussion has been a fairly technical one, while a physician using the MEDICS system is likely to express his needs in terms something like this "I need a section with three parts, the first one of which contains a number of menu screens to be shown at the student's demand. When the student has finished information gathering from these menus, a new screen is to be shown giving some additional information and requiring the student to enter his present hypotheses regarding the final diagnosis. Finally a screen showing alternatives for further action is to be presented."

It has been the intention that the execution types available in the MEDICS system should cover anticipated needs for control specification, e.g. like the one expressed above. Thus we have chosen some of the most common structures discussed above and in essence assigned mnemonic names to them. In practice this is done in such a way that the execution types supported implies a specific structure variant as well as a dialogue mode. In order to make the set of execution types managem-able, we have also introduced the concept of *execution variant* as a way to specify parameters for an execution type (see below).

To summarize, we have found that a few structure variants usually suffice for the description of a large class of simulations. However when the built-in flexibility of the MEDICS approach regarding simulation control is further exploited, it seems advisable to introduce more systematic methods for relating execution types to screen sequencing. The present system organization should provide a good foundation for such enhancements.

CONSTRUCTION OF SIMULATION PROBLEMS

Construction of a PMP simulation within the MEDICS system essentially means storing data (or procedural modules) in a structure, which is partly given beforehand and partly subsequently adjusted to fit the current simulation. What is needed for this purpose is a data editor rather than a programming language. In order to provide guidance for the simulation author, this editor is to be integrated with a program which supervises the construction process and prompts for missing infor-mation.

The algorithmic parts of the simulation are either implicitly defined in the simulation models supported by the system, or specified by the chosen execution type as described earlier in this paper. The simulation model may be extended by storing procedural modules instead of literal data values in item attributes. Since these modules are usually of a limited size, this programming activity does not violate the view of the PMP construction system as a data editor. When completely new execution types are needed, we will have to perform an act of systems programming, which is not regarded part of the construction system.

We presently support two ways of entering PMPs into the MEDICS database. One way is to use a prompting data entry program to enter item by item into the simulation database (see [3]), much like the solution in the GENESYS system described by Harless et al.[13]. A more interesting solution, however, is to construct a new simulation through a top-down specification process.

It is essential that such a process can be carried out in a fashion which closely resembles the mental processes of the PMP author. This means that we should provide a high degree of user initiative in the specification dialogue. On the other hand, this presents a serious problem since we do not want to require proficiency in a complex author language or command language.

Our way to treat this problem is to provide a dialogue interface which integrates a command language facility with the ability to retreat to a fill-in-the-blanks dialogue when needed. The most important assumption, however, is that we may benefit from the interactive nature of our application. The idea is that specification and editing of the data for a PMP are done in the context of a running simulation, which provides a natural frame of reference and allows the effects of specifications and editing operations to be immediately inspected. This approach requires that mechanisms are available for supplying default data, e.g. for simulation of parts not yet defined by the author.

Although it is in principle possible to manage with a powerful PMP editor, which is used step by step to transform a standard simulation to the one to be constructed, we will in practice always have a declaration phase, where parameters for the simulation are specified. From these parameters a skeletal PMP is created and default items (such as physical status, laboratory test values, etc.) are initialized. (In practise initialization is deferred until items are actually selected by the PMP author for inclusion in the current simulation.)

We believe that the ambition should be to reduce such parameter specifications to a minimum and proceed as soon as possible to an executable simulation, which is then further refined with editing operations. The justification for this opinion is mainly that the semantics of a specification language is not a trivial task to learn, while the ability to edit the contents of a PMP section is anyhow essential for a user of the MEDICS development system.

The basic functions of an editor (or a database manipulation language) are to insert, update and delete elements, but also to find the stored representation of a given object. This retrieval process either relies on user specified keys (*get item with key = AB001*) or alternatively on structural relationships (*get next, get first son* etc.). One important reason for performing editing operations during a test execution of a simulation is that implicit access paths for items are provided, without the introduction of a special retrieval language. In fact the MEDICS system also contains an editing subsystem which interfaces the user directly to the stored data structures, but our experience is that this system has hardly ever been used. Another reason for performing editing during test execution is of course that this is when the need to modify a simulation is most often discovered.

In an earlier section we introduced the data structures used in the MEDICS system to represent a simulation problem. Specifically we presented the set of item attributes. /Initialization of new items is discussed at the end of this section. In order to execute a simulation we have to define one or more sets or power sets of items within a section. Such an *item group* also has a number of associated attributes, for instance a TEXT attribute which means that it can be used in menu selection in the same way as an elementary item.

One important aspect of an item group is that it may have an associated layout for presentation as a *screen* (in the sense defined above). A screen typically consists of a *text part* and a *prompt part*. The prompt part may contain a menu showing the text representations of the elements in the item group. The text part is usually divided into a section identification, a screen identification, an informative text and a response instruction. This information may be stored as attributes for the corresponding item group, or else is defaulted. There are presently some fifteen item-group attributes supported by the MEDICS system, the values of which are all generated by default, when a new simulation is constructed. Screen layouts are easily adjusted by editing these attributes.

Activity sections are also described by a set of attributes. Thus sections may have an assigned *management type*. This type defines what kind of activity is performed within the section and implies the availability of a set of standard items with values initialized according to the current global parameter values, which describes the simulated patient. An internal structuring of items in a hierarchy of groups may also be defaulted from the management type (deduced indirectly via the default execution type).

The typical way to construct a new section is thus to select an appropriate management type (if available, e.g. "*Physical exam.*", "*Medical treatment*", etc.; there are presently 10 management types supported in the MEDICS system). Then a restriction from the set of standard items valid in this context may be made and additional items entered. Scores are to be added and new responses provided where the generated "normal" ones are not appropriate. In many cases a different execution type is desired instead of the one assumed by default. It is part of our approach that such an exchange of execution type should be as easy as possible. Sometimes, however, some extra structures or data has to be added to the section, when a new execution type is assigned.

The construction system in MEDICS provides an environment for initialization and editing of sections and items. The construction process starts with a declaration of attributes for the simulation problem to be created, such as:

various descriptive data, e.g. mnemonic *name*, an identifying *description*, a conclusive *comment*, a *teacher's score*, the *medical type* of the case etc.

a list of *sections*, which is specified as a selection from a list of generated section names corresponding to each available management type. A special command may be used at any time to add a new section to a simulation problem.

a list of *decisions*, which are standard decision items to be considered in every section of the simulation problem.

a *characteristics*, which is a list of parameters guiding the generation of default item responses, e.g. stating the sex and/or age of the patient.

When these declarations have been given (most of them may however be defaulted or left undefined initially), the declared sections are traversed in the order of the author's preference for the purpose of providing the opportunity to make a detailed specification of the simulation. The dialogue within sections is executed in a way resembling an ordinary simulation. Screens containing some extra texts instructing the author are presented and local dialogue diversions are provided when ordinary execution is prohibited due to incomplete information. But in all important aspects the author views the sections in the same ways during construction as during final simulations.

The main tool for detailed specification of section contents and structure is the *data editor*. This editor provides basic commands for adding, modifying and deleting attributes for the various objects constituting a section (items, item groups and the section object itself). Objects to be edited may be referenced with its unique identifier, but usually *currency*, as defined by menus shown on the screen etc., is used for selection of the proper object.

There are also a number of editing commands which operate directly upon sets of elements associated with a displayed screen. These commands are used to change the structure of section parts, the clustering of items in item groups and also for the purpose of changing the screen realization of an item group. They implement in principle operations on a macro level, since the same effects may be achieved with sequences of elementary editing commands. Their parameters may be given directly or through a guided dialogue. It is essential that the set of such commands is carefully chosen in order to restrict the number of available options to a manageable minimum.

We will conclude this presentation with a short discussion on item initialization. When a new simulation is to be created, we have to define a large number of items describing the case. Most of them should exhibit values or responses which are normal with respect to the general background and appearance of the patient. Some of them should be significantly "abnormal" as a result of the current disease.

It should be noticed that most items of low relevancy are seldom inquired for in a specific PMP. The work to define these items contributes then comparatively little to the quality of the simulation exercise. Thus it is desirable that the values for those "normal" items, which under the circumstances are irrelevant, may be created with as small an effort as possible.

For this purpose most standard items in the construction database have procedural values, which are evaluated in initialization time with the characteristics of the current patient as parameters. There are however some problems with the treatment of interdependencies between items. We have to enforce consistency when responses to related inquiries are generated automatically. A general solution might employ some kind of semantic network, which is used to derive responses from uniquely stored facts. Since such a solution goes far beyond the ambitions of the current MEDICS system, we have to rely on consistency tests explicitly stored in the response generation expression.

SUMMARY AND CONCLUSIONS

We have discussed educational software from an aspect where we may distinguish between its *contents* and its *realization*. Specifying the contents is very much a question of storing information, but also of defining some basic control patterns or algorithms. Creating a realization means deciding on physical representation of data and the details of the control flow.

This view led us to a perspective where we envisage an application program as a data structure where descriptive data is stored and where subsequently execution control information is attached in appropriate positions. We argued that the proper tool for "programming" in this environment is a powerful data editor, rather than an algorithmic "programming" language. Such a data editor should provide the features of a data manipulation language, with primitives for referencing data objects and structural relationships. For the users convenience, the editor should in addition support more complex higher-level operations, in a way analogous to what may be found in, for example, powerful text editors. This is one way to introduce application dependency in a development system. Another main way is to supply modular default structures and data.

Our presentation has been in terms of the MEDICS system for patient management simulations. We showed that the data editor concept was appropriate for handling a large class of such simulations and that our approach provides good flexibility for extensions in various directions, while still guaranteeing simplicity for regular cases. We think that the integration of editor and program construction facilities with test execution of the program provides a nice solution to the problem of navigating in the data structures, searching for the objects to be edited.

For the class of applications considered here, dialogue management is one important control aspect. Both for the purpose of adapting a program to different run-time environments and to the needs of different classes of users, it is preferable that dialogue control is modular and exchangeable. We have also advocated the utility of control independence for the purpose of having different subsystems driven directly by the data structures, or rather *user views* of this structure, each subsystem imposing its own mode of control for execution as a program.

For the MEDICS application we identified three levels of control. The top level invokes different subsystems, each interpreting the contents of the data structures in its own way as described above. The intermediate level defines how execution within a simulation section is to be performed, especially with respect to dialogue monitoring. The lowest level is defined by the possibility of storing executable program statements instead of literal data as attribute values. This organization is to be understood as an example of how to modularize control and supports the view of control specification as being part of a data structure defining an executable program.

We feel that our experiences of this approach is promising in the sense that considerable flexibility for extensions in various respects is achieved. During the MEDICS system development project some twenty simulation cases were developed. New simulation features, such as non-guided dialogues or intermittent hypothesis interrogations, were easily introduced when needed and applied also to previously defined cases.

REFERENCES

1. Ghesquiere J., Davis C. and Thompson C., *Introduction to TUTOR*. Computer-based Education Research Laboratory, University of Illinois (1975).
2. Elfström J., Gillquist J., Holmgren H. and Hägglund S., Experience with a system for training medical students in patient management. *Proc. 3rd Int. Conf. EARDHE*, Klagenfurt (1979).
3. Elfström J., Gillquist J., Holmgren H., Hägglund S., Rosin O. and Wigertz O., A customized programming environment for patient management simulations. *Proceedings of the 3rd World Conference on Medical Informatics*, pp. 328–332. North Holland, Amsterdam (1980).
4. Sandewall E., Programming in an interactive environment: the Lisp experience. *ACM Comp. Surveys* **10**, 35–71 (1978).
5. Nievergelt J. and Weydert J., Sites, modes and trails: telling the user of an interactive system where he is, what he can do, and how to get to places. In Guedj, R. A. (ed.) *Methodology of Interaction* (Edited by R. A. Guedj), Seillac II, North Holland, Amsterdam (1980).
6. Le Beux P. and Gremy F., A frame selection system for generating queries to a medical data base. *Proceedings of the 3rd World Conference on Medical Informatics*, pp. 1102–1106. North Holland, Amsterdam (1980).
7. Adams, An adventure in small computer game simulation. *Creative Computing* **5**, 90–97 (1979).
8. Hägglund S., Towards control abstractions for interactive software. A case study. Technical Report LiTH-MAT-R-80-37, Software Systems Research Center, Linköping University (1980).
9. Hägglund S., IDECS3 Reference Manual. System-dokumentation 20.1, Software Systems Research Center, Linköping University, 1980.
10. McGuire Ch., Solomon L. M. and Bashook P. G., *Handbook of Written Simulations*. Center for Educational Development, University of Chicago, Illinois (1972).
11. Martin J., *Design of Man-Computer Dialogues*. Prentice–Hall, Englewood Cliffs, NJ (1973).
12. Hoare C. A. R., Notes on data structuring. In Dahl, Dijkstra, Hoare, *Structured Programming* (Edited by Dahl *et al.*), pp. 83–174. Academic Press, New York (1972).
13. Harless W. G., Drennon G. G., Marxer J. J., Root J. A., Wilson L. L. and Miller G. E., GENESYS—a generating system for the CASE natural language model. *Comput. Biol. Med.* **3**, 247–268 (1973).
14. Carlson E. D. and Metz W., Integrating dialog management and data base management. *Proc. of IFIP Congress* 463–468 (1980).

Comput. & Educ. Vol. 6, pp. 77 to 84, 1982
Printed in Great Britain

0360-1315/82/010077-08$03.00/0
Pergamon Press Ltd

TEACHING STYLE AND PROGRAM DESIGN

Hugh Burkhardt,[1] Rosemary Fraser[2] and Colin Wells[2]

[1]Shell Centre for Mathematical Education, University of Nottingham, Nottingham, NG7 2RD
and [2]Investigations on Teaching with Microcomputers as an Aid, College of St Mark and St
John, Plymouth, England

Abstract—We describe an analysis of the spectrum of possibilities open to the designer of class teaching materials based on the use of a microcomputer as a teaching aid. Program design and use are related to the facilities the computer offers, the aspects of teaching to which they contribute, and to the problems of making the materials easy to use. Checklists are put forward as a practical way of bringing essential points to the designer's attention.

The production of computer programs that will help the teacher to be more effective in the classroom is both demanding and time consuming. Though a considerable amount of work has been done over the last decade or so, particularly in providing computer assisted learning material for the individual student, the field of CAL is still in an early experimental stage. This is particularly true for the complex situation which arises when a teacher is using a microcomputer as an aid in the classroom as part of a class or group activity. It is this type of use that this paper considers. We attempt systematically to explore the range of variables in program design, in the use of the programs and in their potential impact on the teaching and learning processes. Our aim has been to begin to provide for designers of educational software some general principles which map help to reduce the cost of producing effective material and, more immediately, a framework for assimilating the experience gained in the classroom use of teaching units that include the microcomputer as a resource.

The full paper "Teaching Style and Program Design"[1] consists of a theoretical discussion of the possibilities available to the designer, grouped under four headings—computer facilities, roles in teaching, the "driving system" for the program, and programming techniques—together with checklists of practical questions in each area which aim to ensure that important things are not forgotten. Here we give a summary of the main arguments, illustrated by extracts from the discussion and examples of the checklists; we aim to let the reader judge whether he is likely to find the complete paper useful or not.

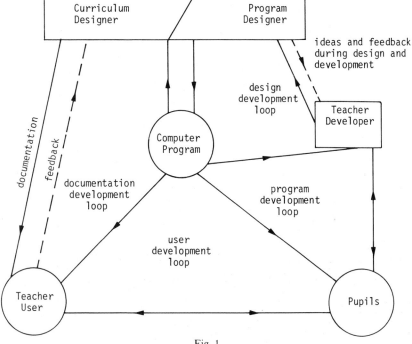

Fig. 1

A later paper "The Classroom Development of Teaching Material"[2] discusses the whole process of developing material so that it will be useful to many teachers with a wide range of styles, preferably in a way that illuminates their teaching beyond the particular lesson or topic covered in the unit.

In developing and using the program teaching units we have a variety of participants playing different roles, with a computer as a new, unfamiliar element. Ensuring easy, effective communication between these participants is crucial in achieving the best results. Figure 1 shows the basic pattern.

The teacher-user, using the program with his pupils in the classroom, (the user development loop of Fig. 1) is at the centre of our interest, with teaching the central communication aim but with the patterns of pupil activity and progress its best measures; although this might be regarded as familiar territory we shall want to discuss teaching strategies and styles in some detail in order to analyse the computer's potential for enhancing them. The design team may have many forms, from a single individual working alone, to a broadly based curriculum development team with specialists in curriculum design, graphics, programming and observation. However, for our purposes it is useful to distinguish three roles—the curriculum designer who has overall responsibility for the program teaching unit and its associated written or audio-visual material, the program designer who realises the computer program and the teacher developers in whose classrooms the material is tried and tuned. In practice these roles may overlap or fuse and contributions in any one area may come from any individual. The design team have a responsibility to help other teachers notice, look at, acquire, study and use the material with a minimum of effort; we take a detailed look at ways of describing to the teacher how to "drive the program" and how to use it in the classroom. Finally, we discuss programming considerations.

PROGRAM DESIGN VARIABLES

We first attempt to produce a taxonomy of some variables of program design and use which we believe are important in creating effective curriculum material; it is illustrated in Fig. 2. We discuss the computer program in rather anthropomorphic terms, referring successively to the **talents, personality** and **style** of the computer program. For different teaching styles and situations certain combinations of these variables may prove more effective than others. Here we first give the checklist C2.1 from Ref.[1] which epitomises the main **talents** to be borne in mind.

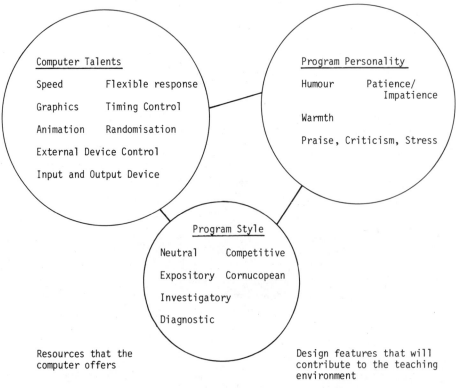

Fig. 2

C2.1 COMPUTER TALENTS CHECKLIST

C2.1s *Speed*

1. Is the current speed adequate?
2. Will transfer to other common micro's cause speed problems?
3. Is the teacher still asked to process things the computer could help with?
4. What related information could easily be provided?
   Does it really contribute?
5. Is the speed of presentation under enough teacher or program control?

C2.1g *Graphics*

1. Do the screen images present all and only the information desired?
2. Does the image clearly focus attention on the essential elements without distraction?
3. Is the size and timing of images such as to make them easily visible to all pupils?
4. Does the computer give information that might better come from the teacher or the pupils? (Consider each point in turn, linking it to the envisaged teacher and pupil activities.)
5. Do the images positively stimulate pupil discussion and pupil activities?
6. Is your use of high resolution or colour essential, or even productive?
7. Is the program written as far as possible in a way that will ease transferability?
8. Have you consulted with a graphic designer on this unit?

C2.1a *Animation*

1. Is animation exploited to give vitality and variety to the images at the best points?
2. Are there concepts that could be better brought out by an animated sequence?
3. Is it well used in providing reward stimuli?
4. Could animation be used to add an extra dimension to the displayed information?
5. Is any of the animation unproductive or over elaborate?

C2.1e *External device control*

1. Would audio output (bell, voice etc.) help the impact?
2. Would other display media (slides, film, video) contribute importantly?
3. Has the unit important conceptual links with apparatus?
4. Is this link clearly established for the pupils?
5. Can this be then demonstrated and how?
6. Could the computer usefully be physically linked to the apparatus in question?

C2.1i *Input and output devices*

1. Has the flexibility of response to any input been explored to make operations simple?
2. Are there any potential benefits from the use of a mouse, touch screen, light pen, graphics pad, voice input, voice output, special purpose devices?
3. In view of the loss of transferability, should these be optional?
4. Does their use compensate for any increased program complexity?

C2.1t *Timing*

1. Is the timing of computer responses adequately controlled at each point?
2. Is the time control left to the teacher appropriate?
3. Is the basic timing resonably stable (e.g. independent of systems software changes), and transferable?

C2.1r *Randomisation*

1. Has the possibility been explored for using computer generated examples, random computer stimuli or realism in simulation?

The **program personality** presented to the student, and to the teacher, need not be that of a neutral machine—it can show a variety of human attributes and a balancing of these in the design of the program is an important matter in which there is room for a variety of approaches. In our experience, the extremes of neutrality ("response incorrect") and folksiness ("aw, c'mon") are equally likely to alienate the student.

Humour epitomises the designer's dilemma—used effectively it can prolong the attention span of the student and enhance the whole of atmosphere of the class, but it needs to be used with a very light touch if, particularly after using the program many times, disenchantment is to be avoided.

Warmth of program image is an asset to be sought in a whole variety of ways, e.g. the facility for using the actual names of the children in the class (input in advance by the teacher) can be effective. Fundamentally, the program should present the demands it makes on the class as worthwhile, achievable and, preferably, enjoyable.

Praise and *Criticism* are an obvious part of any interactive teaching material, but the balance must be carefully adjusted both in the initial design and the classroom development of the program unit. The value of praise in providing encouragement has to be blended with the instructional benefit that criticism can bring to the pupils; we believe there is room for experiment in this area in particular. Eventual guaranteed success is often a very desirable aspect, especially for young or slow learners.

Stress can easily be generated in a class by a teaching program, through the use of competitive situations, for example. This can be used to obtain responses from the pupils beyond what they would otherwise achieve. However, undue pressure may result in actual distress for some pupils and, much more likely, a general rejection of the program by the class. Stress can also be placed on the teacher by careless program design or careless program use—this has no benefits.

Patience and *Impatience* are key ways in which the pressure a program puts on pupils can be adjusted. Control of the rhythm of the lesson will depend partly on the structure of the program and how easy it is for the teacher to use.

Program style is obviously related to how the teacher and program operate together to create the learning environment. We are concerned with the micro being used with a class or a group of children. Observing in the classroom, we have been very encouraged to see that many programs that were originally designed and written to be used by a whole class are very effective with groups of pupils working on their own, either with the same approach or when a subset of the possible activities offered by the program is being used, PIRATES, JANE and TRANSPOTS have all been found effective in this way. In the same way, material written for the individual child is often used with one child operating the keyboard and a group of children involved. In all situations the communication between pupils themselves, and between pupils and the teacher appears to increase.

Interactive computer programs can present ideas, facts and basic techniques in a powerful way, aiming for their assimilation and the development of conceptual understanding of the more strategic skills. Exercise and testing play an important part at all levels. Program design can aim to aid all of any of the these activities by:

> actual presentation—sowing seeds;
> generating a supportive environment—producing curiosity in an atmosphere of enjoyment;
> stimulating pupil participation—setting up situations or exploiting them, providing a structure
> for investigations, or examples or exercises.

The following program styles at least are available; a single program may employ more than one:

Neutral—the micro is used simply as a device for presenting information as requested by the teacher, an electronic variant of the blackboard or overhead projector which uses the computer's talents, e.g. to do graphs, display pictures, record and reproduce data or perform calculations.

Expository—the program "teaches" a topic itself, presenting ideas in a straightforward didactic way and initiating pupil activity and specific tasks. Here the teacher's role is mainly managerial and supportive.

Investigatory—the program provides a system for the teacher to explore with the class. Computer simulation of physical or social systems are the best known examples of this mode, but the possibilities are much wider—in particular, programs which illustrate theoretical concepts directly in numerical, graphical or symbolic terms can provide a powerful "bridge" in the development of abstract concepts. The teacher's role here in providing the right amount of guidance in the investigation is most important, with room for wide differences of approach, particularly on the levels of demand to be placed on the pupils.

Competitive environments have a powerful stimulant effect on a class. The swift interactive response of the micro and its flexibility within a well defined set of rules make it particularly effective in setting up game situations. its data holding potential allows it to be used to help ensure that all pupils are involved in the games as well and the traditional competitive classroom activity—testing.

Cornucopean—the prolific production of examples (which is an essential element of the investigatory style) can also be used to provide a multitude of practice exercises. The polishing of basic technical skills in this way is well known; more work is needed to learn how to provide good problems for the development of higher level problem solving skills in all subject areas.

Diagnostic—although it is possible when a program is used for individual tuition for it to collect data on pupils' performance, this is only one mode of diagnostic use. Indeed this mode should be used with care as it may well be the non-judgemental personality of the machine that motivates a child to persevere with a problem. We have observed in a classroom that many programs help the teacher to understand the pupils' level of comprehension through the pupil response that they provoke. The observation so far is with programs where the designer has not concentrated on this aspect at all, but it seems very hopeful that work in this area can be developed.

The **program in action** brings in the whole range of variables related to teaching. Here, rather than give too brief a discussion of the possible roles in teaching a program may play, and the documentation that might support each, we again simply reproduce a brief checklist from Ref.[1].

C3 TEACHING CHECKLIST

1. Have you a clear view of how the teaching unit may be used by a variety of teachers?
2. How can you help the teacher to use the unit effectively?
3. Which of the following activities will the program help the teacher with
   (a) introducing a new topic
   (b) exercises to help strengthen understanding
   (c) progression through a topic
   (d) revision of a topic or topics
   (e) problem solving activities
4. What age and ability range of pupils is the material suitable for?
5. Will it appeal to some teaching styles rather than others?
6. Does the program try to assume ideas that would be best left to the teacher?
7. Can the program contribute to the teacher's education?
8. Can the program be used in more than one subject area?
9. Can the program be used to produce teacher material?
10. What concepts does the program tackle?
11. Does the program link different aspects of the curriculum together?
12. Does the program cater for different levels of presentation?
13. What type of flexibility does the program offer to the teacher?
14. Does the program provide aids to memory; if so how, through visual impact, mnemonic aids etc.?
15. What motivation does the program offer?

The amount of space devoted to it here does not reflect our view of the importance of this aspect of program design. A clear view of the role of a particular program in the classroom and of *the pupil and teacher activities the unit is designed to stimulate* is central—indeed we believe it is the most important single factor in promoting effective unit design and will lead to programs quite different from those designed, e.g. simply to illustrate the topic involved; often there will be surprising omissions and inclusions which relate directly to intended pupil or teacher behaviour.

Driving the program—the aims and potential objectives for the teaching unit will be built into the teaching material, the computer program being a part of this material; their successful realisation by a wide range of teachers will depend crucially on the driving system of the program and the image of the unit that it presents to the user. This should be at the centre of the designer's attention through the development of the unit—indeed starting with preliminary ideas of what options the program should present to the user and then refining and extending them, the program will develop in tune with the feedback received from the classroom [2].

There is an inherent tension between range and flexibility of options on the one hand, and their simplicity and clarity on the other. It has several aspects including:

(a) the range of options offered to the teacher is crucial in fitting the program to his style and enabling him to contribute effectively, but too many options will be confusing;
(b) the designer may see a whole range of possible extensions to the teaching possibilities of the program. The lengthy development process of all good teaching units make such extensions attractive, but trying to include them in one program will tend to make it difficult to "see through" and to use;
(c) the desire for compatibility with different hardware configurations often inspires programming constraints that can be severe; conversely programs that fully exploit the facilities of a particular microcomputer are likely to be difficult to transfer to others.

In defining the program image and writing the documentation, the designer has to draw a balance in all these dimensions, informed by development trials in the classroom. It is important always to consider the probable roles of teacher, pupils and program to ensure that the partnership is a productive one. Checklists are an aid towards this end.

The driving system then is crucial in making a program that will be effective in the hands of a lot of teachers. What elements are important in its design? The novice teacher will require careful guidance through the options structure of the program with clear explanations and very limited demands in terms of making choices, if he is not to be distracted from the normal demands of teaching, or even put off completely. The more experienced teacher who has used the program several times, on the other hand, will not want to go through lengthy explanations and interrogations by the program amid the pressures of the classroom. He will be able to handle a wider range of options with only mnemonic guidance. For him the minimum number of key strokes for program control is appropriate. It is our view that designers should generally pursue such an economical, even terse, style but with a clearly defined choice structure, regarding "initial training" as a separate task.

The best way to define the choice structure remains a matter for research. However, it is likely to be preferable to limit the range of choices facing the teacher at any moment and to group them in a natural way from a teaching point of view. Various sorts of logical structure, with branching and loops, will achieve this—in general we see great advantages in presenting them to the user in graphical form.

There are of course, no unique prescriptions for realising these principles but we think it worthwhile to examine a few possible approaches in more detail. The traditional form of interaction with the user is purely through dialogue in which written messages present him with immediately available choices, or ask him to supply values for parameters in the program; this approach has grown from individual tutorial CAL. It has the advantage that the user is given a feeling of security by being concerned only with a limited range of immediate decisions. There are at least two disadvantages from the class use point of view. The lengthy explanatory messages required take time to read and absorb and are a potential distraction to the class. In addition, and this also applies to tutorial CAL, the user is given no help in forming a global picture of what the program can achieve.

The topological structure of the decision space can be quite complicated even in a fairly simple program. Such structures are best displayed graphically. The DRIVE CHART which we have described fully elsewhere[3], is an example of this approach being specifically adapted to the sorts of decision that are characteristic of a program used in class or group teaching. We shall outline their main features here. Figure 3 shows the DRIVE CHART for the program JANE+ which aims to

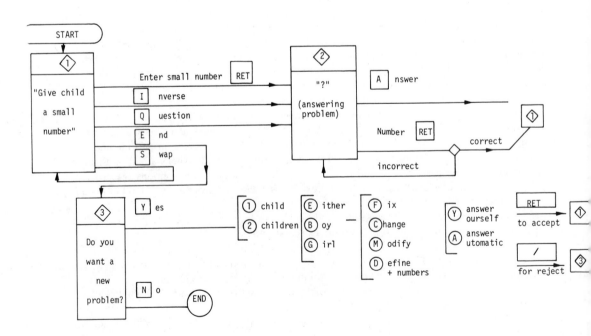

JANEPLUS DRIVE CHART

Fig. 3

introduce pupils to the idea of mathematical functions by displaying *named* figures each of which either adds or multiplies by a particular small whole number—which number the pupils must discover by trial, hypothesis and check. On the drive chart, the DECISION POINTS represented by square boxes each offer a natural group of alternative ROUTES for the teacher, who chooses one by pressing a single key, e.g. I selects the *inverse* problem where the computer provides the "output" number from the named function and invites the class to guess the "input" number. Along certain routes there is a "menu" of FEATURES that may be set—one being chosen from each vertical group or "course" of the menu. It is easy to see from this DRIVE CHART that the number of modes of operation is large, but that the choice facing the teacher at any given moment is among only a few possibilities. The global structure of choices is clearly displayed. The price paid for this powerful system is the introduction of the new unfamiliar notation with its associated fear factor for many teachers, particularly those unused to mathematics or flow-charts. This is the "initial training" problem referred to above. It can be met in various ways. The written material for the unit should contain a detailed guide to the DRIVE CHART, including key-by-key sequences to take the teacher through simple and commonly used options. Such training sequences can also be included as an optional part of the program, which should also contain "help" routines to feed information to the teacher who is having difficulties. Such a training system has been found in practice to be very effective with a wide range of teachers.

Simpler systems are possible, e.g. all the options in the program may be available at any time, and in certain circumstances this may be preferable. The price of this simple structure is that there is no framework to help the teacher make the choices from the large total number that are often, in principle, available. The balance between these factors needs further research. The more complicated the decision space for the program, the more sophisticated will be the optimum driving system which may ultimately need most of the features of a full graphics oriented data-base management system. Perhaps the most highly developed example currently available in an educational context is the DYNABOOK system developed by Adele Goldberg and others at Xerox' Palo Alto Research Center. Although this was designed for individual use its flexibility and generality are such that it may well have wider applications. However, at the present time it requires a highly skilled and sophisticated programmer to use it. We regard it as unlikely that many teachers in the near future will be able to handle facilities of this range and power amid the pressures of the classroom. However, it is important for the designer to be aware of the nature and extent of the possibilities that are in principle available so that he may be able to exploit some of them when it seems appropriate.

Programming usually occupies the major part of the time spent in developing a unit. It is crucial to the educational success of the unit that the program be robust and educational demands will often stretch both the programmer's ingenuity and the resources of the microcomputer being used. Nonetheless, we believe it appropriate to mention it last for various reasons. It is the *servant* of the educational design of the unit. Most of the time is absorbed in skills which are essentially of craftsmanship rather than design nature. This is particularly true in the languages (BASIC and various machine codes) in which we are now forced to write teaching programs; higher level languages allowing better design and more clearly structured programs are on the point of becoming available and technological developments, including the 16-bit microprocessor, will allow the educational aims to be more often met even with the loss in run-time efficiency that such languages tend to imply. For the present situation, we illustrate the balance of considerations that should be borne in mind using the programing checklist.

C5 PROGRAMMING CHECKLIST

1. For which system or systems has the program been developed?
2. Are these systems available for schools now or in the near future?
3. Have you chosen a system because of the peculiar non-transferable features? If so, would you consider modifying the requirements to make them more transferable?
4. Do you know details of the ROM monitor of the system and what this implies?
5. Do you know the version of BASIC to be used?
6. Do you know how much memory will be available for the program?
7. Is the suggested program likely to fit into this memory size?
8. What additional storage facilities are provided for the machine?
9. What additional hardware devices are provided for the system?
10. Are you fully aware of the facilities provided by the 'standard' machine?
11. Are you aware of the range of facilities which can be added through software routines in machine code?

12. Are you aware of additional facilities provided by hardware?
13. Do you know the overheads of using standard software, special software and hardware in terms of speed, memory use and transferability?
14. Have you established which facilities will be *necessary* for the successful implementation of the program?
15. Are they likely to produce sufficiently good performance for the user?
16. Does the necessary set of facilities exist on a system which is practicable for schools?
17. Is the speed of the program fast enough but not too fast?
18. Is the program logically crash proof?
19. Are all possible user errors trapped and help messages provided?
20. Are there any operations in the use of the program which would be at all complicated to a user inexperienced in the use of a computer system?
21. Is the internal structure of the program as efficient as it needs to be for good performance?
22. Which are the critical routines to optimise for speed and for memory size?
23. Is the program logically structured?
24. Is the program easily understood by the author and by the others?
25. Is there an available "library" of sub-routines which may help towards meeting the requirements of this program?
26. Are there any conventions for variables or routines agreed for this program unit to aid readability, set by yourself, your establishment, a national body or publishers?
27. Is the program adequately documented for the user to be able to feel at home with it from the start?
28. Is the program adequately documented for the author and other programmers or interested people clearly to understand its operation?
29. Are any 'special' routines documented in detail?
30. Is the program intended to be portable or transferable, if so, have common characteristics been established as being practical, are all machine dependent routines written and clearly documented subroutines, and do the equivalent routines on the other systems perform adequately?
31. Have you discussed any possible areas of difficult in implementation with the others in the design team so that alternative approaches could be considered if necessary?
32. Are you sufficiently confident about being able successfully to complete a program which will perform well enough to meet the design specifications and which will thus justify the time you spend?

REFERENCES

1. Burkhardt H., Fraser R. and Wells C., Teaching style and program design. Council for Educational Technology. To be published.
2. Burkhardt H., Eggleston J. F., Clowes M. and Fraser R., The classroom development of teaching material. Council for Educational Technology. To be published.
3. Fraser, R., Wells C. and Burkhardt H., *TESTDRIVE—A Handbook for ITMA Units.* Longmans, London (1981).

Comput. & Educ. Vol. 6, pp. 85 to 91, 1982
Printed in Great Britain

0360-1315/82/010085-07$03.00/0
Pergamon Press Ltd

TEACHING MATHEMATICS THROUGH PROGRAMMING IN THE CLASSROOM

J. A. M. Howe, P. M. Ross, K. R. Johnson, F. Plane
and R. Inglis

Department of Artificial Intelligence, University of Edinburgh,
Edinburgh EH12QL, Scotland

Abstract—An experiment in teaching mathematics to nearly 90 secondary school children, with the aid of microcomputers, has been running in an Edinburgh classroom since August 1980. The 6 TERAK microcomputers are being used in a way that is unconventional in CAL terms; they are being used by the children themselves to experiment with mathematical processes, in a new version of the LOGO language specially written for this investigation. Using these microcomputers in such a way allows the children to develop useful planning and 'debugging' talents, as well as helping them towards an understanding of the structure implicit in particular mathematical topics.

This paper describes the early stages of the investigation, and argues in favour of using microcomputers in schools to provide pupils with constructive general-purpose modeling tools, in addition to the more conventional type of CAI program that is directed towards a particular topic in a particular subject. The description of the investigation falls naturally into three parts: details of the version of LOGO being used, a short account of the background to the whole project and an explanation of how it fits, in practice, into the childrens' normal mathematics lessons.

INTRODUCTION

The essential principle underlying the teaching of programming in a mathematics class is that the pupils can use the computer as a mathematical "laboratory" in which to experiment. Devising a program to experiment with a mathematical concept, in effect "telling the machine how to do it", not only involves the child in the discipline of stating his thoughts in a precise (programming) language, but also involves him in the cycle of modifying his ideas as a result of seeing what the computer does with his descriptions, and this is potentially a formative experience in developing problem-solving skills.

Feurzeig *et al.*[2], the original proponents of the idea of teaching programming in mathematics classes, claimed (amongst other things) that doing so would provide pupils with an excellent environment for mathematical exploration and a context for getting to understand the general ideas necessary for problem-solving. Research during the past decade has gone some way towards justifying this. For example, there have been encouraging results from studies by Statz[5] on whether learning to program improves problem-solving and from Howe *et al.*[4] on the links between programming and mathematical ability.

Of course, there are vital prerequisites for the success of the idea: reliable computer hardware with good graphics, and powerful and easily usable software, so that the effort of using the computer does not obscure the general aims. The chosen programming language must be powerful, flexible and relatively "characterless"; that is it must not make certain kinds of operation easy and others hard, which would tend to impose certain kinds of approach to problems. It must also embody a simple and believable model of how the computer works, and give meaningful error messages expressed in terms of that model. To give a counter example, some versions of BASIC have opted to provide graphics commands compatible with the SIGGRAPH specifications, which require the idea of mappings from "windows" to "viewports" and from "viewports" to the screen, a notion much too bewildering for a tyro. Until recently, the hardware requirements have only been available on time-sharing mainframe systems, and so the approach has been impractical except in educational research laboratories. Now, microcomputers are powerful enough, and almost cheap enough, for the idea to be feasible in a school mathematics class room. The software requirements have been avilable, on certain large machines, for about ten years in the form of the LOGO language. It is not (yet) commercially available on any microcomputer, and so we have written a new version for the TERAK machine, a particularly versatile microcomputer.

Our current investigation is attempting to study some of the difficulties of integrating programming work into mathematics classes for half of the first year group in a secondary school (the other half being a control group). For instance, merely learning to use a computer will take up a part of the mathematics timetable— does the constraint of the syllabus allow enough time for worthwhile kinds of experimentation? This project is the natural continuation of a 2-yr study conducted within the Department of Artificial Intelligence. However, before describing the results of that study and the early stages of the present one, we shall first describe the version of the LOGO language that we are using.

ABOUT LOGO

Operational aspects

LOGO is an interactive, graphics-handling, list-processing language, originally based on another called LISP. Its most publicised feature is an orientable graphics cursor, called the "turtle", which can be controlled by body-centred commands such as FORWARD ⟨a distance⟩ or LEFT ⟨an angle⟩. The turtle can also be controlled by Cartesian commands. However, there are other general characteristics of LOGO that are less remarked upon but are much more important. One is that the language is genuinely extensible, another is the list-handling features.

To the experienced user the TERAK version of LOGO is a collection of about a hundred procedures that he can employ for such tasks as drawing on the screen, manipulating numbers and printing out text. (It is worth noting that only twenty of the hundred have anything to do with "turtle geometry".) In particular a certain few of them give the user the power to extend the language by defining new procedures, in terms of the existing set, that are syntactically indistinguishable from the existing set and can have the same syntactic possibilities. The mechanism for doing this is a simple screen editor, and the definition of a new procedure is superficially similar to a program in BASIC. The only requirement is that everything in the definition is known to the system *at the time the procedure is run*. This means that procedures can call each other, and be recursive. For example, the factorial function when defined in LOGO might look like this (with comments in lower case):

```
FACTORIAL 'N      N is the name of the input for the purposes
                  of the definition.
10 RESULT (IF ZEROQ :N THEN 1 ELSE
   MULTIPLY :N (FACTORIAL SUBTRACT :N 1))
                  :N is the value of the input.
```

This procedure can then be used anywhere, e.g. PRINT FACTORIAL 7 will print 5040. This is shorter and much more readable and comprehensible than what many versions of BASIC will allow:

```
50 N = 7
60 GOSUB 1000
70 PRINT X

....

1000 X = 1
1010 FOR J = 1, N
1020 X = X * J
1030 NEXT J
1040 RETURN
```

In our microcomputer version of LOGO, there is enough space to have about twenty average-sized procedures co-existing with the initial set.

Clearly there are many mathematical topics with which one might experiment whose concepts are rather distant from those dealt with by the hundred built-in procedures. If one were restricted to using only those, the system's usefulness would be very limited. However, the normal way of using the system is to build and use an additional set of procedures that are appropriate to the topic. For example, in set theory one might extend the language by building two procedures called UNION and INTERSECTION, that manipulate representations of sets appropriately, and then use these to verify or predict relations such as the distributive law. Of course, building the language extension must happen before one can use it, and this step may be too difficult or disproportionately time-consuming for a schoolchild. Because of this there is, besides a long-term procedure filing system, a mechanism by which a teacher (or whoever) can create a new system that incorporates any particular set of language extending procedures. When the pupil starts the new system, the extension is there waiting to be used.

The LOGO system, as described so far, would still not be particularly adaptable or useful were it not for the list-handling procedures. The built-in procedures each manipulate one or more of three data types: words, which are just text strings without spaces, numbers (including decimal parts if needed), and lists. A list is an ordered set of numbers, words or lists. Because lists can contain lists, and can be expanded or contracted at will, they can represent almost any kind of structure. Common examples include sentences, co-ordinates, general sets, tree structures, networks and symbolic descriptions of geometric figures.

Educational aspects.

It should be clear from the foregoing description that LOGO can be used in two distinctly different ways. In the more conventional of the two, the child is provided with one or more procedures and merely runs them in order to see a concept demonstrated in an unusual or graphic manner. As an example of this, we shall describe the procedures that we have used to introduce children to the topic of bar charts.

The first is called TYPIST. It is used with a worksheet that introduces simple experiments with letter frequencies. Essentially it is useful for taking the tedious bit out of an otherwise useful and instructive activity. When run, it clears the screen, draws a line across it halfway up, and sets up a bar for each letter of the alphabet at the bottom. When the user types, the letters appear in the top half and the appropriate bars grow at the bottom. The letters are in the graphics display, so that the pupil can have a copy of the whole display on the printer.

The second is a procedure called CHOOSY, with one numeric input. It selects a random digit the given number of times, and grows a bar chart on the screen which shows how many times each digit has been chosen so far. We have used it to make some points about randomness. Both CHOOSY and TYPIST are merely simple games, useful because they present an idea in a powerful and unusual way. (Each is about 25 lines long.)

In addition to these, the pupil can experiment with random walks and random numbers by using procedures built permanantly into LOGO. For example, the command.

REPEAT 100 (FORWARD 5 AND RIGHT PICK 360)

will draw a random walk of constant step size. A pupil of about 14 or more could easily experiment with this idea—by making the step size vary as well, for instance, or restricting the random angle to multiples of 10. Questions they might ask are "does a constant step size make it more likely for the walk to leave the screen?"; "does a restricted choice of angle make the turtle stay on the screen, and if so, what are the restrictions?"; "does the turtle always return to the centre in a 2-D walk, or only in a 1-D walk?". Of course, it is possible that a pupil might never think of such experiments—it seems sensible to seed the imagination by asking one or two questions on a worksheet that can be solved without too much (or too little!) effort, and suggesting one or two open-ended projects.

A procedure such as TYPIST could equally well be written in BASIC, since only the author of the package needs to know what is happening inside it. This "black box" approach is relatively undemanding of the user, as opposed to the "glass box" or "kit of parts" approach. In this latter style, the user is given, or has to build, a language extension that contains the "atomic elements" for the topic under study. If the learner has to build his own "kit of parts" out of the existing set, such a UNION and INTERSECTION in set theory, then his noetic task is essentially one of clarifying and extending his existing understanding of the topic, since he has to translate the processes into procedures, and the objects into a representation suitable for the computer. As Howe [3] points out, this places considerable cognitive demands on him. Not only does he need to be at least partially familiar with the mathematics aspects, he also needs to know what computing procedures are available to him and to have some sense of what their potentialities are, besides having a vocabulary of computing constructs. For example, when constructing a drawing that includes circular arcs, he may need to know:

  (i) that procedures ARCL and ARCR, that draw leftward and rightward arcs, exist;
 (ii) that they each take a radius as first input, and an angle through which to turn as the second;
(iii) that the angle of turning is necessarily the same as the angle subtended by the arc at the centre;
 (iv) that neither input need be an integer;
  (v) that the procedures do certain sensible things if either or both of the inputs are negative.

A sensible alternative is to provide the learner with a prewritten "kit of parts", but this does not remove the load, merely lessens it. He still has to become familiar with what the component procedures do and how they may be written using these components. We shall describe two examples of how this might work out in practice in a mathematics class. They are taken from the first- and second-year syllabuses, and concern the topics of number bases and of geometric transformations.

Example 1. Number bases

In this topic we have chosen to provide a set of LOGO procedures that allow a user to perform calculations in any number base, and to convert numbers from one base to another. The choice of representation is, as always, of paramount importance—in this case, the representation should

(a) make it clear which base a number is in (EVERY time it is seen)
(b) make the idea of columns (or digits) clear
(c) be usable in ANY base. In particular, this means avoiding the artificial conventions for digits, such as the common one of using A–F for hexadecimal digits.
(d) be very readable!

The one we chose is a list, essentially a list of the digits together with a final element which is itself a list and contains the base as a number in base 10. For example, 31 (decimal) would be represented as

   [3 1 [10]]

in base 10, and in base 16 as

   [1 15 [16]]   (meaning $1 \times 16 + 15$)

and -256 (decimal) would be written in base 16 as

   [$-$ 1 0 0 [16]]

This notation has the advantage of being recognisably different from the normal, so that any integer is definitely in base 10.

There are six procedures in the set, and the base in use at a given time is determined by a global variable called **BASE**. The procedures are

(a)   CONVERT. This takes a number or list, and turns it into a list expressing that number in the given base. Thus, if BASE is 7,
       PRINT CONVERT 16 will print [2 2 [7]]
       PRINT CONVERT [3 3 [8]] will print [3 6 [7]]
(b)   DEC. This turns a list into a decimal number, so that
       PRINT DEC [3 6 [7]] will print 27.
(c)   SUM. This takes two arguments, each either lists or decimal numbers, and returns their sum in the current base.
(d)   PRODUCT. This is similar to SUM.
(e)   DIFFERENCE. This is similar to SUM.
(f)   QUOTIENT. This is similar to SUM.

Because the procedures will accept numbers either as normal decimals or in the list notation, it is easy to make the point that a number is the same whatever notation it happens to be expressed in. Doing simple sums makes the idea of columns and the idea of carrying fairly clear, e.g.

        PRINT SUM [1 5 [8]][1 4 [8]]
        prints the 'number' [3 1 [8]]

and this can be verified by using DEC to turn these back into decimal numbers and doing a normal addition.

It is worth noting that, written in LOGO, the procedures CONVERT and DEC are about 6 lines long, and the other four are each 3 lines long. A pupil who used these to become familiar with the idea of number bases could then look inside these procedures to see how they are implemented, thus learning the simple algorithm by which a number can be converted from one base to another. (If such an algorithm is too complex or not clearly expressible in LOGO, there is a mechnism by which a teacher can prevent pupils from ever seeing inside a procedure). These procedures could be used at various levels in secondary school maths. Clearly they can be used in S1 and S2, but a pupil in S3 or S4 could use them to study the question of whether the idea of a fractional or negative base is at all sensible—this might involve rewriting the CONVERT algorithm, as the provided one might not be general enough.

The above procedures, written in LOGO, look like this (comments are given in lower case):

```
CONVERT 'I
10 IF LISTQ :I THEN MAKE 'I DEC :I          If the input is a list, use DEC
                                            to turn it into a number.
20 NEW 'L AND MAKE 'L [ ]                    L will hold the final result.
30 NEW 'NEG AND MAKE 'NEG 'FALSE             NEG holds the sign temporarily.
40 IF (LESSQ :I 0) THEN MAKE 'NEG 'TRUE
   AND MAKE 'I SBT 0 :I
```

```
50 WHILE (GREATERQ :I (SUBTRACT :BASE 1))
   MAKE 'L PUTFIRST (REMAINDER :I :BASE) :L
   AND
   MAKE 'I (SHARE :I :BASE)                          SHARE = integer division.
60 MAKE 'L PUTFIRST :I :L                            Insert remaining digit.
70 IF :NEG THEN MAKE 'L PUTFIRST '— :L               Insert sign if negative.
80 RESULT JOIN :L ⟨⟨:BASE⟩⟩                          Attach list giving base.

DEC 'L
10 NEW 'B AND MAKE 'B :L{COUNT :L}{1}                B = base of input.
20 NEW 'I AND MAKE 'I 0                              I will hold final result.
30 NEW 'NEG AND MAKE 'NEG 'FALSE                     NEG holds the sign temporarily.
40 IF (EQUALQ :L{1} '−) THEN
   MAKE 'NEG 'TRUE AND MAKE 'L REST :L               Prune off any sign.
50 WHILE (GREATERQ COUNT :L 1)
   MAKE 'I (ADD (MULTIPLY :I :B) :L{1})
   AND MAKE 'L REST :L                               Assemble no. from digits.
60 RESULT IF :NEG THEN SUBTRACT 0 :I ELSE :I

SUM 'A 'B
10 IF LISTQ :A THEN MAKE 'A DEC :A                   Make first input a number.
20 IF LISTQ :B THEN MAKE 'B DEC :B                   Make second input a number.
30 RESULT CONVERT (ADD :A :B)                        Convert their sum!
```

The other procedures are nearly identical to SUM.

Example 2. Geometric transformations

In this topic we have written a set of procedures that will allow a child to experiment with linear and rotational transformations and reflections. The set is a nice example of the toolkit idea—it consists of the following:

(a)   two procedures called AHEAD and TURN, which can be used to create geometric patterns e.g. one might define TRIANGLE as
       TRIANGLE 'SIDE
       10 REPEAT 3 (AHEAD :SIDE AND TURN 120)
   These are used instead of FORWARD etc., so that drawings can be rescaled by changing a global variable called SCALE. The definition of AHEAD shows how this is done:
       AHEAD 'N
       10 FORWARD (MULTIPLY :N :SCALE)
   If the value of SCALE is 2, the figure drawn by TRIANGLE 20 will be twice as large as when the value of SCALE is 1.
(b)   a procedure called AXES which draws co-ordinate axes with the origin in the centre of the screen (and labels them).
(c)   a procedure called DRAW, that takes two inputs. The first is the name of a procedure defined by the user using AHEAD and TURN, and the second is a list giving X and Y co-ordinates relative to the displayed axes. The command DRAW 'TRIANGLE [50 10] would draw the triangle at the current SCALE starting at X = 50, Y = 10.
(d)   REFLECT, which takes one number. It draws the reflection of the shape most recently DRAWn, in a mirror inclined at the given angle to the X-axis. It also draws a dotted line to represent the mirror.
(e)   ROTATE, which rotates the turtle about the origin by the given number of degrees. Hence.
       DRAW 'TRIANGLE [50 10] followed by
       ROTATE 90 AND TRIANGLE
   will draw the triangle rotated through 90 degrees about the origin, therefore starting at X = −10, Y = 50.

With this set, it is possible to experiment with compounding sequences of rotations and reflections, such as trying to find how to reflect any shape in the origin. The shapes do NOT have to be closed shapes! The set is introduced to S1 pupils in the course of several worksheets, again leading towards potentially interesting experiments. A pupil higher up the school might choose instead to reproduce how, for example, REFLECT works, learning some ideas in trigonometry in the process.

We use worksheets together with the language extension for any topic, so that that learner can assimilate the knowledge gradually and in a structured way. The worksheets contain information and exercises, and "seeds"—suggestions for open-ended experimentation. They have a further important function, not explicit, which is to introduce the learner to the parallels between the computer representation and the mathematical one—for instance, the list representation in the number bases example. The choice of representation in LOGO is a very important one, with major repercussions. In particular it sets limits on what the user can do at his level of competence, and these limits may be too narrow to allow him to draw adequate mathematical parallels. An interesting example of this is given by du Boulay [1], in a study that attempted to use LOGO to re-teach mathematics to a group of primary school teacher trainees who had self-confessed "blocks" about mathematics. When studying the topic of fractions, his volunteers started by trying to represent fractions as pie-charts. However, they were thwarted by the technical difficulties of constructing drawings of pie-charts, and so never got to grips with ideas about fractions. Even when they were given procedures that did the drawings, the task of interpreting the drawings proved too hard, especially in the potentially interesting cases of combining fractions with unequal denominators and of vulgar fractions. The unfortunate general conclusion that may be drawn from this is that only in those cases in which the choice of representation is simple and obvious can the learner be allowed to indulge in unprompted experimentation. The pedagogical and time penalties may otherwise be too great.

It might be suggested that, since worksheets and prewritten procedures steer the user towards particular discoveries, experimentation in this LOGO "mathematics laboratory" raises questions similar to those that used to be asked about work in physics laboratories. Why have pupils "discover" things when it is quicker to tell them or show them the "discovery" process? Clearly one answer is that there is a tremendous psychological advantage in the user doing it himself, even if fairly unproductively. There are also very important differences between the two kinds of laboratory: physics experiments are aimed at the discovery of a (finite) number of laws, whereas mathematical ones are aimed at the discovery of an infinite number of patterns—discoveries can be genuinely personal! There is also as much to learn from designing the apparatus as from using it, something rarely true in physics at a school level.

BACKGROUND TO THE PRESENT STUDY

The evidence from a two-year evaluation study within the department suggests that this approach to mathematics can benefit the less able child. Our pupils were 11—13 year old boys from a local school, divided into two groups of 11 each. The experimental group, of lower initial ability compared to the others, came to our LOGO classroom during normal school hours, and the control group followed a normal timetable. The boys' performance on various tests was recorded at several stages during the two years.

In this study, the experimental group spent the first year learning computing concepts and techniques. The worksheets introduced the boys to computational ideas such as procedures, variables and recursion; problem-solving tactics like decomposition, and the use of debugging skills such as using a trace facility. In the second year, the emphasis shifted to using programming to explore school mathematics topics in arithmetic, geometry and algebra. From the results of the study[4], we concluded that the experimental group's ability to do maths and their understanding of maths had improved relative to the performance of the control group. In particular an item analysis suggested that their grasp of algebraic topics was marginally better than that of the control group. Moreover, the class teachers were of the opinion that the experimental group pupils "could argue sensibly about mathematical issues" and "explain mathematical difficulties clearly", but rated the control group poorly for this. Although these results were encouraging, there are many uncontrollable factors that could account for them. For example, the experimental group might have benefited by the closer personal attention they received, or the extra time they spent on mathematics. The results might also be explained by a Hawthorne effect. For these reasons we moved the work into a school classroom, where the pupils could be taught by their normal class teachers as part of the normal timetable.

THE PRESENT STUDY

In the state secondary school in question, mathematics classes in the first year are of mixed ability. We have installed 6 microcomputers and 2 printers in one room, and 3 of the 6 first-year classes come to it for their normal maths lessons. The other three classes act as a control group, and never see the computers. The class teachers, each of whom had an initial course on programming in LOGO, are now solely responsible for the teaching; our own role is now one of observers, responsible for producing teaching materials and maintaining the equipment. The school uses a modular maths scheme, in which each fortnight is devoted to a particular topic, and pairs of pupils work their way at their own pace through a series of workcards and worksheets. Because there is not enough time to teach programming first and mathematics second, we are trying to introduce both in parallel, using our own worksheets containing LOGO-based material introduced at appropriate points in the sequence of normal workcards.

The main problems are practical, related to classroom management. With only 6 machines, and 24—30 pupils in each class, each pair can spend rather less than half of the five available half-hour lessons each week actually working at the machine. In order to prevent bottlenecks, the LOGO-based worksheets include a proportion of material that should be done away from the machine. However, this is hard to enforce, and demanding on the teacher. The children are now fairly adept at starting the system and using their own floppy disks—the first fortnight of the year was devoted to the rudiments of using the machines. Their most serious difficulty lies in seeing the computer-based work as a genuine part of mathematics; this has meant giving them tests on LOGO material, it order to allay anxieties about the control group getting "more marks".

The results of the project will be judged on several sets of information. We gave all six classes two standardised NFER tests at the start of the year; there will also be two post-tests, besides the results of the school's own tests set occasionally throughout the year. In addition, the LOGO system keeps a record of whatever is typed on the keyboard, together with timings, on the user's floppy disk; these are read and printed in the department at the end of each fortnight. Thus we have some record of what each pair has done at the key board. The impression at present is that the statistical distribution of childrens' progress is settling into a bimodal shape. This is more or less as expected—the interesting question is that of the correlation with initial ability in mathematics. On the practical side the bimodal distribution is emphasising the perpetual problems of managing a class of mixed and widely-varying ability. Ideally we would like to be able to introduce programming into mathematics classes S1, S2 and S3, and follow individuals' progress over several years, to observe any effects on mathematical and problem-solving skills.

SOME CONCLUSIONS

It seems likely that computers will spread their effect throughout schools in the next decade or so, making the benefits from computer modelling tools more apparent. One effect will be that teachers will have to cope with many levels of sophistication in computing and it seems sensible to use a language such as LOGO that can be tailored to many ability levels. This would reduce the demands on teachers to be familiar with two or more conventional languages such as BASIC or PASCAL, that are suited to particular age bands within the school. The knowledge required to be able just to run a simulation package is soon likely to increase greatly, as packages begin to take advantage of the power of currently available microcomputers. In addition to this, we foresee a demand for the teaching of the concepts and techniques of modelling and of computing, for which the current set of "educationl" languages will be inadequate. We believe that the results of our present project will provide valuable information about the feasibility of this.

Acknowledgements—The authors would like to thank the staff of James Gillespie's School for their co-operation, assistance and enthusiasm in their current project. All the authors, apart from J. A. M. Howe, are supported by a grant from the Social Science Research Council of Great Britain.

REFERENCES

1. du Boulay J. B. H., Learning primary mathematics through computer programming. Ph.D. Dissertation, Edinburgh University (1978).
2. Feurzeig W., Papert S., Bloom M., Grant R. and Solomon C., Programming languages as a conceptual framework for teaching mathematics. Report No. 1889, Bolt Beranek & Newman Inc., Cambridge, MA, (1969).
3. Howe, J. A. M., Learning through model building. In *Expert Systems in the Micro-electronic Age* (Edited by D. Michie). Edinburgh University Press (1979).
4. Howe J. A. M., O'Shea T. and Plane F., Teaching mathematics through LOGO programming: an evaluation study. In *Computer-Assisted Learning—Scope, Progress and Limits* (Edited by R. Lewis and E. D. Tagg). North-Holland, Amsterdam (1979).
5. Statz, J. Problem solving and LOGO. In *Final Report of Syracuse University LOGO Project*. Syracuse University, New York (1973).

Comput. & Educ. Vol. 6, pp. 93 to 98, 1982
Printed in Great Britain

0360-1315/82/010093-06$03.00/0
Pergamon Press Ltd

LOGO BUILDING BLOCKS

STUDENT TEACHERS USING COMPUTER-BASED MATHEMATICS APPARATUS

J. B. H. du Boulay[1] and J. A. M. Howe[2]

[1]Department of Computing Science, University of Aberdeen, King's College, Aberdeen AB9 2UB
and [2]Department of Artificial Intelligence, University of Edinburgh, Forrest Hill,
Edinburgh EH1 2QL, Scotland

Abstract—We describe experiments in which student teachers, who have been identified by their college of education as needing mathematical help, undertook a computer-based elementary maths course. Our objectives were to assess the effect of this work on the students' mathematical performance and attitude.

The students were given hands-on experience of the programming language LOGO, which included both writing simple programs and running pre-defined procedures, such as those for illustrating the multiplication of fractions pictorially. The computer was used as a piece of mathematics apparatus with which the students could experiment: it did not take any tutorial or managerial role.

A variety of mathematics performance and attitude tests were administered pre and post, and the results are described and analysed. Some evidence for the success of the approach is shown, though the experiments underline the enormous difficulty of helping this kind of student.

INTRODUCTION

Colleges of Education have mixed success in ensuring that their students are fit to teach mathematics in primary school[1–4]. As a result, there are some teachers who lack confidence in their mathematical ability, teach the subject poorly and pass on their distaste for mathematics to their pupils.

One approach with potential is to give student teachers access to a computer equipped with the programming language LOGO. This allows them to conduct mathematical experiments appropriate to their level of ability, and to their individual needs[5–8]. For example, many students have difficulty with the multiplication of fractions. In the computer, a fraction can be used as a ratio to change the size of a drawing. So a student can get an intuitive feel for fraction multiplication by predicting and observing the size change produced when a drawing is re-scaled.

PRELIMINARY RESEARCH

We tried out the approach in a preliminary study working with 15 student primary teachers who were attending a local College of Education[9,10]. Using case studies, we showed that programming as a method of learning mathematics had a number of benefits. For example, the requirement to make each problem explicit before it could be turned into a series of program instructions to be executed forced the students to acknowledge weaknesses in their mathematics, and to explore these weaknesses. In other words, they were confronted by their own inadequate grasp of mathematics, and had to come to terms with it in a practical way.

Initially, we followed a two-part teaching strategy. Students were taught LOGO programming, then went on to use programming to explore troublesome maths topics. However, we quickly discovered that they worried about spending time learning LOGO and then writing programs, even though they enjoyed it, because of the many other demands on their time and because they could not easily see how the activity related to classroom teaching.

We increased the perceived relevance of the programming by linking it more directly to mathematical topics that the students were finding troublesome and by providing new LOGO procedures, making it easier for them to explore such topics. Besides saving time, the provision of new procedures, rather than expecting students to write them for themselves, helped them concentrate on mathematical as opposed to programming issues.

The close involvement with each participant in this study—almost evocative of the analyst–patient relationship—made it difficult for us to gauge how much of the benefit was due to the computer-based work and how much was due to our intervention as teachers. Notice, too, that the participants were volunteers. So we embarked on two new studies, embedding the approach within the mathematics regime of a local College of Education, and explored its effects on student teachers' attitudes to mathematics and on their mathematical performance.

TWO STUDIES

In both studies, students in experimental groups followed work modules exploring shape and number concepts. The shape work dealt with angles and their measurement, the angle and symmetry properties of regular polygons, states and transformations. The number work dealt with topics such as place value, multiplication and division of decimals, operations on whole numbers and fractions.

The students' work was highly structured and involved only a small amount of program building. The main reason for this was that we wanted to avoid the problem of the students perceiving the work as fun but irrelevant, which we had encountered in the preliminary study. But they were expected to put a lot of effort into explaining how and why basic mathematical processes worked, by trying to describe the algorithm used by the computer program or, in some cases, by writing a program for themselves. In other words, the work was much more concerned with *explanations of processes* than with the practice of those processes. So the course continually faced the student with the problem of trying the "unpick" and understand basic mathematical notions that she had learned to take for granted.

(i) *The second year study*

The College identified students who might benefit from the computer-based approach. These were 12 second year students who had not reached the required standard in their first year mathematics course, and consequently were required to take a remedial course during their second year in College. The students were randomly assigned by the College to an "experimental" group of 6 students and a "control" group of 6 students. The "rest" of the second year consisting of 36 students had performed satisfactorily in their first year.

Students in the experimental group travelled to the University once per week for 17 sessions spread over an academic year. The average time per student spent at the University was 26.3 h. While these students undertook the LOGO-based course outlined above, the control group remained in the College and covered the same mathematical topics in a more traditional, and less demanding manner under the guidance of a member of the College's staff. So both groups were taking extra mathematics by comparison with the rest of their year who only sat the pre- and post-tests. Also all the students took a common mathematics course whose content was entirely under the control of the College and which played no part in the study.

The following tests were given to all the students. Two tests, matched for content and difficulty, were made up from items drawn from NFER's Secondary Mathematics Item Bank. One was used as a pre-test, and the other as a post-test. Four attitude tests were used, the same tests being employed both pre and post. Three of these tests were taken from Lumb and Child[4]. The fourth consisted of a set of 5 questions about how the student had enjoyed mathematics at various stages of her education. In addition, two tests of shape and number were given to the experimental and control groups, the same tests being employed just before starting a module and just after completing it. Part of the number test was taken from Rees[3].

(ii) *The third year study*

Two groups of students were involved. One was an "experimental" group of 9 students who were judged to need mathematical help despite the efforts of the College to provide remedial tuition during the students' previous year. The other group, the "rest" of the third year, contained 25 students who took no mathematics courses either as part of this experiments or within the College.

Students in the experimental group travelled to the University once per week for 17 sessions spread over an academic year. The average time spent per student at the University was only 13.9 h. The experimental group followed the same course of work as the second year study and the same tests were administered.

RESULTS OF THE ATTITUDE TESTS

(i) *Second year study*

Detailed analysis of the results of the attitude tests are presented elsewhere[11]. What follows is a brief description. Although students were assigned randomly to experimental and control groups, the experimental group enjoyed school and College maths less than either the control group or the rest of the year group. The attitude data also suggest that at the start the experimental group's attitude to maths was more favourable than the attitude of either the control group or the rest group. It was viewed as an awful, unenjoyable, uncomfortable activity. By the end of the study, the experimental group had moved more negative on most dimensions. So facing up to thier mathematical difficulties did not endear the subject to them, even though its perceived value increased.

As for attitude to teaching, the situation was reversed. On a number of dimensions, the control group was significantly more negative at the start than the rest group whereas the experimental group's view was close to that of the rest group.

The overall picture suggests an imbalance between the experimental and control group with the former liking teaching more and disliking maths more than the control group at the start. By the end of the study the students in the experimental group seemed to have grown in their dislike of maths, while increasing their liking of teaching, whereas the control group had a somewhat ambivalent but more neutral attitude to maths and a much improved attitude to maths teaching.

(ii) *The third year study*

On the whole, the third year students' enjoyment of maths remained stable throughout the year. The only exception was that the experimental group changed its perception of primary school, remembering maths as less enjoyable at the end of the study. As might be expected, the experimental group enjoyed maths at secondary school much less than the rest of the third year.

Dealing with attitude to maths first of all, the rest group was more positively disposed to the subject than the experimental group. In general terms, the attitude of the experimental group was closest to that of the second year experimental group, but whereas that group became more negative over the year, the third year experimental group became more positive, ending up close to the position taken by the control group in the second year study.

Turning now to attitude to teaching mathematics, both groups started off with a favourable view, which became more favourable over the year. When we compare the two studies, we find that the attitude of both rest groups was similar, but that the attitude of the third-year experimental group to maths was more positive than that of the experimental and control groups in the second year study.

RESULTS OF MATHS TESTS

(i) *The second year study*

The mean scores in the general maths pre- and post-tests, each worth 39 marks are given in Table 1.

The scores show that both the experimental and the control group scores were hovering around the pass mark whereas the rest group was performing at a much more acceptable level. In general, the values of the standard deviations were large, suggesting considerable variability within all three groups. In practice, scores for the remedial groups ranged from 16 to 28, with 8 members of the rest group achieving scores within that range. This indicates a discrepancy between this test and the tests used by the College to decide which students needed remedial help.

Because the groups were less homogeneous at the start of the study than we might have wished, the chance of identifying significant shifts in performance as a result of the intervention was much reduced.

The general maths tests contained questions covering algebra, geometry and arithmetic. Breaking down the data into these three categories showed that over the year the experimental group's algebra performance declined to the control group's level of performance, its geometry was static but its arithmetic improved. But the control group's arithmetic and geometry performances also improved, bringing them closer to the performances of the experimental group which started out at a significant advantage in the pre-test.

A shape test was given to the control and experimental groups, pre and post. The data are given in Table 2.

Table 1. Mean scores in general maths tests

	Pre		Post	
	Mean	SD	Mean	SD
Exp. ($n = 6$)	22.3	4.53	22.5	5.08
Cont. ($n = 6$)	18.8	2.92	21.8	3.87
Rest ($n = 36$)	29.4	5.29	30.4	5.05

Table 2. Mean scores shape test, pre and post

| | Pre | | Post | | |
	Mean	SD	Mean	SD	Sig.
Exp.	3.67	2.48	9.5	3.93	1%
Cont.	3.00	2.19	7.83	3.96	5%
Sig.	NS		NS		

Given that the test was worth 21 marks, their performance in the pre-test was extremely poor. However, as a result of the intervening teaching, both groups' performance improved. In the case of the experimental group, the improvement was significant at the 1% level by t-test, bringing them close to a pass score in the test, whereas the control group's improvement was significant at the 5% level by t-test, leaving the average performance still well below a pass mark.

We turn now to look at the results of the number test, worth 45 marks, that was given to the experimental and control groups pre and post. The data are given in Table 3.

Again the performances of both groups were very poor. Also, contrary to our expectations, the control group performed better than the experimental group on the pre-test to the extent that their mean performance was significantly better compared to the experimental group. But whereas the remedial number work in College had little effect on the mean score of the control group, the computer-based number work boosted the scores of the experimental group, the increase being significant at the 5% level.

The number test contained three different batches of questions (a) calculations e.g. $\sqrt{1000}$; (b) explanations, e.g. "in dividing 53.26 by 2.7, explain why one is allowed to change 2.7 into 27", and (c) illustrations, e.g. "draw a picture to illustrate 3/8". Breaking down the scores into these categories showed clearly that the control group were better at tackling pre-test questions which called for an explanation, but that the gap had narrowed after the intervening activity. Since the computer-based work forced the students to give explanations, this improvement is consistent with that strategy.

(ii) The third year study

The mean scores for the general maths pre- and post-test, worth 39 marks, are listed in Table 4.

As might be expected, the initial difference between the performances of the two groups was significant at the 1% level. The performance of the rest group was similar to the performance of the rest group in the second year study, while the performance of the experimental group lay mid-way between the performances of the control and experimental groups in the second year study. The actual scores for members of the experimental group ranged from 10 to 29, with 10 members of the rest group achieving scores in that range. Again, this indicates the discrepancy between the general maths test and the College's method of assessment.

In the post-test, the difference in performance of the two groups was still significant. Both groups improved in performance. The improvement was greater for the experimental group but was not significant due to the high variance in the scores.

Table 3. Results of number test, pre and post

| | Pre | | Post | | |
	Mean	SD	Mean	SD	Sig.
Exp.	20.75	2.38	26.17	4.89	5%
Cont.	26.1	2.13	28.2	4.32	NS
Sig.	1%		NS		

Table 4. Mean scores of third year groups in general maths pre- and post-test

| | Pre | | Post | | |
	Mean	SD	Mean	SD	Sig
Exp. ($n = 9$)	20.9	6.53	24.7	5.41	NS
Rest ($n = 25$)	28.6	5.67	30.5	4.46	5%
Sig.	1%		1%		

Table 5. Mean scores on shape test, pre and post

| | Pre | | Post | | |
	Mean	SD	Mean	SD	Sig.
Exp.	3.00	1.94	6.22	2.11	1%

The scores were broken down into areas of mathematics, as in the second year study. The performance of the experimental group on algebra questions was stable, like that of the control group in the second year. Improvements in performance by the experimental group were recorded for both geometry and arithmetic topics. But the rest group also improved its geometry and arithmetic performance which might suggest that the post-test questions in arithmetic and geometry were easier than those used in the pre-test. Since the pre- and post-tests were constructed to be of equal difficulty using items from NFER's item bank, it is more likely that the improvement was a real one. For example, we cannot neglect the effect of teaching practice on post-test performances.

The shape test was administered to the experimental group only. The scores are shown in Table 5.

The weaker geometry marks in the general maths pre-test were reflected in the shape test. The experimental group's performance was inferior to that of the second year experimental group, but the same as the second year control group. However, the improvement in performance, although also significant at the 1% level, was poorer than that of the control group in the second year study, and still fell well short of an acceptable standard.

The results of the Number test are given in Table 6.

The test was worth 45 marks, so the experimental groups's performance was poor, being similar to the performance on the control group in the second year study. Moreover, there was no improvement as a result of the intervening activity. Breaking down the test into calculations, explanations and illustrations showed that there had been no significant shift in favour of a particular question type.

DISCUSSION

In the second year study, each student spent 26.3 h working with the computer-based shape and number modules. This is somewhat less than the estimated completion time for the two modules (30–40 h), so not surprisingly few completed either one. In each case most omitted the latter sections, dealing with transformations and fractions. Despite this, the experimental group made significant gains in the shape and number tests. Curiously, this improvement was not reflected in the experimental group's performance in the general maths test. It started at a significant advantage over the control group, and advantage which largely disappeared by the end. This appears to be due in part to a relative deterioration in the experimental group's performance on algebraic topics, and in part to the control group's relative improvement in both shape and number topics. Of course, the experimental group's negative attitude to the subject was a factor that might have depressed performance in the post-test. Indeed, the gains recorded in the shape and number test were remarkable when viewed against a backcloth of growing dislike of the subject.

Students in the third year study spent only 13.9 h on average working with the computer-based shape and number modules. This was about half the estimated time required. While they covered approximately the same number of sections in the modules, they did so in a much more superficial way. Whereas the second year students were able to think about mathematical issues, due to the time restrictions the third year students had to skim the modules, and concentrated on answering the questions at the expense of thinking about issues. This would account for their poorer performance on the shape test. Although the third year students' performance on the general maths test showed a 20% improvement on geometry and number topics, this improvement was not significant due to the high variance in the scores.

The fact that neither experimental group made dramatic gains in performance after working with the computer-based materials might seem to be a disappointing outcome. But while we would have

Table 6. Mean scores on number test, pre and post

| | Pre | | Post | | |
	Mean	SD	Mean	SD	Sig.
Exp.	26.56	4.71	27.89	5.54	NS

welcomed clear-cut evidence, it would be quite unrealistic to expect that 10–20 h of computer-based instruction, spread over a year, would produce a startling improvement in students who had struggled with the subject in the classroom for many hundreds of hours.

CONCLUSION

Our objective was to find out if a short remedial maths course based on programming would help trainee primary school teachers whose mathematics was known to be weak. While some of the test results indicated enhanced performance after taking the course, other results did not bear out this finding. Factors which could not be properly controlled included students' attitude to taking part in the experiment, the allocation of students to experimental and control groups and the amount of time spent working with the computer-based materials. Undoubtedly these affected the outcome and ought to be controlled before a final judgement is made about the value of the computer-based approach.

Encouraged by the positive remarks made by students who took part in the studies, the College of Education is continuing the work during 1981/82, using a Terak micro-computer, lent by the Scottish Microelectronics Development Programme. Besides removing the stigma associated with travelling to the University for help, working in College eases the access problem since students are able to work through the modules in their own time, days or evenings, and at their own pace. Performances recorded under these conditions are a much better measure of any benefit accruing from the computer-based intervention. We await the outcome with interest, but for the moment, LOGO's value to student teachers must remain an open question.

Acknowledgements—We thank the staff of Craiglockhart College of Education, especially Mrs Greta Clarke, for all their help in setting up and conducting these studies. Also, we are grateful to the students who took part for their patience and good humour. This work was funded by a research grant from the Social Science Research Council.

REFERENCES

1. Lumb D. Student teachers and mathematics. *Math. Teach.* **68,** 47–50 (1974).
2. Kerslake D., Attitudes 1974. *Math. Teach.* **68,** 47–48 (1974).
3. Rees R., An investigation of some common methematical difficulties experienced by students. *Math. School* **3,** 25–27 (1974).
4. Lumb D. and Child D., Changing attitudes to the subject, and the teaching of mathematics amongst student teachers. *Educ. Stud.* **2,** (1976).
5. Feurzeig W., Papert S., Bloom M., Grant R. and Solomon C., Programming languages as a conceptual framework for teaching mathematics. Report no. 1889, Bolt Beranek & Newman Inc., Cambridge, MA (1969).
6. Papert S., Teaching children to be mathematicians vs teaching children about mathematics. *Int. J. Math. Educ. Sci. Technol.* **3,** 249–262 (1972).
7. Papert, S., *Mindstorms: Children, Computers and Powerful Ideas.* Harvester Press, Brighton (1980).
8. Howe, J., O'Shea T. and Plane F., Teaching mathematics through LOGO programming: an evaluation study. D.A.I. Research Paper no. 115, Department of Artificial Intelligence, University of Edinburgh (1979).
9. du Boulay B., Learning primary mathematics through computer programming. Ph.D. Thesis, Department of Artificial Intelligence, University of Edinburgh (1978).
10. du Boulay B., Teaching teachers mathematics through programming. *Int. J. Math. Educ. Sci. Technol.* **11,** 347–360 (1980).
11. du Boulay B. and Howe J., Student teachers' attitudes to maths: differential effects of a computer based course. *Proceedings of IFIP 3rd World Conference on Computers in Education.* To be published.

Comput. & Educ. Vol. 6, pp. 99 to 104, 1982
Printed in Great Britain

0360-1315/82/010099-06$03.00/0
Pergamon Press Ltd

ADAPTIVE FEATURES OF A CAL SYSTEM BASED ON INFORMATION RETRIEVAL

Gösta Grahne

University of Helsinki, Department of Computer Science, Tukholmankatu 2,
SF-00250 Helsinki 25, Finland

Abstract—A CAL system named STUDIO is presented. The system is under development and is being implemented on a Burroughs B1700 computer using the DMSII data management system.

STUDIO is an information retrieval system provided with a teaching strategy. The instructional material to be presented is divided into frames, which are regarded as retrievable documents. The frames are classified with weighted index terms describing the contents of the frame. The index terms used within a course form a course thesaurus. The thesaurus is used when designing the structure of the course and in each individual run-time instructional decision in the course.

After giving a general presentation of some methods of information retrieval, this paper shows how these methods are utilised in the STUDIO system, especially in the individualisation of instruction. Some aspects of student modelling are also discussed.

INTRODUCTION AND MAIN OBJECTIVES

One of the widely recognised problems in CAL is that of writing the instructional material. Using the traditional author-language approach the effort of producing one hour of CAL tuition is considerable —according to [1,2] up to 500 h. Since not all pedagogues have programming ability, or the willingness to learn it, a team approach to courseware production is often required. This makes the process stiffer and more complicated. Furthermore almost every author-language is machine dependent [1]; thus the painstakingly obtained courseware is not portable. This calls for the development of methods to facilitate the courseware production process. The possibility of utilising information retrieval techniques in CAL was first recognised by Osin [3] in his SMITH system. Our aim is to explore this potential further.

Another point of interest is the individualisation of instruction. The author-language approach to CAL is intuitively based on the branching program concept of Crowder. The computer, however, with its massive capacity to store and manipulate data, offers more sophisticated scope for adaptation. This has been recognised in the Artificial Intelligence (AI) approach to CAL (e.g. [4]), but in exploring curriculum structure with their semantic and procedural networks, AI workers tie their systems to that curriculum. Our objective is to develop a context-free CAL system, in which the individualisation of instruction is not based only on the intuition of the author-language user. Information retrieval techniques are inherently well suited to these ends also. A third objective is to utilise standard database management systems in file operations in CAL.

INFORMATION RETRIEVAL

The discipline of information retrieval deals with the storage and retrieval of documents. The documents are classified for this purpose by attaching index terms to them. The index terms, or keywords, of a document describe its content. For instance, the classification COMPUTERS,EDUCATION means that the document deals with both computers and education. This is an example of a binary classification, i.e. a term is either present or absent in the classification of a document. A finer classification is obtained by using weighted indexing. A weight, for instance between 0 and 1, is attached to each index term in the classification. COMPUTERS, 0.2, EDUCATION, 1.0 means that the document deals mainly with education and to a lesser extent with computers.

The index terms of all the docements in a collection form a thesaurus. The thesaurus is stored in the computer files along with the documents (or sometimes with just the titles or abstracts of the documents). The user of such a system can retrieve documents by making queries specifying the content of the documents he is interested in. The queries are compared with the document classifications, and the documents believed to be relevant are retrieved. Exact match retrieval means that only documents exactly matching a query are retrieved. In partial match retrieval this condition is relaxed by defining a similarity between the queries and the documents on the basis of the co-occurrence of index terms. For instance, the query COMPUTERS,EDUCATION could have a

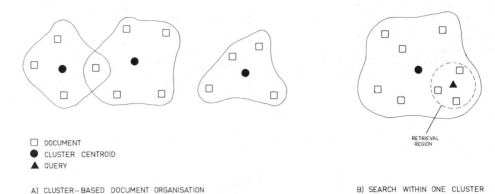

DOCUMENT
CLUSTER CENTROID
QUERY

A) CLUSTER–BASED DOCUMENT ORGANISATION   B) SEARCH WITHIN ONE CLUSTER

Fig. 1. Cluster-based document organisation and search.

similarity of 1.0 with a document classified by COMPUTERS,EDUCATION and a similarity of 0.5 with a document classified by TEACHERS,EDUCATION. The value of the similarity of course depends on the way it is computed; different computation methods give different values. The user can choose his level of relevance (cut-off value), for instance 0.6. Documents with a similarity higher than 0.6 with the query are then retrieved. Retrieval performance is measured by recall and precision. Recall is the proportion of relevant documents actually retrieved, precision is the proportion of retrieved material actually relevant.

The document files can be arranged to facilitate the search for and retrieval of documents in the partial match case. Similar documents are grouped together in clusters. The clusters can be overlapping. The similarity between documents is measured, as is the similarity between queries and documents, by the co-occurrence of index terms in their classification. For instance, a document classified as COMPUTERS,CAL,INTERACTION could have a similarity of 0.7 with a document classified as COMPUTERS,CAL, and a similarity of 0.3 with a document classified as COMPUTERS,TUTOR, PROGRAMMING. A cluster is classified by a cluster centroid, which is some average of its document classifications. A search is conducted by comparing the query with the cluster centroids. The clusters having the highest similarity with the query are examined in detail. Documents with a similarity with the query above the cut-off value are retrieved. Figure 1 illustrates the cluster-based document organisation and retrieval. The distance between the objects (documents, centroids and queries) is inversely proportional to their similarity.

The standard treatment of the discipline of information retrieval is Ref. [5], while Ref. [6] provides an up-to-date survey of the field.

THE STUDIO CAL SYSTEM

The initial plans for the STUDIO system were outlined in [7]. STUDIO is an information retrieval system provided with a teaching strategy. The instructional material is divided into frames, which are regarded as retrievable documents. The frames are classified by weighted index terms. The index terms used within a course form a course thesaurus. The instructional process can be regarded as a series of queries, some made by the system, some explicitly by the student.

A frame is the smallest instructional unit. The frame can be textual, i.e. contain textual information to be displayed on the terminal screen. The use of graphics is restricted by our current alphanumerical terminals. The frame can also be procedural, i.e. contain a computer program which conducts some tutorial dialogue or drill; in this case the program is activated instead of the display of the frame. The procedural frames are programmed by the course author in a standard programming language (BASIC, COBOL or FORTRAN). It must, however, be emphasised that the procedural frames are optional. If a course contains only textual frames the teaching strategy and instructional dialogue are conducted completely by the system's software and no programming is involved in the production of a course.

The author classifies the frames using weighted index terms. The index terms describe the contents of the frame, and the weights make the classification even more specific. For instance, a frame classified as CONTROLSTATEMENTS, 0.1, PROGRAMFLOW, 0.8 emphasises program flow and only touches upon control statements, whereas a classification CONTROLSTATEMENTS, 0.8, PROGRAMFLOW, 0.1 indicates the opposite situation. Up to nine terms can be used to classify one frame. If the frame contains an exercise the author provides a grouped list of predicted answers. The first group consists of correct answers, the following of wrong answers. The wrong answers are grouped according to the type of misconception or lack of information or skills they represent. Up to four groups of wrong answers can be formed. Each group of wrong answers is classified with up to nine index terms from the course thesaurus. These index terms reflect the need for revision. This classification is binary, i.e. the index terms are not weighted. Consider for instance the question "What is the value of C after the execution of the following ALGOL statements:

    A := 2;
    B := 5;
    IF A+B < 10 AND B > 4 THEN C := A+B*5 ELSE C := 20;

                                                                                                    ?".

The answer "20" would show a lack of understanding of the boolean expression and it could be classified with the index terms BOOLEANEXPRESSION, RELATIONALOPERATOR, while the answer "35" would show the understanding of the boolean expression, but a lack of understanding of the arithmetic expression. The answer "35" could thus be classified with the index term ARITH-METICEXPRESSION.

If the author requires a more sophisticated answer validation procedure than just comparison with predicted answers, this is obtained by attaching an answer analyser to the frame. The answer analyser is a computer program which takes the answer given by the student as input, and returns an alternative: right, wrong1, wrong2 etc. The alternatives are treated as answer groups and classified in the same way. Before coming to a conclusion, the answer analyser can communicate interactively with the student. The answer analyser can be programmed by the author, or it may be a modified compiler added with an interface, for example. This compiler could analyse statements and programs made by the student. The same analyser can be used in different frames.

Course design starts with assembling the required frames. The author designs and adds frames to the STUDIO database. He can also explore the existing database by making queries, and if suitable frames are found they can be included in the course. A frame can be shared by a number of courses, and the goal of the system is a large database of related instructional information, from which different courses can be assembled. When all the frames for the course are assembled, STUDIO produces a hierarchic course thesaurus of the index terms included. The hierarchy is at present on two levels, i.e. the index terms are grouped. The author may also use a pre-coordinated classification, i.e. select and arrange the index terms before including the appropriate frames.

With the help of the course thesaurus a static sequence including all the frames in the course is produced by interaction between the author and STUDIO. The static sequence corresponds to a logical order for presenting the instructional material. The strategy of the system is to put similar frames close together in the sequence. The similarity between the frames is measured by their classification, as described in the preceding chapter, and clustering techniques are used for the sequencing. Since this is not an optimal instructional strategy, participation by the author is needed. An example of a resulting sequence is shown in Fig. 2. The sequence is indicated by the arrows and the distance between the frames is inversely proportional to their similarity. The sequence consists of both similar and less similar frames next to one another. When the sequence has been obtained the frames are divided into basic and additional ones. The basic frames contain the nucleus of the course, and they are presented to all students. The selection of additional frames to be presented is a run-time adaptive decision which depends on the state of knowledge acquired by the student up to that moment. This is considered in the next section.

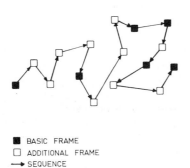

■ BASIC FRAME
□ ADDITIONAL FRAME
—▶ SEQUENCE

Fig. 2. A sequenced course.

ADAPTIVE BEHAVIOUR OF THE STUDIO SYSTEM

The run-time adaptive instructional decisions involve selecting the additional frames to be presented, presenting remedial material when exercises are answered wrongly, and presenting remedial or additional material according to the students' own requests. These decisions depend on the students' state of knowledge up to that moment.

The students' state of knowledge is registered in the student thesaurus, which can be regarded as a student model. The student thesaurus consists of the same index terms and logical structure as the course therausus. Each index term in the student thesaurus reflects the students' knowledge of the topic(s) described by that term. The knowledge is quantified by a weight, ranging from 0 to 1, where total ignorance is indicated by 0 and complete knowledge by 1. The weight is computed from a group of descriptors assigned to each index term. The descriptor group includes the presented amount of material classified by the index term, the time spent with this material and the number of correct and wrong answers to exercises classified by the index term. The amount of material presented is obtained from the classification of the frames presented and is proportional to the weights of the index terms. For instance, a frame classified with the term CONDITIONALSTATEMENTS, 0.8 contributes more to the corresponding amount than a frame classified with the term CONDITIONALSTATEMENTS, 0.3.

The descriptors are continuously updated throughout the instructional process. The presentation of a frame causes a small increment in the knowledge weights of the index terms that occur in the frame classification, a correct answer to an exercise causes a bigger increment and a wrong answer causes a decrement in the knowledge weights. As the instructional process continues, and more evidence of the students' behaviour is obtained for the descriptor group, the changes made to the knowledge weights become smaller. The initial values of the knowledge weights are approximated by the student himself. He estimates his *a priori* knowledge of each index term group. This value is then used as the initial weight for all the index terms in that group.

A similarity between the students' state of knowledge and each frame in the course can be computed on the basis of the knowledge weights in the student thesaurus and the frame classification. This similarity lies between 0 and 1, and it quantifies the need to present the frame to the student. 0 means that the student already knows the topics in the frame, and that no presentation is needed; 1 means that he does not know them at all, and that presentation is urgently required. This similarity corresponds to the similarity between queries and documents in information retrieval. If, for instance, a student has a knowledge of 0.9 of CONDITIONALSTATEMENTS and 0.2 of ASSIGNMENT-STATEMENTS a frame classified as CONDITIONALSTATEMENTS, 1.0, ASSIGNMENTSTATE-MENTS, 0.3 is not very relevant to him, whereas a frame classified as CONDITIONALSTATE-MENTS, 0.3, ASSIGNMENTSTATEMENTS, 1.0 is very relevant to him.

The run-time presentation of frames corresponds to the static sequence of the course. The inclusion of additional frames in the run-time sequence is decided successively according to the similarity between the students' state of knowledge and the frame. If the similarity exceeds a cut-off value the additional frame is presented. The cut-off value is computed successively from the students' performance during the course. A good performance raises the cut-off value, while learning difficulties lower it. The cut-off value is computed from the global proportion of correct answers to exercises, the time spent with the frames and the use of help-type commands. The use of the cut-off value is based on the concept of precision and recall of information retrieval. A low cut-off value implies high recall and low precision, a high cut-off value implies the opposite. The pedagogical strategy is to present the "less bright" students with more and broader material, and the "brighter" students with less and more precise material. This is illustrated in Fig. 3. Case (A) illustrates the region of presentation of frames implied by the state of knowledge of a "less bright" student at a specific moment, Case (B) is the same situation for a "brighter" student with the same knowledge profile at the same moment.

If the student answers an exercise wrongly he will be presented with a revision sequence. The content and the extent of the revision sequence depend on the students' state of knowledge and cut-off value. When an exercise is answered wrongly the assigned list of index terms is weighted with the corresponding knowledge weights of the student thesaurus and a remedial loop of frames is generated. The loop consists of frames previous to the exercise in the static sequence, whose similarity with the weighted index term list exceeds the students' cut-off value. The order of the frames in the loop is obtained from the static sequence of the course, and the loop ends with the frame which caused it. The index term list can be regarded as a centroid of a remedial cluster. By weighting it with the students' knowledge weights a query is obtained. The region of retrieval (presentation) depends on the students' cut-off value. The situation is illustrated in Fig. 4 for two students with different knowledge

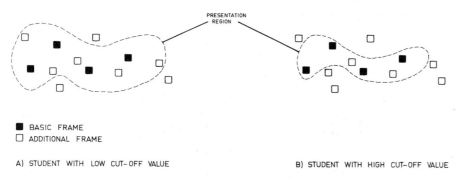

BASIC FRAME
ADDITIONAL FRAME

A) STUDENT WITH LOW CUT-OFF VALUE   B) STUDENT WITH HIGH CUT-OFF VALUE

Fig. 3. Adaptation with the students' performance.

profiles and cut-off values. The student in Case (A) has a lower cut-off value, and is presented with a wider revision sequence than the student in Case (B).

At any moment in the course the student may feel a need for revision or additional material. He then states the index terms (weighted or unweighted) describing his need, and a loop of frames is generated according to the request. The loop consists of frames in decreasing order of similarity with the request, and the student can return from the loop as soon as he feels that his need is fulfilled. If the course does not contain relevant material the request can be extended to the whole STUDIO database. The student can obtain a list of the index terms in the classification of the present frame by a special command. The list can help him define his need for revision or additional material. Another command gives him the list of all the index terms in the course, a third command the list of all the index terms in the STUDIO database.

ON STUDENT MODELLING

Every CAL system or program makes use of a student model, even if it is only an implicit and intuitive one. Constructing an explicit and cognitive student model involves difficulties, some of which are outlined in [8]. This chapter focuses on these difficulties from the point of view of the STUDIO student model.

The representation and content of the STUDIO student model is analogous to the course thesaurus. The representation and content of thesauri is a central issue in information retrieval, and the results of that research are utilisable in a STUDIO type system. Skills and cognitive knowledge may, however, require different representations, as in the BIP system [9], and this is recognised as a possible source of problems in the STUDIO system. When a student is assigned to a course his model has to be created. This is handled in the STUDIO student model by copying the course thesaurus and having the student estimate his own *a priori* knowledge. If the system contains several courses then

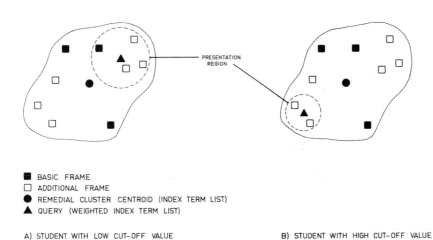

BASIC FRAME
ADDITIONAL FRAME
REMEDIAL CLUSTER CENTROID (INDEX TERM LIST)
QUERY (WEIGHTED INDEX TERM LIST)

A) STUDENT WITH LOW CUT-OFF VALUE   B) STUDENT WITH HIGH CUT-OFF VALUE

Fig. 4. Individual revisions.

measures from related index terms from courses previously taken by the student can be used as initial knowledge weights.

When the student learns during the instructional process, his state of knowledge is changed by updating the knowledge weights. As psychologists gain more insight into the learning process the computation methods for the knowledge weights can be developed without changing the foundations of the model. Since the STUDIO student model covers the content of the course the problem of the growth of the model does not arise. After the learning process has been modelled, the model has to be used, or executed, during the instructional process. The STUDIO student model is executed through the similarity between the model and the frames and by the cut-off value. The problem of comparing the student model and the students' behaviour does not arise since behaviour is not modelled. As pointed out earlier this is recognised as one restriction of the model. The main direction of the teaching process is determined by the author through the static sequence. Thus the STUDIO student model is not directly used for planning; this may also be considered a restriction of the model. The STUDIO student model could be used for monitoring by suggesting requests or by encouraging the students' requests for information on topics that he has less knowledge of according to the model. The cost of implementation of the STUDIO student model is not of the same order as that of many AI systems, and the response times are quite fast according to our preliminary experience.

CONCLUSIONS

The use of information retrieval techniques may contribute to the solution of some central problems in CAL. Courseware production is facilitated since no programming is necessarily required. Large banks of data can be utilised and shared by many CAL courses. With the development of videotex networks[10] and the increasing use of information retrieval systems this will be an important alternative for CAL. By utilising information retrieval techniques the adaptivity of the CAL system can be made quite sophisticated by uncomplicated means.

The STUDIO system is still under development and has not yet been fully implemented; hence evaluative data is not yet obtainable. When fully implemented the system will run on a Burroughs B1700 computer using the DMSII data management system.

Acknowledgements—I am indebted to Mr Olavi Maanavilja from the Technical Research Centre of Finland for many valuable ideas and fruitful discussions. I would also like to thank Dr Hannu Erkiö and Mr Harri Laine for their comments on an earlier draft of this paper.

REFERENCES

1. Chambers J. and Sprecher J., Computer assisted instruction: current trends and critical issues. *Commun. ACM* **23**, 332 (1980).
2. Fielden J., The cost of CAL. In *Learning Through Computers* (Edited by D. Tawney), pp. 159–170. Macmillan, London (1979).
3. Osin L., SMITH: How to produce CAI courses without programming. *Int. J. Man-Machine Stud.* **8**, 207 (1976).
4. *Int. J. Man-Machine Stud.* **11**, no. 1 Special issue on intelligent tutoring systems (1979).
5. Salton G., *Automatic Information Organisation and Retrieval*. McGraw–Hill, New York (1968).
6. van Rijsbergen C., *Information Retrieval*. Butterworths, London (1979).
7. Maanavilja O., Database system for CAL (STUDIO). In Finnish. Unpublished technical report. University of Helsinki, Department of Computer Science (1979).
8. Self J., Student models and artificial intelligence. *Comput. Educ.* **3**, 309 (1979).
9. Barr A., Beard M. and Atkinson R., Information networks for CAI curriculum. In *Computers in Education* (Edited by O. Lecarme and R. Lewis), pp. 447–482. IFIP, North-Holland, Amsterdam (1975).
10. Ball A., Bochman G. and Gescei J., Videotex networks. *Computer* **13**, (1980).

Comput. & Educ. Vol. 6, pp. 105 to 112, 1982
Printed in Great Britain

0360-1315/82/010105-08$03.00/0
Pergamon Press Ltd

REMEDIAL AND SECOND LANGUAGE ENGLISH TEACHING USING COMPUTER ASSISTED LEARNING

Gary Boyd, Arnold Keller and Roger Kenner

Audio-Visual Department, Concordia University, Montreal, Quebec, Canada H3G 1M8

Abstract—The problem addressed is that of teaching collegial and entering level university students the requisite skills to write intelligible papers and reports in English.

This is a real problem in Montreal because a high proportion of the students have English as a second or third language in which their proficiency is limited or, though English may be their native language, their training in it is not adequate for the pursuit of further education.

Several hundred students have worked through 20 or more CAL lessons each year for 3 years, and appreciable gains in skills have been measured. However, where it was possible to duplicate the CAL lessons as programmed texts, equal gains were achieved by those using the programmed texts.

Current work is in two divergent directions:

(i) providing simple template software for ESL and other teachers to write lessons;
(ii) providing a measure of artificial intelligence and auto-adaptation, via a student-constructed sentence diagnosis and remediation package.

A service and record system in CDC BASIC was produced to support the grammar lessons. However, a more powerful language is needed for the sentence diagnostician/remediator. This was initially written in APL but used too much CPU time in that language and is now being re-written in NATAL (the Canadian standard CAL language).

Three quasi-technical questions which also have paedogogical implications occurred and are answered:

(i) To what extent can access procedures and frame formats (typography, etc.) be standardized for all studyware on the system?
(ii) How much data needs to be collected automatically to ensure that studyware is working properly and to identify needed improvements?
(iii) To what extent should self-documentation of source-code be used, and to what extent should it be in a standardized format?

Although a CAL language, CITCAN, was used initially on the CDC system, the level of expertise required to maintain it was too high, and subsequently the present system, written in BASIC, was developed. Personal computers, although available in this environment, are not as yet cost-effective when compared to time-shared access.

We expect to move to a hybrid system, with studyware and records stored on the maxi-system, but actual "delivery" being provided by personal computers to which the studyware will be downloaded in blocks and from which the usage data will be collected back at sign-off.

THE PROBLEM AREA

Effective, clear, coherent, concise, and logically correct written English is essential if students are to establish credibility and be productive in any profession. The circumstances of the contemporary world being what they are, about half the students entering colleges, and about one third of the students entering universities in Canada, lack such capabilities[1]. We have a particularly severe problem at Concordia University because about half of our (approx. 25,000) students have learned English as their second or third language.

Many sections of conventional classes in English as a Second Language (ESL) and in remedial English are run; typically 300 students per term take such courses. These classes do help some students. But despite research which indicates that classes become much more effective when size is reduced below 15 to about 5 or 6[2], our budgets dictate classes of about 20 students.

The problem is really one of "requisite variety". The variety of students' learning styles and rates, and the variety of their writing deficiencies, is much greater than can be matched by the variety of learning activities which can be provided in a 13-week, 2-h per week, group-instruction course.

OPPORTUNITIES

The Graduate Programme in Educational Technology at Concordia has an enrolment of about 130 students, and in a given year, typically about a dozen of these are professionally concerned with language teaching. Over the past decade both the University and the Québec Ministry of Education have made available access to large timesharing computer systems for instructional purposes at no direct cost to academic departments. (In the case of the Ministry, rather high service charges have recently been instituted.)

The conjunction of these conditions constituted an opportunity for developing CAL packages for ESL and remedial English teaching and for conducting research in this area.

HISTORY

At the suggestion of the ESL Department at the Sir George Williams Campus, our first foray into this area involved the development of a CAI lesson on the "continuous present progressive" verb tense for English as a Second Language students. Two versions of this lesson were produced, one for the MITSI/SINTRA teaching machine and another version written in our own CAI dialect, CITCAN, which ran on the CDC Cyber 74 KRONOS/NOS timesharing system. About 20 students used the CITCAN version of the lesson, and exhibited appreciable skillgains. Computer access was limited by a shortage of funds at that time, so that other means of delivering the lesson were sought. This led to the development of a board game, to teach the use of the "present continuous" tense which proved quite successful with adult ESL trainees [3].

Two directions of development were then followed. On the one hand we continued to develop packages to teach specific grammatical/syntactical skills, while on the other we sought an approach to "whole composition" writing skills.

A group at the University of Michigan had produced a successful précis-writing CAI program for Journalism students [4], and this led one of us (G. B.) together with Professor George Huntley and several graduate students, to develop a learning activity package for teaching précis-writing skills for remedial English classes [5]. The package was initially developed as TAI (Teacher Assisted Instruction), and the CAL version is not yet operating. One of us (A.K.) has largely concentrated on work at the sentence-building skills level. This has resulted in both CAI and PI materials which have been used successfully by upward of 500 students at both Vanier College and Concordia University [6]. Over the past 2 years another of us (R.K.) has developed a template approach for the production of language skills CAI lessons, which has been employed by a number of ESL instructors to add new studyware to our CDC based language laboratory library at Concordia.

METHODOLOGICAL AND CONCEPTUAL PROBLEMS

Mastery of effective writing, when analysed, resolves into both component skills and global skills (which continuously interact with the component skills). My use, or non-use, of the semi-colon depends on the conditions in the sentence I am now writing; also it depends on the degree and kind of stylistic coherence I feel to be appropriate when addressing an audience of British educators. The elementary component skills can nicely be represented by algorithms [7], but the ways in which these algorithms should be altered or extended, to take into account the global considerations of effective and efficient (potent, timely, and valuable) communication, are as yet largely unknown. Such skills are usually taught by providing models, and by extensive correction of compositions; the understanding then remains tacit and, in a sense, inaccessible.

There is a dearth of good research on the psychology of the process of composition and writing. (One book nominally on the subject [8] actually is a collection of papers nearly all on other topics. Some of the pertinent theory and research is reviewed in *Schooling and the Acquisition of Knowledge* [9].) The formalized conversation theory of Gordon Pask provides a potential route for rendering these processes ostensive [10].

Writing is a form of communicative control of a "conversation" in the Paskian sense. It is more difficult than ordinary conversation because in ordinary conversation a biological individual can manage by playing the rôle of only one "p" individual (persona), but the biological individual, when writing, should play the rôles of both writer and reader [11]. This is of course even more difficult if the intended readers have had a different cultural-linguistic socialization from the writer. Potent writing is the recorded remains of a conversation among six "p" individuals: (1) the strategic planner; (2) the imaginative illustrator; (3) the sentence builder; (4) the details critic; (5) the rapt reader; and (6) the analytical critic. They should cyclically take turns on the stage of the mind in roughly the above order to shape effective prose. Teaching writing may then be envisaged as training each of these personae.

Our work in developing a précis-writing skills package was an attempt to train the "analytical critic", the "strategic planner", and the "sentence builder" personae. The CAI lessons are to train the "sentence builder" and the "details critic". We have not made any attempts yet to develop CAL to train the "imaginative illustrator", the attentively "rapt reader" or the "argument-analysing critic" personae, since their nature is intimately connected with subject area considerations which an all-faculty service facility cannot adequately explore.

Our practical aims have forced us to narrow our concerns in several ways, but we have tried to keep the fundamental (cybernetic) problem of teaching the process of communicative-control called: "writing English" in mind in connexion with each practical venture.

Effective writing implies effective thinking and feeling and the possession of a "good" model of one's audience. The full entailment mesh (in the Paskian sense) for effective writing capability must be a very extensive and complex thing indeed; in fact too complex to be worth attempting to construct at present. On the other hand the process of making a précis of what someone else has written, as-it-were to you, is a more limited and better defined task, yet it does involve some of the global strategic and tactical skills as well as all the purely grammatical and syntactical component skills. Content is specifically stated; intent can be inferred when the audience is specified. Précis-writing skills and hypothetical sub-optimal sequences for employing and for learning them can be identified and verified empirically. And there is some evidence that these précis-writing skills do transfer to composition-writing of other kinds [5].

THEORETICAL CONSIDERATIONS RELATING TO CAL

Both a paedagogical strategy and a dialogue control strategy are involved in CAL, though often there seems to be no awareness of their separate natures. (The main change which should be made to an earlier APLET paper on this subject [12], is to add this distinction [cf. Ref. [13].) The dialogue control strategy does have educational implications being related to objectives such as fostering autonomy or teaching people to learn how to learn. These were not main objectives of this operation, and consequently we have employed highly directive pre-programmed control of the dialogue in our studyware. (The term "studyware" is preferred to "courseware" since the programs do not constitute a formal course but rather are a library of optional modules available to students.)

Written (typed) English can be dealt with very easily at the level of computer input and output and by the procedures of character-string matching and the selective presentation of stored text. Parsing and semantic processing are much more difficult. Consequently it seemed sensible to see how much could be taught effectively and efficiently without resorting to syntactical and semantic processing. It turns out that many sentence-building and detail-checking skills can be taught well by quite simple Crowderian CAI or PI [6]. The combination of these skills and their transfer to habitual use in essay and report writing does not occur automatically once the individual skills are learned and does seem to require something more than a conventional programmed instructional approach to teaching.

THE DELIVERY SYSTEM CONFIGURATION

We have tried four delivery system configurations and are now proposing a fifth. The main trade-offs are between accessibility, reliability, and cost. The most accessible system is a telephone-accessible timesharing system—because there are many ASCII terminals and personal computers with 300 baud modems in existence, and in Canada local area telephone calls are not timed. Such a system can be fairly reliable. What we have found is a cyclic behaviour with these big systems swinging from high reliability (after a new extension has been worked in and before the traffic has built up too much) to low reliability, with a period of about 2 years. We have been using both the University's CDC Cyber system and a Government IBM 370 system with similar results (except that the Government system was shut down by a strike for several weeks).

We have also been trying out personal computers (Apple II, TRS 80). These would have to be purchased in large numbers to give the same accessibility as is available via the timeshared system. Moreover the personal computers are frequently subject to idiosyncratic faults which are difficult to locate and simply come and go almost whimsically. Keyboards are easily wrecked by static electricity, and disc drives and their controllers fail fairly frequently when subjected to student use. However, when a timesharing system fails nothing can be done on 20 dumb terminals, but with 20 personal computers it is unlikely that more than 4 of them will fail at a given time. Consequently we believe that a better configuration will be one in which we "download" studyware from a timeshared system to personal computers via a telephone and send back results and comments at the end of each user session.

After some years of experimentation with fairly complex CAL service software (CITCAN/TUTOR) we have settled on the simplest possible suite of programmes which permits access and keeps minimal records.

```
8/02/12. 18.48.06.
PROGRAM   RINDEX
```

```
FIRST FRAME         *********************************
                    *  EFFECTIVE ENGLISH PROGRAMME  *
                    *********************************

                    CHOOSE FROM AMONG THESE TOPICS
                        1.  COMMAS            (5 LESSONS)
                        2.  CAPITALIZATION    (2 LESSONS)
                        3.  PRONOUNS          (2 LESSONS)
                        4.  VERBS             (1 LESSON)
                        5.  APOSTROPHES       (1 LESSON)
                        6.  SYNTAX            (1 LESSON)
                        7.  GAMES             (2 GAMES)
                        8.  MISCELLANEOUS     (LOOK & SEE)


                    TYPE A NUMBER (1-8)
student chooses:    ? 6
```

```
SECOND FRAME        SYNTAX
                    ------
                    ------

                    RDANGLE          DANGLING AND MISPLACED MODIFIERS

                    COMMENT          YOUR COMMENTS, PLEASE!



                    A.  TYPE THE NAME OF THE LESSON YOU WANT
                    B.  TYPE 'B' TO CHOOSE ANOTHER TOPIC
                    C.  TYPE 'QUIT' TO STOP
student chooses:    ? comment
```

Fig. 1. Menu of lessons and options as seen by a student.

All students use the same account number and password to log-on to a transaction account which contains only one file, an automatically invoked procedure. This procedure calls files from another service account and runs or writes in them. (In the personal computer configuration this procedure file will always be locally resident and will telephone the mother system to obtain studyware and send back usage-data.)

In operation the procedure calls a file of student names, asks the current user for his or her name, checks the file, and adds the name if it is not already there. A menu of lessons and service options (Fig. 1) is then presented to the student who chooses one. The chosen lesson is called by the procedure and run interactively. If the student types "QUIT" or works through to the end of the lesson he is taken back to the menu and can exit the system from there by typing "QUIT" again. The lesson used and the score on any questions is recorded with the date and the time and the student's name, and the terminal is then logged-off. The most important service option on the menu is the comment procedure which enables a student to write, and modify, a comment about a lesson he is using and then return to the lesson, or "QUIT".

When new lessons are being developed we add a routine which records all wrong or unrecognized answers and each student's trail through the lesson. But such procedures produce too much undigestible output if left in indefinitely [14]. The only data which are always kept is: date/time, user's name, score, completion or not, and comments as made. A report-generator program tabulates this information in different forms to suit: the lab manager, the teacher/professor, and the lesson developer (see Fig. 2). This proves to be quite enough information to justify the programme and to enable the manager to tell whether he needs to repair or replace studyware or hardware. If a specific research project needs more data it is collected only for that project.

TERMINALS AND OTHER DELIVERY CONSIDERATIONS

The best arrangement paedagogically turned out to be the use of printer-type terminals with the learners' being encouraged to keep the printouts and use them as reference material [Dennis, 1979]. However, the noise of the printer-terminals made it necessary to use CRT-type terminals in the

TOTAL SYSTEM DATA
==============

SYSTEM ='VAFFI32--REMEDIAL ENGLISH' ON DATA FILE 'RUSERS'.

FROM 80/12/20. TO 81/02/09. OR 11 USER DAYS.

1. THE SYSTEM WAS ACCESSED 66 TIMES.
    FOR AN AVERAGE OF 2.2 TIMES/DAY.

2. A TOTAL OF 85 LESSONS WERE ACCESSED.
    FOR AN AVERAGE OF 1.3 LESSONS/STUDENT SESSION.

3. AN AVERAGE OF 2.8 LESSONS PER DAY WERE ACCESSED.

4. THE SYSTEM 'QUIT' PROCEDURE WAS USED 13 TIMES.
    THIS MEANS STUDENTS LEFT ABRUPTLY 53 TIMES?

DATA TABULATION FOR SPECIFIC LESSONS
=================================

LESSON NAME	X ACCESS--FINISHED--QUIT--STOPPED	MEAN TIME ON	MEAN SCORE	MEAN QUIT	REASON	A	B	C	D
2. RCINTRO	3 1 1 1	.48 MIN.	0/ 0	3		0	0	0	0
	TOTAL TIME ON THIS LESSON	1.4 MINUTES							
3. RCOMENT	4 1 1 2	.00 MIN.	0/ 0	0		0	0	0	0
	TOTAL TIME ON THIS LESSON	.0 MINUTES							
4. RCSER	3 1 2 0	3.00 MIN.	0/ 10	3		1	0	0	1
	TOTAL TIME ON THIS LESSON	9.0 MINUTES							
5. RCMAIN	3 1 1 1	4.82 MIN.	10/ 10	0		0	0	0	0
	TOTAL TIME ON THIS LESSON	14.4 MINUTES							
6. SCRAMBL	17 2 7 8	11.08 MIN.	84/100	8		0	0	3	4
	TOTAL TIME ON THIS LESSON	188.3 MINUTES							
7. RAPOST	3 2 1 0	7.71 MIN.	12/ 20	0		0	0	0	0
	TOTAL TIME ON THIS LESSON	23.1 MINUTES							
8. RNOCOM	6 1 2 3	2.37 MIN.	0/ 0	12		0	1	1	0
	TOTAL TIME ON THIS LESSON	14.2 MINUTES							
9. RCPAIR	4 1 2 1	10.93 MIN.	9/ 10	14		0	0	0	2
	TOTAL TIME ON THIS LESSON	43.7 MINUTES							
10. RVERB	8 1 3 4	17.64 MIN.	18/ 20	18		0	1	2	0
	TOTAL TIME ON THIS LESSON	141.2 MINUTES							
11. COPMENT	2 1 1 0	.00 MIN.	0/ 0	0		0	0	0	0
	TOTAL TIME ON THIS LESSON	.0 MINUTES							
12. RDANGLE	5 1 2 2	13.28 MIN.	0/ 0	24		0	0	1	1
	TOTAL TIME ON THIS LESSON								
	TOTAL TIME ON THIS LESSON	66.4 MINUTES							
13. RPRCASE	4 2 1 1	13.82 MIN.	15/ 20	0		0	0	0	0
	TOTAL TIME ON THIS LESSON	55.3 MINUTES							
14. RPROGRE	4 2 1 1	8.75 MIN.	8/ 10	0		0	0	0	0
	TOTAL TIME ON THIS LESSON	35.0 MINUTES							
15. RCAPIL	5 1 3 k	12.04 MIN.	0/ 0	14		1	0	0	2

TOTAL STUDY TIME ON LESSONS COMPLETED OR QUIT IS 11.2 HOURS.

DATE TAKE 81/02/10.

Fig. 2. Report as obtained by language laboratory manager.

language-laboratory carrells to avoid disturbing other students. Students have access to a wide variety of terminals and some even have computers with modems so that it has become necessary to employ the television-producers' concept of "safe-area" and to format the studyware so that it can be used on any commonly available terminal. The smallest screen we have encountered is a 32-character by 16-line display (LEK103) but this is exceptionally cramped. There are, however, many units with 40 characters per line since this is the maximum which can be displayed on an ordinary (NTSC) television set.

Our studyware has consequently been paged in terms of 40-character by 16-line pages where the ends of the lines are assumed to be unsafe so that all important material is within a 32-character by 16 line area. This cramps the instructional designer somewhat but being forced to be succinct and coherent does greatly improve readability.

The length of all packages has been arranged to take the slowest learners no longer than 40–45 min to complete, while aiming for 15–25 min for average students.

Many students will do 2 or 3 lessons at a sitting but we do not encourage this, as Sumi et al.[15] found that performance falls off after 40 min of interaction and our own observations bear this out.

STUDYWARE

There are four classes of studyware: (1) the remedial grammar lessons; (2) the template lessons; (3) the sentence diagnosis and corrector modules; (4) vocabulary and other games.

The Remedial Grammar Lessons by A. Keller are simple CAI lessons written in CDC BASIC (and also in PAL). They consist of: a statement of objectives, a series of sub-concept or sub-skill rule, example, test and remediation-if-necessary cycles, followed by a criterion test for the whole lesson. The lessons, and content covered, are:

CINTRO   The comma to separate introductory elements from the rest of the sentence;
CPAIR   The comma to enclose nonessential elements of a sentence;
CSER   The comma to separate items in a series;
CMAIN   The comma to separate two main clauses joined by a coordinating conjunction;
NOCOM   The conditions governing the omission of the comma;
APOST   The use of the apostrophe;
DANGLE   Identification and correction of dangling and misplaced modifying elements of a sentence;
VERB   Verb tense and agreement;
PRCASE   Pronoun case;
PROGRE   Pronoun agreement;
CAPI   The principles of capitalization;
REVIEW   A 50 question summary of all other lessons.

The template lessons are written for the most part by teachers of English as a Second Language who have no familiarity with computers and who simply fill in a form to be coded into a lesson with a predesigned control strategy. The form requests: opening documentation (not seen by student), a presentation, exercise instructions, three sets of exercise questions with answers, and a criterion test and three replies depending on test scores. The actual flow of these lessons is as in Fig. 3 (from Kenner, [16]).

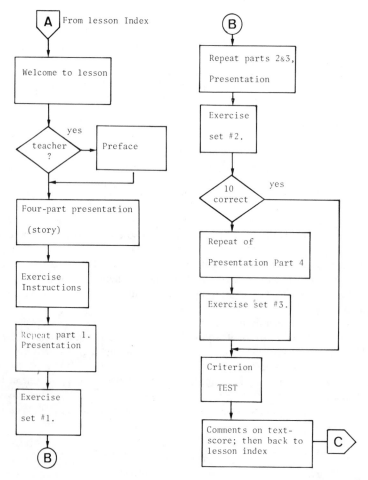

Fig. 3. Flow diagram of the simple template lessons, showing the "boxes" which are filled by teacher-authors.

The sentence diagnosis and corrector lessons are currently being developed by Keller. These lessons provide structural models of correct usage and then accept (compound/complex) sentences constructed by the student, and print out a diagnosis of certain classes of faults occurring in them. Neither an English lexicon nor the usual sort of sentence-parser is used to assess these sentences. Rather specific word and punctuation structures, which are known to occur frequently as faulty forms, are checked for, and a diagnosis and corrections are made accordingly. The special knowledge of the English teacher–researcher, concerning the variety of likely-to-occur faults, is used to reduce the diagnosis and remediation problem to a manageable size.

The method of detail analysis which is used is called "IDT". It involves: first, making an inventory (I) of structures found in the sentence input by the learner; secondly, discrimination (D) between correct and incorrect usage of the algorithms governing the structures found; and third, should the discrimination have revealed a discrepancy, a transformation (T) adds or removes the necessary elements (commas, etc).

After being shown a corrected version of his sentence, the learner is asked why sho [sho ≡ she or he; possessive: sho's] thinks sho made the mistake; whether(a) sho didn't consider it a possible mistake, or (b) sho considered it but thought it was right, or (c) sho though it was wrong but didn't know how to correct it. These choices correspond to Inventory, Discrimination, and two kinds of Transformation errors. By this means the learner's view of sho's mistake can be juxtaposed against the machine's procedure [17].

The game lessons are fairly straightforward and mostly aim at building vocabulary with correct usage. The learner normally plays against the machine rather than against other learners.

Formal experiments have been run on the 12 details-critic lessons and will eventually be conducted for the IDT module [17].

The results of the one experiment on the 12 detail lessons are as follows. 20 subjects were given a standardized pre-test covering the skills involved. They then worked through the lessons over a three-month period and took a matched post-test.

	Mean	SD	Min.	Max.	$n = 20$
Pre-test	45.1	11.6	30	68	
Post-test	59.3	11.6	35	79	

Computed t value (equal var.) = 5.7 which has a $P = 0.001$.

It is evident that the lessons do enable learners to make appreciable improvements in their detail-critic skills.

USE AND RESULTS

Usage

Approximately 100 students each term at Vanier College are required to work through the lessons. At Concordia it is a voluntary situation; an invitation is extended to about 300 students each term who have been identified as needing these kinds of skills. About half of these students try one CAI lesson and, of these, about half continue and work through most of the lessons.

Results

Nearly all those who complete lessons pass the criterion tests at the end of the lessons. Most of the lessons have gone through three revisions to achieve this level of effectiveness. What remains less satisfactory is the transfer of "detail-critic" skills to the composition-writing activities of the students. Consequently new modules to draw together a number of skills, in particular the sentence diagnostic programme currently under development by Keller, should help students integrate and improve their sentence building and detail diagnosis skills.

There remains the need for a module to teach the student to cyclically assume the succession of six viewpoints which are needed to produce potent writing.

Since the system is working in two institutions and involves half a dozen active contributors it is to be expected that these problems will, in time, be solved, although this may mean that certain, probably synthetic, skills and structured dialogues will be referred definitively to classroom teaching.

REFERENCES

1. Priestley F. E. L. and Kerpneck H. I. (Eds), Report of the Commission on Undergraduate Studies in English in Canadian Universities. Association of Canadian University Teachers of English, Toronto (1976).
2. Smith M. L. and Glass G. V., Meta-analysis of research on class size. *Am. Educ. Res. Jl* **17**, 419 (1980).

3. McAlpine L. C., The use of games in second language teaching. Educational Technology Research Memorandum 73–34, Concordia University Montréal (1973).
4. Bishop R., Journalism: a programme to provide assistance in the analysis of newspaper writing. In *Project EXTEND: an Introduction* (Edited by W. K. Davis *et al.*). Centre for Research on Learning and Teaching, University of Michigan Ann Arbor (1972).
5. Siliauskas G., Learning transfer from précis-writing skills to a composition task in undergraduate composition courses. Master of Arts in Educational Technology thesis, Concordia University Montréal (1977).
6. Keller A., An experimental comparison of CAI and PI for teaching the mechanics of writing. Master of Arts in Educational Technology thesis, Concordia University Montréal (1979).
7. Gerlach V. S., Reiser R. A. and Brecke F. H., Algorithms in education. *Educ. Technol.* **17**, 14 (1977).
8. Hartley J. (Ed.), *The Psychology of Written Communication.* Nichols, New York (1980).
9. Anderson R. C., Spiro R. J. and Montague W. E., *Schooling and the Acquisition of Knowledge.* Erbaum Associates, Hillside, New Jersey (1977).
10. Pask G., Developments in conversation theory. *Int. J. Man–Machine Stud.* **13**, 357 (1980).
11. Olson D. E., Comprehension of written and oral language. Paper given at McGill University 23 January (1978).
12. Boyd G. M., The appropriate level of sophistication of computer languages for the writing of tutorial modules and courses. In *Aspects of Educational Technology V* (Edited by D. Packham, A. Cleary and T. Mayes), pp. 449–455. Pitman, London (1971).
13. Richards G. and Boyd G., Authoring and control strategies using NATAL74. In *Proceedings of the Third Canadian Symposium on Instructional Technology*, pp. 241–246. National Research Council, Ottawa (1980).
14. Romaniuk E. W. and Montgomerie T. C., After implementing your CAI course...what's next? In *Proceedings of the Second Canadian Symposium on Instructional Technology*, pp. 377–389. National Research Council, Ottawa (1976).
15. Sumi H., Itaya H., Shimada M. and Yagi K., A study on instruction programs for CAI system—problems of fatigue. Japan Society for the Promotion of Machine Industry, Tokyo (1973).
16. Kenner R. and Richards G., Report on the first year of development of the language laboratory's CAL programme. Audio-Visual Department, Concordia University, Montreal (1980).
17. Keller A., The design of an adaptive CAI program for the teaching of writing skills. In *Computer Based Instruction: A New Decade*, pp. 41–44. ADCIS, Washington, DC (1980).

Comput. & Educ. Vol. 6, pp. 113 to 116, 1982
Printed in Great Britain

0360-1315/82/010113-04$03.00/0
Pergamon Press Ltd

COMPUTER BASED EXERCISES FOR LANGUAGE LEARNING AT UNIVERSITY LEVEL

BRIAN FARRINGTON

Kings College, University of Aberdeen, Aberdeen AB9 2UB, Scotland

Abstract—The changing emphasis of language teaching in schools away from old-fashioned grammatical accuracy, combined with a serious shortage of staff in University French Departments, has meant that an increasing proportion of academic staff time is now, and will be in the future, spent bringing First and Second year students up to that standard of accurate usage that a University still requires of its language graduates. If some degree of mechanisation were to be introduced, it seemed wisest, for reasons which will be outlined, to keep to a form of exercise which was already familiar to both students and staff. The material consists therefore of exercises in computer-based French prose composition. There are linguistic reasons also for preferring material which is text-based in contrast with the mode adopted by some CAL materials in language learning which are open to criticism in the light of applied linguistic theory. Similar reasons can, in my view, be advanced for maintaining that it is at this level, and for this sort of work, that CAL can make its most useful contribution to language learning. Beginners progress fastest, and in a manner more in tune with the most pressing of their usual requirements, if they concentrate on the spoken language in interaction with live, and preferably native, speakers.

The aim of this paper is to describe a CBL package devised for teaching French to First and Second year undergraduates and therefore at a somewhat higher level of proficiency than most CBL language materials. The approach is unashamedly empirical; the material has been designed to produce in the student, as closely as possible the same operations and thought processes that she goes through when engaged in doing the standard language practice exercises used at this level, and to cut out the least useful of these operations. I propose to discuss the context in which this package was designed, and then describe certain of the traps into which it seemed that such a technological innovation in the field of language learning might be in danger of falling, and finally outline some of the main features of the program.

The package came into existence for the simplest and most unadventurous of reasons. It struck me that a great part of a university language teacher's work consists of a mechanical routine which could certainly be done as well by a machine, namely the marking of written exercises, usually prose composition and translation. This was the starting point. Soon it was clear that to write a CBL program to deal with natural language at this level raised a number of theoretical questions that would have been of sufficient interest in themselves, even if there had not been the stimulus of the challenge of producing something that students would actually be able to learn more French from than they could from the hand-made alternative.

As the work developed it became apparent that in several ways language instruction at this level and at University is particularly well suited to CBL. This is so far for two reasons. The first is that in First Year University language teaching we are above all concerned with the written code of the language. The extent of the difference between the written and the spoken codes varies for different languages; in the case of French it is quite large, even larger than it is in English. Now, in the present state of the technology, and though some interesting work has been done in Computer Aided Learning of spoken language, it is I think true to say that most Computer Based language learning materials have been and are being produced to teach via the written medium. However, they are almost all designed to teach beginners or elementary, rather than advanced learners. Now it is sure that beginners progress fastest, and above all in a way most suited to the most pressing of their needs if they concentrate on the spoken language, and in interaction with human, and preferably native, speakers. Since at the moment at any rate CBL may be better adapted to the learning of the written code rather than the spoken, it would seem to be better suited to the needs of other learners than complete beginners.

Since university courses are above all literary, the correct handling of the conventions of the written language is essential for any student embarking on a university course in French. And this brings me to my second reason. Any learner of a language has to weigh the relative importance, for her, of accuracy and fluency. They are in fact complementary; you can learn a language very fast if you are only concerned with the latter. For example, you could ignore all gender differences in French, or the -s of the third person singular of English verbs. All teachers, of course, try to encourage both, but there can be important differences of emphasis. The trend, which is only appearing now, towards communicative, situational, teaching of languages in schools, will probably accentuate a tendency that we in universities are already conscious of towards the cultivation of fluency rather than accuracy. However universities still, and rightly in my view, attach great importance to accuracy. It follows that the university teacher of French must now, and increasingly in the future, spend a lot of time correcting mistakes of detail which do little to obscure the general drift of meaning but are unacceptable in any learner aspiring to an 'academic' knowledge of the language. The learning of this part of the language seems particularly well suited to unsophisticated CBL methods using keyboard and VDU.

There was another and maybe more sophisticated idea behind the elaboration of this package. To explain it I shall start off, if you will bear with me, with some generalities about Educational Technology. Now it is common with new inventions for their inventors not to realise what it is that is new about them, taking the object for a mere modification of some existing device. When Richard Trevithick first thought of putting a steam engine on wheels, railway engines having until then been stationary, pulling the train along by winding in a rope, he seems to have been unaware of the perspectives that this opened up. With Educational Technology it somehow seems to be the reverse that happens. You think you have got something original when you have not. In other words technical innovation gets harnessed to backward educational thinking. The most striking example of this depressing phenomenon seems to me to be the Language Laboratory; it is a precedent which we would do well to bear in mind. I have a long experience of the Language Lab, having worked in one of the first to be built outside the U.S. in the early fifties. I have been involved with the thing ever since the Language Laboratory was a cloud no bigger than a man's hand on the language teacher's horizon, right up to now when the instrument is widely discredited and the most influential courses in Applied Linguistics in the country teach that a single tape recorder is likely to be more effective as an aid to language learning. Now, I am not just underlining the danger of seeing every novelty as a breakthrough. The main mistake as regards the Language Laboratory was, apart from the oversell, in allowing the technology to dictate the theory behind its use. It seems to me that this could be a danger in CBL, where it could take the form of allowing the ingenuity behind the technology, the designing of software and so on, to dominate and overshadow the educational, and in this case linguistic preoccupations which ought to come first.

We do not know very much about how people learn language. To quote Howatt[1]

> What we require is not so much a technology of language teaching as an understanding of language and language learning.

A successful CBL package will have to take account of the specificity of language as a thing to learn. Two facts about language might be pointed to here. First there is the trouble that, if it is abstracted from its normal role and function of communication, language virtually stops being language. The fact that sulphuric acid and lead react to produce an electric potential is as true in a laboratory as it is in a car battery; the difference between the Imperfect and Past Definite tenses in French is only "knowable" to the extent that they are realised in words belonging to a context and in a context of situation. It follows from this that relatively little useful purpose is served by presenting the learner with a job lot of disembodied contextless utterances to work on. The second fact is that consciously knowing the grammar or vocabulary of a language is not the whole battle; this is knowledge about the language. Learning and acquiring language are different things, and the end product that both teachers and learners desire is not knowledge *about* the language but knowledge *of* it. They are not the same thing, and how one leads to the other is something we do not yet know.

What, therefore, is the best line to follow? Newmark[2] in one of a series of articles on language learning writes:

> Our experiments... suggest that the most dramatic improvement in students' abilities to use the language come from increasing our sophistication about how to induce (them) to *attend to* instances of language use.

I think that if people are going to learn language usefully from a computer, then ways must be found to get the computer to induce them to do this: to attend to instances of language use. It goes without saying that this "use" needs to be contextualised, situational. It is better sentence-based than word-based, better text-based than sentence-based. It seems also that not only do people learn at different speeds, they learn in different ways, and they learn different things. Probably, therefore, a successful CBL package will not set out too clearly designed a set of aims to be achieved by a certain point. In other words it will be cyclical rather than linear. It will be open-ended in a number of ways, so as to allow for the haphasard unpredictable and irrational nature of language, and of human behaviour when coping with it. The material I want to describe now was put together with these considerations in mind.

The package called TEACHER, which has been used with First and Second Year undergraduates taking French in Aberdeen, is designed to take the student through a piece of continuous text, answering questions as she goes. The text can of course be in French or English. The questions can require the student to translate or to suggest alternatives or substitutions for things in the text. The students are given the text to prepare a week before doing the exercise, and they are set a written exercise on the same material in the week after. I would underline the fact that the exercises used are very conventional—the most successful so far has been a traditional prose composition—and also that the student encounters the material to be treated in a customary manner, i.e. printed on a page. The package consists of a program and a set of data files.

The program consists of 2 or 3 pages of FORTRAN, mostly taken up with one long loop. Subroutines in the program cope with problems caused by numbers of students accessing the package at the same time, and also control messages written to the Reports file, the use of which I shall explain later.

The data files consist of four parts. These could be labelled INSTRUCTIONS, QUESTIONS, ANSWERS and COMMENTS. Each "frame" so to speak, that is each pass round the loop, presents a QUESTION and an INSTRUCTION. There are up to 100 QUESTIONS for an average session lasting about 1 h. The INSTRUCTIONS are however standardised and consist of sentences like *Translate the next word, Fill in the blank* etc. For reasons of programming simplicity the QUESTIONS are limited to one 80 character line each. Each QUESTION is followed in the file by up to 20 ANSWERS.

The program compares the student's REPLY with each of these ANSWERS in turn until an exact match is found. If it has not been able to match the REPLY, the program prints the message *Sorry, I can't cope with that, try something else.* The student can go on trying REPLIES indefinitely if one doesn't match one of the ANSWERS. I shall discuss this in a moment. Each ANSWER controls three separate instructions to the program which function when the student's REPLY matches that ANSWER. They are labelled LINK, NEXT and INDX. LINK refers to a small memory file which can hold a record of a student's choice at any point in the program. This is so that two questions can be linked, and is necessary if one is using a continuous text, since the choice of answer made at one point can decide whether or not a later choice is right. There are two separate linkings, in fact, one which works over the whole exercise is used to "remember" for example which tense was chosen for a given verb. This will obviously be relevant in all questions about the tense of other verbs later in the text. The other type of link only relates two questions which occur quite close together, and copes with such matters as noun and adjective agreement or lexical collocations. The way LINK works is that a given ANSWER can only match the student's REPLY if the LINK for that ANSWER is null, or if the memory has not picked up a relevant number earlier on.

NEXT, the second instruction, is simply the number of the next QUESTION to be taken. Since it can be any question in the file the student can be easily sent forward or backward, and along a multitude of pathways through the program. Finally, INDX: every wrong answer, and some right ones, have a number here which is the number of one of a series of comments listed at the end of the file. There are about 100 of these. Like the QUESTIONS they are limited to 80 characters each, a limitation which, if brevity is the soul of wit, is probably salutary. About half of these COMMENTS are only used once, the others appear over and over again and relate to the more obvious errors. These COMMENTS explain, praise, encourage correct or hint according to the student's REPLY.

I must explain a little more about the 20 ANSWERS for each QUESTION. So far as possible, the QUESTIONS are worked out so that there are not more than 10 or so likely answers to be expected. This leaves some room for adding the inevitably unexpected ones later. Some of the more obvious mis-spellings and typing errors can also be included. However there are usually more than one acceptable or "right" answer. Words like HINT can also be included among the ANSWERS, so if a student types HINT it will call up a COMMENT designed to help her to make an intelligent guess. In some cases all or most of ANSWERS are right, but the NEXT instruction sends the learner along different pathways according to which she chooses. In other cases all the ANSWERS are wrong. This will happen if the QUESTION itself misrepresents the problem. In this case the brighter student will, at least after a few tries, refuse the question, and ask for a different one by typing OTHER. In a translation this happens when a learner insists on trying to translate word for word; there will be no right answer, and she will eventually be forced to try HINT or OTHER.

I said a moment ago that when a student's REPLY cannot be matched by any of the ANSWERS in the file, the message *Sorry, I can't cope with that, try something else.* appears on the screen. When this happens the REPLY typed by the student is copied to a file called REPORTS. This file is added to at every session, and periodically printed out. I use it to improve the list of ANSWERS. When a new exercise is introduced it is quickly improved by the REPLIES which it was not possible to anticipate. In this way the package gets better all the time. Most of the unmatchable REPLIES are of course mere mistypings or mis-spellings. It would probably be possible to bypass these, and make them acceptable as correct answers, but I am afraid I consider that a case of mistaken ingenuity: correct spelling is one of the things that I should like this program to encourage.

The QUESTIONS and COMMENTS are couched in a style that is intended to be polite and neither peremptory nor jokey nor exaggeratedly pally. The program does not call the learner by her first name. This is part of a conscious attempt to avoid the anthropomorphism of some interactive programs, but also to demystify the whole process. Care is taken to make it clear to the students that they are not "talking to a computer" they are simply consulting a file of questions and answers put together by me.

What is more, the learner is put in control of her own progression through the exercise. Now, it is common to speak of CBL as having the great advantage of enabling the learner to work at her own pace, and that it individualises instruction. I am afraid that I think this is rather a con-trick. Usually it is the program that decides what the student will learn and when and how. In most of the programs I have seen, the amount of liberty she has is fairly limited. In TEACHER I have tried to rectify this in various ways. First of all at any moment the student can get out of the exercise by typing EXIT. Then in any QUESTION if she types HELP she is immediately given the, or a, right answer, and moved on to the frame following that answer. But this will not happen unless she asks for it by typing HELP. I find it a little presumptuous, those programs that automatically dish up *the* right answer the moment the learner makes two mistakes or otherwise take it upon themselves to decide how many tries a learner may have. More importantly, it is possible at any moment to skip forwards at will, or to go back to an earlier QUESTION. To do this, the student types NEXT whereupon the program will ask what number question she wants. This enables a learner to go back and go over a part of the program a second time, answering the questions differently or choosing a different pathway. Or she can decide that the next bit is too hard or too easy and skip past it. This is useful because if the text is a piece of natural language the standard of difficulty will vary constantly all the way through it. Most of these features of TEACHER, incidentally, were suggested by my students, who have been my most helpful collaborators.

The program has been used, after being tried out with groups of volunteer students, as part of a regular language course. It is too soon to speak of results, and the novelty of CBL in a conventional French course at this level may explain why the general response was favourable. Most of the students remarked that they found working at the CBL exercises quite fun, and also that the time spent seemed to pass quickly. Many students took written notes as they worked through it, and some remarked on the usefulness of gathering information in this way, i.e. by using the program to try out their own suggested translations or ideas. The principal criticism made of the material was that it was too procrustean. In spite of the efforts made to ensure maximum flexibility and variety of pathway through the exercise, it seems that it still needs improving in this respect.

REFERENCES

1. Howatt A. P. R., *Programmed Learning and the Language Teacher*. Longmans, London (1969).
2. Newmark L., How not to interfere in language learning. *Int. J. Am. Ling.* **32,** 77–83 (1966).

Comput. & Educ. Vol. 6, pp. 117 to 120, 1982

Printed in Great Britain

0360-1315/82/010117-04$03.00/0

Pergamon Press Ltd

A MANAGEMENT SYSTEM FOR FOREIGN LANGUAGE TESTS

Robert Ariew

The Department of French, The Pennsylvania State University, 316 Burrowes Building,
University Park, PA 16801, U.S.A.

Abstract—Two of the more difficult and time-consuming problems facing the foreign language teacher is the preparation and administration of quizzes and examinations. Since testing is an integral part of teaching, the problem of designing and implementing accurate, valid examinations is a crucial one. Computers are known for their speed, accuracy and repeatability. The use of the computer solves several problems inherent in test preparation. One can, given a well designed program, relegate the tasks of item selection and the producing of duplicating masters to the computer. Of course, the test items must be entered on the machine originally and proofread, but once the procedure is done, the computer becomes an ideal storage medium: editing the items is quickly and easily performed. And, since all test items are stored in one place, it is possible to improve the test quality (both by increasing the quality of the test items themselves and by reducing the number of typographical errors) through repeated use with students and the subsequent modification of the computers "item bank" based on the students' performance on the tests.

Two of the more difficult and time-consuming problems facing the foreign language teacher are preparing and administering quizzes and examinations. Since testing is an integral part of teaching, the problems of designing and implementing accurate, valid examinations are crucial ones. Until now teachers have had to rely on index-card filing systems such as the one described in Valette [1]. However, such systems have proven inadequate primarily because they require the teacher to assemble, type, and proofread the test each time it is administered, and, because any new retyping generally introduces typographical or omission errors, tests prepared in this manner are usually deficient in some respect.

Obviously, a medium for rapidly preparing numerous high quality tests is needed. The medium must fulfill two main objectives: (1) to make preparing tests less time-consuming by reducing the mechanical (stenographic) process; and (2) to maximize the quality of the tests.

Because it is a storage medium and an information manipulator, the computer was identified as the medium through which these objectives could be fulfilled.

The computer is known for its speed, accuracy, and repeatability. The computer therefore has the potential to solve several of the problems inherent in preparing tests. One can, given a well-designed program, relegate the tasks of selecting items and producing duplicating masters to the computer. Of course, the test items must be entered on the machine originally and proofread, but once these steps are complete, the computer becomes an ideal storage medium: the items entered can be quickly and easily edited. Since all test items are stored in one place, it is possible to *improve* the test by improving the items themselves and by reducing the number of typographical errors through re-working the test items. If one modifies the computer's "item bank" in accord with students' performance each time a test is given, tests eventually reach a very high level of quality.

In heeding the old adage, "look before you leap," a careful analysis of the types of items which would eventually be stored on the computer and of the computational resources at hand was undertaken. It was important to avoid an error which would waste time and energy.

ITEM TYPES

Modern foreign language tests are typically complex. They usually include items designed to measure the students' mastery of or achievement in 3 of the 4 language skills: (1) items dealing with listening comprehension and audio discrimination test the students' ability to decode or to recognize utterances; (2) writing ability, including the ability to handle grammatical problems, is normally tested; (3) items testing the students' reading ability and their ability to identify and understand certain structures and vocabulary items are also included*. Clearly, a large number of areas are tested and a great variability exists in the types of items.

---

* Testing the fourth skill, speaking, is of course possible, but would not generally occur in the testing situation described here. It would be limited to "private interview" tests.

The item format also varies greatly. The cue (stimulus) for a test may be given either orally, graphically (that is, visually, through a picture, diagram or sketch), or it may be written. The student's response may be written or graphic. While the latter type of response is relatively rare, it is possible to ask the student to draw, sketch, or otherwise illustrate an answer.

When a written response is required, it can have two distinct formats. The student may be asked either to provide an answer in prose or to make a choice, as in multiple choice and true/false questions. If the answer is to be in prose, the number of words or the amount of free expression used may vary from one word to a paragraph, or even to a complete essay.

Any storage design would have to take into account the types of item: fill-ins, translations, transformations, and questions-answers are but a few of the most common item types. The storage design would also have to accept oral cues or graphic cues. All these formats should be adequately handled to achieve an effective computer testing program.

COMPUTATIONAL RESOURCES

Requirements in hardware and software must also be identified. An easy, effective means of managing information must be used to store a large number of test items on a computer. The ubiquitous computer card could serve in this capacity, but it is very cumbersome, difficult to edit, and generally inconvenient for storing large scale information. Fortunately, there are other means of inputting information.

Most computer installations support a file management system. The Pennsylvania State University, for example, supports its own Remote Job Entry (RJE). The system, which allows the user access to the computer from keyboard terminals located at several sites on campus, is file oriented. That is, all types of data are collected in a file which can be stored and retrieved as a unit. The information contained in a file may be manipulated; the user can, for instance, edit a specific line, delete or add lines, save or delete whole files, and so on.

The RJE system has several types of terminal. Generally, most are equipped with television monitors, while others feature typewriter-like printing devices. The typewriter terminals are the more useful types for storing tests as they allow the user both to input information and to print it. In addition, since the terminal is similar to a typewriter, printing may be done on various types of paper or on duplicating masters*. Some typewriter terminals also have interchangeable typing elements. A variety of typefaces are available for these, including elements with foreign language characters and diacritics. This type of terminal is obviously the most useful for storing foreign language data.

Implementing a foreign language testing system involves not only hardware, but also software. In other words, one must have on hand a means of altering the stored data, as well as a means of printing them.

Rather than try to provide a completely new data management program, readily available programs were sought that would be potentially useful for storing tests. The RJE system was identified as the best available means for storing and maintaining test data. Another program deemed useful in this context was SCRIPT.

SCRIPT is a text formatting program written at the University of Waterloo. Given any text with imbedded instructions, the program paginates, footnotes, justifies, indents, and offsets the text according to the instructions. A small number of different instructions perform most of the formatting functions. The program is easy to use and flexible enough for most applications. Its usefulness with tests is apparent: it will perform stenographic functions so that the final copy is printed in a clear, well laid-out format. Because SCRIPT was specially written to handle textual material, and because it is dependable, flexible, and well documented, it is the ideal program to use in this situation.

STORAGE CONFIGURATION

There are potentially many ways in which test items can be stored on a computer. Two main approaches were considered. Test components such as test items, directions, and associated item analysis information, can be stored either according to their content, where items are stored by their grammatical category, for example, or they can be stored as an integral test, where all of the questions pertaining to a given exam are stored in the same computer file.

Storing items by grammatical category is desirable in some ways. Given this storage configuration, one could request that a certain number of items with a specific level of difficulty, and dealing with a

---

* While some of the functions can be obtained on line printers, duplicating masters are not generally available for these.

particular grammatical category, be selected from a "bank" of items to make up an individual test. For example, the instructor could request that four items dealing with the formation of the future tense from chapters one through four of the text used be selected from all the stored items. The computer would undertake the search and print only those fulfilling the requirements.

However, a storage configuration of this type poses several problems in searching and retrieving. In order to retrieve the items, they must be coded by (a) grammatical category, (b) item type, to avoid the retrieval of dissimilar items such as, for example, a fill-in, a dictation, and a multiple choice item for one grammatical category, (c) difficulty, to avoid selecting both simple and complex concepts from widely different parts of the text used. Such a multi-leveled coding scheme quickly becomes complex; consequently the retrieval programming becomes cumbersome.

A less complex configuration for storing the tests was therefore adopted: the tests are stored in computer files where each file represents one test. All the information pertaining to a particular test is stored in the same file. This one-test-one-file format was chosen because of its simplicity in retrieving and assembling the tests. Since each test is complete in itself, problems of searching and retrieving are eliminated.

The test file holds all items for a particular exam; it contains directions to the student, directions to the teacher (for orally cued items), and answers or possible answers as well as item analysis information. In addition, each test item may have several alternates associated with it. The alternates are considered corollaries of the test item, varying in the choice of vocabulary, with the person with which the verb is used, etc. All the information is submitted as a computer "job" to prepare a test.

PROGRAM DESCRIPTION

Two software packages used with the test storage system were previously identified. They are RJE, a file management system, and SCRIPT, a text processing system. RJE is used to input and maintain the item bank, while SCRIPT serves as a formatter for the clean test copies which are finally printed on the typewriter terminal. Between input and final output, some other processing must be performed on the test files.

Since the test files should contain all test information, including teacher's directions, answers, alternate items, etc., a program is needed to perform two additional functions: (a) to select one of the alternate items to be presented to the student; and (b) to separate teacher information from student information.

A program randomly selects the alternate item. It counts the number of alternate items; then it chooses a number between one and the number of alternates from a random number list. The program next directs the randomly designated item to an output file which is printed later. Of course it sends all directions and related information to this same output file.

After all items are selected, the program performs its second function. It creates *two* new files from the output file. The program scans the items selected and places in one file all data relevant to the student's copy and in another the data relevant to the teacher's copy. Directions are printed on both copies. The program sends oral cues to the teacher's copy alone, while sending written cues to both. Item identifications, the answer (or possible answer), item analysis data, and other pertinent information are directed to the teacher's copy.

Once alternate items are selected and the information is divided between the two files, a second phase begins. Both files are submitted to SCRIPT for final formatting and output. SCRIPT rewrites the files, taking into account any formatting instructions: the files are dated, properly indented, spaced, and paginated. These files will subsequently be printed on duplicating masters. The duplicating masters are then used in the normal fashion to produce the required number of test copies.

TEST PREPARATION

Operationally, preparing a test becomes a relatively easy task with this system, involving few steps: (1) Test items, directions, and relevant data are prepared in a traditional way. Alternate items may also be prepared at this time. (2) All information pertaining to the test is entered on a computer file. (3) The file is submitted to the computer as a "job." A program selects from among alternate items and then separates the information onto two separate files—the student's copy and the teacher's copy. Both copies are then formatted by SCRIPT. (4) Duplicating masters (spirit masters or stencils) are inserted one at a time in the typewriter terminal and both the student's and teacher's test copies are printed on them.

The process becomes much simpler with subsequent use. As a bank of alternate items is built up, a large number of different tests can be produced and printed from the same set of items. For example, one can request a separate test for a student who misses class. It is even possible to provide each student with his/her individual test. Each test would be different since alternate items are randomly selected. Each test would also have its own answer sheet (the teacher's copy).

As the number of alternate items increases, preparing tests becomes nothing more than a "maintenance" process; that is, it becomes a process whereby one needs only to add new alternate items from time to time, or to modify or improve existing items.

There are other benefits to be gained from such a system: secretarial functions are minimized, as are the number of proofreading-retyping cycles, thereby reducing the possibility of introducing errors. Once the test items have been entered on the computer file and proofread, they need not be further manipulated. Correcting and altering can of course be done at any time. More important, the tests can be improved. Instead of preparing and assembling each test from "ground zero," the storage can be used to progressively improve the test by noting the students' performance with each item and by modifying or discarding items that do not meet minimal criteria.

In addition, it is possible to use the storage system to prepare the test with a computer system that grades the test, and thereby computerize the process of administering the test. One need only write tests that are entirely composed of multiple choice items and store these on the computer, along with the customary answers, directions, and other associated information. The system for preparing the test would be used to generate a test and a teacher's copy, which would serve as the answer key. The students would then be directed to mark a response sheet which would be optically scanned and graded.

CONCLUSION

Since accuracy, speed, and the need to handle large amounts of data are necessities for preparing foreign language tests, the computer is a useful tool in this context. It should be noted that though the storage system has only been implemented for examinations in French, its applicability to other foreign languages and, indeed, to other disciplines, is evident.

REFERENCE

1. Valette R., *Modern Language Testing.* Harcourt Brace Jovanovich (1977).

Comput. & Educ. Vol. 6, pp. 121 to 125, 1982
Printed in Great Britain

0360-1315/82/010121-05$03.00/0
Pergamon Press Ltd

AN EXPERIMENT IN COMPUTER ASSISTED LEARNING OF ENGLISH GRAMMAR AT THE UNIVERSITY OF PARIS VII

FRANÇOISE DEMAIZIERE

DRL Université Paris VII, Tour Centrale 8e étage, 2 Place Jussieu,
Paris 75005, France

Abstract—This paper discusses various aspects of an experiment in Computer Assisted Learning (CAL) of English Grammar which began in 1969 at the OPE Laboratory of the University of Paris (VII) (OPE = Ordinateur Pour Etudiants, Computer for Students).

THE OPE LABORATORY

Hardware

The laboratory was opened in 1967 by Professor Y. Le Corre. It has an IBM 360-40 computer (256 K byte core memory). The terminals are 20 teleprinters to which random access slide projectors have been connected (a few terminals located outside the University are connected by phone). The connection of a random access tape recorder was completed in 1980. All the hardware and software design necessary for these connections was done at the laboratory.

Software

The OPE system was designed for CAL. It evolved from a constant exchange between the computer specialists and the various teams writing CAL materials (biology—2 teams; chemistry, English—2 teams; genetics, physics—2 teams; pedagogy). Two authoring languages, "langage auteur" and "langage de description associé" have been written at the laboratory[1–3]. They give the teacher a wide range of facilities, especially for the analysis of verbal answers (which is most important in our case) and do not require any special knowledge in computer science. They enable the teacher to concentrate on pedagogical problems since their structure limits technical coding to a minimum for the author.

Here are two examples of their use taken from our material.

(1) In order to check that the meaning of *must* and its possible French equivalents is understood, we ask the learners (pupils of about 14 yr) to give a possible French equivalent for *we must hurry up*. There is a great variety of acceptable answers to the question. *We* can be rendered by *nous* or by *on*. *Must* can correspond to a form of *devoir* (*devons* or *doit* depending on the pronoun chosen), to the phrase *il faut que*, or even to phrases with *obligés, forcés* (*nous sommes obligés de...*). As for *hurry up*, it can correspond to *se dépêcher, se hâter, se magner, se presser, se grouiller*. Answers like the following must all be accepted as equivalent: *nous devons nous dépêcher, il faut qu'on se presse, il faut que nous nous hâtions, on doit se grouiller*. By using the key word system of "langage auteur" and two of its functions, "or" and "and", we were easily able to gather all the possible right answers within one "answer type" (réponse type) written:

⁻FAU⁻ // ⁻DOI⁻ // ⁻DEVON⁻ // ⁻OBLIGE⁻ // ⁻FORCE⁻

—   ON // ⁻NOUS⁻ // SE

—   ⁻DEPECH⁻ // ⁻GROUILL⁻ // ⁻HAT⁻ // ⁻PRESS⁻ // ⁻MAGN⁻

CJD   Bonne suggestion.

// indicates the function "or".   — indicates the function "and".

One element in each of the three lists must be found. The order of the elements is irrelevant (code D). The J indicates that in the records the answer will be filed as "right" (*Juste*). C signals a text of comment. The arrows which stand for an optional sequence are used to accept variations like DEPECHIONS/DEPECHER, spelling mistakes like DEPECHEZ instead of DEPECHER and typing errors, omitting to leave a space between words, for example. We decided not to comment on such details here. (It is also possible to indicate a single optional character or optional blanks when one wants to control the spelling and the typing more strictly. A third function also exists to indicate an absence of key words.) Seven other "answer types" analyse the various mistakes (e.g. confusion between *must* and *can* or *want*, use of an imperative, a future, a conditional, bad translation of *we* or *hurry up*). The answers of more than 200 pupils were analysed. (All learners' answers are recorded, sorted and printed out by the OPE system.) Seventy-six different answers were given. Only about 15 cannot be treated, e.g. because they cannot be connected at all to the question (answers like "I'm tired"). The flexibility of the OPE "langage auteur" makes it possible to ask fairly open questions: why...?, what's the difference between...?, make up a question about the slide... The "langage de description associé" is used to manage the various branchings, flags, counters, slides, or to suppress the automatic loop checking. It is also written with very few codes and its structure can be quickly mastered by a non-specialist. Eighty slides, 16 flags and 8 counters are available for each package. We use the flags and counters to diversify comments and questions according to certain variables. For instance, if a learner makes a mistake, the testing of a flag enables us to know whether he made the same mistake before. We can then send him comments reminding him he had given the correct form so far or had already had the mistake explained to him. We can also give him additional exercises corresponding to his type of mistake, later on, whereas another learner will be given another exercise or go directly on to the next point.

(2) Our second example shows the use of flags and tests in order to take previous answers into account. The learners are 12–13 yr old pupils. They have been shown various interrogative sentences. Here is the translation of the text of the question.

> "WHERE ARE YOU GOING?
> WHAT'S HE WEARING ON HIS JACKET?
> WHO ARE YOU GOING TO COMPLAIN TO?
> WHEN DID YOU GO TO WASHINGTON?

THERE ARE AT LEAST 3 COMMON POINTS IN THE STRUCTURE OF THESE QUESTIONS. GIVE ONE"

We want the pupils to find the three important common points one by one, so we suppressed the loop checking and used only one block for the analysis. We used 6 flags and tested then two by two in six different double tests so as to send appropriate comments. When a pupil has just given one of the common points, it is important to know whether this is the first, second or third common point given so as to either tell him to give another common point, a last one or to congratulate him for giving the three expected ones. It is also necessary to take previous answers into account when dealing with calls for help (they are automatically detected from a pre-established list). We wrote three different help comments corresponding to each of the three expected common points and had to make sure we did not send a help comment corresponding to a common point already given.

Figure 1 shows the flow chart corresponding to this question.
Here is a possible resulting dialogue (translated into English):

pupil (R6)	THE STRUCTURE OF THESE SENTENCES IS THE SAME
computer	TRUE, THESE QUESTIONS HAVE THE SAME STRUCTURE.
	BUT YOU WON'T GET AWAY WITH IT SO EASILY...
	WE WANT DETAILS ABOUT WHAT IS COMMON.
	TYPE HELP OR ANSWER AGAIN.
pupil (R4)	THERE IS A ? AT THE END OF THE SENTENCES
(5TD:00)	
computer	YES, THE QUESTION MARK IS ONE OF THE COMMON POINTS
(C 21)	NOW, TRY TO GIVE ANOTHER COMMON POINT.
pupil (H)	I DON'T KNOW
(1TD:00)	
Computer	LOOK AT THE BEGINNING OF THE QUESTIONS.
(C 23)	
	NOW, TYPE HELP OR HAVE A GO
pupil (R5)	THERE IS ALWAYS AN AUXILIARY
computer	YES. THERE'S AN AUXILIARY IN ALL THESE QUESTIONS
(C 21)	NOW, TRY TO GIVE ANOTHER COMMON POINT
pupil (H)	HELP
(1TD: ≠, 2TD: ≠ ; 3TD: 00)	
computer	THINK OF WHAT IS BEFORE AND AFTER ONE
(C25)	ELEMENT IN THE SENTENCES. HAVE A GO

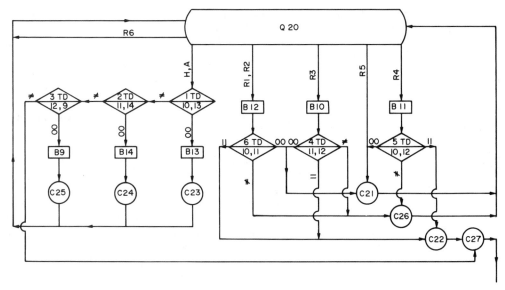

Fig. 1. Flow-chart to question 20. R = answer type; TD = test double; B = flag position;
C = comment; H = help; A = unpredicted answers.

Pupil (R2)	THERE ALWAYS IS AUXILIARY + SUBJECT + VERB
(6TD: ≠)	
computer	YOU'RE RIGHT, THE ORDER OF ELEMENTS IS COMMON
(C 26)	NOW, TRY TO GIVE A LAST COMMON POINT
pupil (H)	HELP
(1TD: ≠; 2TD: ≠; 3TD: ≠)	
computer	HERE ARE THE 3 COMMON POINTS TO REMEMBER
(C27)	THE ORDER OF ELEMENTS IS THE SAME
	ALL THESE QUESTIONS BEGIN WITH A WH- INTERROGATIVE WORD
	THEY END WITH A QUESTION MARK

Figures

About 2500 learners come to the laboratory each year for CAL sessions which corresponds to about 700 h per week and 12,000 h per year. More than 300 h and 400 packages of CAL are available. About 1000 learners come each year for English (secondary school pupils and trainee teachers mainly). About 25 h of English grammar are offered to them.

ENGLISH AT OPE

Background

The theoretical grammatical framework adopted was that of Professor A. Culioli (Linguistics Department, Paris VII): the "théorie des opérations éconciatives". One of the aims of the project was to adapt this linguistic theory for incorporation into CAL material. This is why we started writing English grammar materials, using an analytical approach as a basis of the teaching. We had set ourselves fairly ambitious goals from the start. We did not consider language teaching as based mainly on drill and practice, for instance. And, all too often, drills seem the obvious thing to do with a computer. We did not set out to write a computer based course but considered CAL as a complement to other modes of teaching.

CAL and language teaching

When one uses CAL to teach a foreign language one should be fully aware of the type of communication it implies. The complexity of the relationship between the three elements involved in the interaction (teacher, programmes—computer, learner) the special conditions imposed on the production and analysis of messages make it impossible to consider that any real dialogue takes place in the language taught. CAL can only provide an analytical situation. On the other hand (and this is all the more true if one is interested in having the learners analyse the language they are learning) there are obvious and invaluable advantages to be gained from individualized work, especially when sufficient technical facilities are easily available. We always lay great emphasis on the diversification of paths and comments. (And, in the comment sheets they fill in after their sessions at OPE, a majority of learners mention that what they most liked was the detailed analysis of their answers and the way it helped them to find the right answers.)

CAL and methodology

Considering the analytical situation created by CAL, the possibilities of the OPE system, and observing the learners' difficulties, we soon came to the conclusion that CAL is especially useful when methodology is a prominent component of the teaching. By methodology we mean both the methodological component of the subject taught, learning a certain approach to the description of linguistic phenomena, and methodology in a broader sense, learning to carefully read the texts, to carry out the instructions given. . . . We were struck by the fact that a large number of learners' mistakes were due not to erroneous reasoning or to ignorance of the necessary elements but to faults in their methodological approach of the problem to be solved. Quite often, the learner is just not trying to do the task the teacher wants him to do, hence the "mistakes". We tried to design our materials so that they help the learners to become aware of some of the attitudes that regularly lead them to failure (presentation of the information, progression, type of questions and exercises).

A first point we keep insisting on in our materials is the proper carrying out of instructions. We know that each time a new activity is required some of the learners will not realize the change and keep trying to do the previous type of exercise. For instance, if one asks learners to complete several sentences with a question tag (e.g. you'll be coming, *won't you?*) and then goes on to the question "what's the auxiliary in the above sentence?" one gets a few "isn't it?" as answers. In the same way, for the following exercise:

"Complete the sentences using MUST and the words in brackets.
Example: Captain Double Scotch wants to see you. . . .(come with me)
answer: You must come with me.

(1) The passage is very low.   . . . . . .   (get off her horse)
(2) Percival:—. . . . . .?   (change your clothes)

   Linda: —yes, I must. I can't go to a banquet with these dirty clothes on."

We get answers like: She must come with me, you must get off your clothes. Such mistakes—caused by picking up the wrong elements, looking too far ahead or not far enough—are constant and we always try to comment on them. (After a session at OPE, the most common initial reaction is something like: "I realized I was not careful enough, I did not read well enough").

We also tried to observe the learners' reactions to the information presented (by interviews in particular). We noticed several phenomena that we now try to take into account: inability to make the necessary links between various elements presented; inappropriate memorization of rules (simplifications, overgeneralizations); illicit deductions, interference due to the mother language; inability to perceive the structure of the lesson. For instance, we found that when we gave the rule "In the case of an imperative, LET US can be found with a short form of US: LET' S" (let's get in), it was often remembered as "LET US can become LET' S" (overgeneralization through not remembering the beginning of the text). So, we then ask whether a short form may be introduced in "They won't let us get in if we are late", and, of course, we get "They won't let's get in" which enables us to send the learners back to the rule. At the end of a lesson about *must* and its meaning of "obligation", we mention the other value of *must* (probability) and give this example: *Listen, a horse is entering the courtyard. It must be Lord Neverlate.* (negation: *It can't be Lord Neverlate.*)

This remark often induces reactions like: "So, must and can sometimes mean the same". Here again, we force the learners to analyze what they have been told by asking them to judge this assertion: "what is said in point 20 means that MUST can mean the same as CAN"*.

We also found out that quite a few problems arose from our own presentation of the material. Here again, the instructions are most important. In a lesson about interrogative sentences, we first thought that it would be a good idea to check whether the learners knew when to use *where* by telling them "Ask a question about a place". But we soon found out that about 10% answered with sentences like "what's the name of the town? which is indeed a question about a place! In numerous other cases, we again realized that mistakes or inconsistencies were in fact due to our terms. When we presented the following text: "Must you take me to him now?—Yes, I must. dans la réponse, on reprend MUST mais pas le reste (take you to him now)" and when some learners maintained that this assertion was wrong, we had to admit they had got a point. We had used *reprend* as meaning "repeat" but it is also

_____

* For more details about these phenomena see Ref.[4].

quite possible to interpret it as meaning "take back" (cf. Je reprends le livre que je t'ai prêté) and then the assertion is wrong: must is not "taken back", it is repeated! The importance of metalanguage in teaching is emphasized in a CAL situation: definition of the scope of terms, use of terms associated with technical terms but not defined as such; previous habits in the use of terms; interference between everyday language and metalanguage; use of symbols and visual elements*. The problems we have just mentioned are central to any teaching situation and CAL is one of the best ways of bringing them into the open and helping both teachers and learners to overcome them.

CONCLUSION

We tried to link an experiment in CAL to more fundamental research in applied linguistics. We also tried to design CAL materials that would help the learners for any learning situation. In these respects our results are encouraging. It is possible to elaborate a version of the materials that analyses a great variety of possible answers satisfactorily. The results of the CAL sessions and the teachers' reports about their long-term influence, as well as the learners' reactions, are on the whole positive. Our hope is that such experiments will be developed elsewhere (even though it is sometimes difficult to obtain the facilities we have) and that the problems we have treated will be taken into account: the quality of the materials written is crucial at a time when microcomputers are spreading quickly without proper attention being always paid to the specific requirements of CAL, especially in terms of software.

REFERENCES

1. Jacques M., *Acta electron.* **14**, 369 (1971).
2. Jacques M., *Automatisme XVI*, 328 (1971).
3. Jacques M., *Acta electron.* **17**, 319 (1974).
4. Demaiziere F., *Champs Educatifs* **3**, (1981).
5. Demaiziere F., *Les Langues Modernes* **LXXIV**, 85 (1980).

* For details about this analysis and examples see Ref.[5].

Comput. & Educ. Vol. 6, pp. 127 to 132, 1982
Printed in Great Britain

0360-1315/82/010127-06$03.00/0
Pergamon Press Ltd

A STUDY OF AN APPLICATION OF COMPUTER AIDED LEARNING TO BUSINESS SIMULATION

J. DRISCOLL

Department of Industrial Studies, University of Liverpool, PO Box 147,
Liverpool L69 3BX, England

Abstract—The inherent inability to transfer the real business scene into the teaching environment has led to the increasing use of simulation exercises or games as a means of student centred learning. This paper describes the historical development of one such business exercise, Hogwash Ltd, which has been used over 60 times in the past decade both in universities and industry for teaching undergraduate, postgraduate and managerial level participants.

In describing this development, which was planned around one of the new generation of small computers, the progressive role played by educational and computing objectives in the selection and application of computing equipment will be outlined as a means of drawing out general conclusions that may be of use in the development of similar exercises.

THE HOGWASH LTD BUSINESS EXERCISE

Hogwash Ltd is a completely self-contained competitive business exercise for between 16 and 64 participants which lasts for 3 continuous days. Concerned with the volume manufacture and trading of a low-technology cleaning fluid by up to 8 independent companies, the educational objectives of the exercise are:

1. To provide self-teaching in accountancy practices including the preparation of cash flow accounts, trading accounts, profit and loss accounts and balance sheets.
2. To develop an understanding of the major functional roles within a manufacturing company i.e. Production, Marketing, Finance and Planning.
3. To introduce, through experience, a basic understanding of the effect of industrial relations, marginal trading and environmental considerations on the effective organisation of companies.
4. To develop an appreciation of the role of forecasting and the evaluation of alternative strategies in selecting and implementing company policies.

The programme of events for Hogwash Ltd is illustrated in Fig. 1 and involves the three distinct stages of preparation, trading and debriefing.

Preparation

Preparation starts with an initial training period giving an outline of the objectives and form of the exercise accompanied by a brief lecture on basic accounting routines and is followed by a period of accounting practice as the accounts left by previous company management are brought up to date. A second briefing follows in which the market model is explained and the limitations imposed on each of the major company functions of production, finance and marketing are given.

Using the second briefing as a basis each company then prepares and submits to the exercise controllers an individual, detailed, policy statement to be followed in the light of individual forecasts of market sales over the 4-year trading period. Acceptable 4-year plans can range from high price–low volume Rolls-Royce policies, through middle road approaches, to low price–high volume Woolworth strategies. In each case it is the appreciation of the need for profitability and a realistic approach to planning company development that is stressed in approving policies.

Trading

After the acceptance of policies company trading commences on the basis of the need to satisfy one of eight possible pre-determined markets which are not revealed to participants prior to the 16 cycles, each of which represents one quarter in a 4-year trading programme. Subject to a strict timetable during each cycle, companies are required to attempt to implement their selected policies by producing:

1. Quarterly decisions on publicity, salesmen, price, production, capacity expansion, labour-saving plant and the raising of loan stock, each decision being subject to budgetary and market limitations.

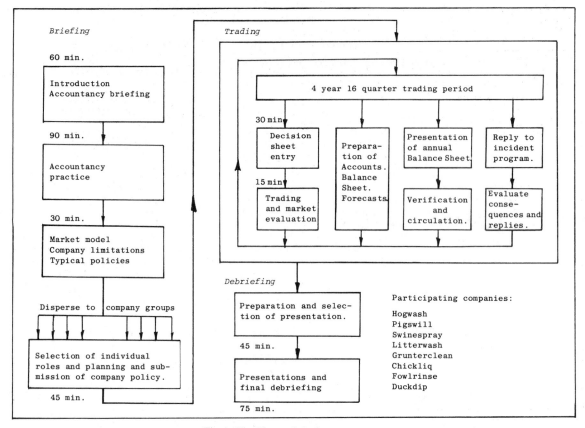

Fig. 1. The Hogwash Ltd programme.

2. Correct quarterly cash flow, trading, profit and loss accounts and balance sheets along with provisional projections of cash flows for future trading periods.
3. Approved Annual Balance Sheets at the end of each financial year for publication and circulation to each company.
4. Estimates of future market and company behaviour on the basis of control charts for stock control, production planning and cost control, cash flow control and by the use of charts recording market sales and profitability.
5. Realistic responses to a portfolio of industrial relations, environmental and marginal trading incidents selected to suit the market being satisfied.

In attempting to implement their selected policies the aim of each company is to make the maximum total profit in relation to the capital it employs throughout the 4-year period, without prejudicing future operations by failing to retain an adequate market share or a sound financial position.

The key to the Hogwash Ltd exercise is the adherence to a strict timetable throughout the 16 trading quarters. The time pressure produced creates a greatly accelerated rate of learning for participants with respect to the educational objectives.

Debriefing

On completion of the 4-year trading programme the final stage of debriefing takes place with each company preparing and presenting a short talk on a selected subject related to their performance, followed by an explanation of the actual market played, individual company responses to the incident programme and by summary comments on the relative performance of each company.

APPLYING COMPUTERS TO HOGWASH LTD

The outline of Hogwash Ltd just described represents the current state of the business exercise after a decade of academic and organisational development. In reviewing this process of improvement and the role eventually played by computers, three periods of change as illustrated in Fig. 2 can be identified for discussion:

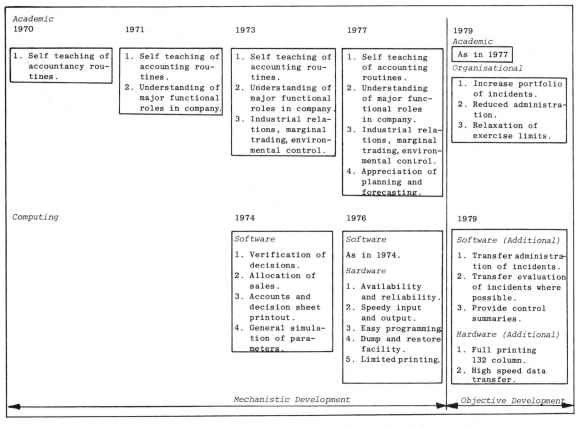

Fig. 2. The development of academic and computing objectives in Hogwash Ltd.

1. Early academic and organisational revisions to the manual form of the exercise.
2. Mechanistic conversion to computer simulation.
3. Objective development of computing and educational aims after conversion to computer simulation.

Early academic and organisational revisions

Hogwash Ltd was first introduced in 1970 as a training exercise in basic accounting set in the context of an operating company but with the emphasis substantially on student-centred accountancy practice, the simplified market model being used to generate the information for completing 16 sets of accounts. With five companies participating and approximately four participants in each company, each of whom produced the required set of accounts, supervision of the exercise was relatively easy and was undertaken by one controller. Experience obtained in the first year of use indicated however that greater understanding of accountancy practices was achieved if accounting was seen within the context of equality with the other functional roles; production and marketing. Furthermore the development of an understanding of all three functional areas and their interaction was an equally worthy academic objective. In consequence student roles within each company were diversified between the major functions, and participants rotated from role to role at intervals within the 4 year cycle. The act of diversifying activities within companies whilst still maintaining continuous paced learning was however to create problems of supervising both the companies and the control of the exercise and was to lead eventually to the use of a computer simulation model.

To understand the new organisational problems encountered in controlling the exercise consider the tasks that had to be completed by the controller within a 15 min spell of each cycle:

1. Decisions made by each company had to be checked against the acceptable range of possible answers. The decision sheet submitted by each company contained 7 decision and 24 pieces of information that had to be checked before market sales could be calculated.
2. The allocation of sales required the totalling of each companies individual sales effort, known as "market score" and distributing sales in proportion to market scores.

3. Where any company had insufficient production and stock to meet sales a complicated procedure for evaluating intercompany sales and purchases was evoked, working on the basis of buying shortfalls from the cheapest market price company and ending with importing for large market discrepancies.

Every figure submitted by companies and calculated by the controller has theoretically to be correct or unfair trading will take place and where such an error occurs, and is detected, the process of allocating sales must begin again.

Similar problems of accuracy were being encountered within each company where the now limited number of accountants available were required to maintain accurate accounts from quarter to quarter, each set of accounts containing 86 pieces of information needing balancing within each 45 min cycle. When failure to balance occurred tutor and accountants would be involved in time consuming backchecking over values whilst decisions by other company participants on marketing and production would have to continue without the necessary financial information, an act which often lead to future cash flow crises.

The response to these organisational problems was to increase the number of personnel involved in supervising the exercise from one to four, comprising an exercise director and three skilled umpires practiced in the accounting routines used.

In 1973 a second major change was made in the academic objectives by introducing a limited set of incidents to test each company's ability to respond to typical industrial challenges, thus providing through experience, an understanding of industrial relations, marginal trading and environmental considerations.

The mechanism for introducing this experience was to launch a selection of incidents over the 4 years of trading on the basis of a prearranged incident programme. The effect on supervision of Hogwash Ltd was considerable for in addition to the regular routine of market sales distribution that took place in the fifteen minutes available it was now necessary to supervise the incident program. For each possible incident this could involve:

1. The issue of information memoranda at appropriate times in the 4 year cycle.
2. The collection and scrutinising of replies from companies.
3. The despatch of results back to companies and the amendment of company information as required.
4. Supervision of further correspondence with companies and amendment of information if required.

The result of this extra administration on top of the existing 15 min routine was to increase the need for supervision and a further chief umpire was introduced to supervise the incident program, acknowledging that a further strong source of potential errors had appeared.

Conversion to computer simulation

With the method of manual operation and academic content stabilising by 1974 but subject to the need for high accuracy within limited time the first attempt at specifying and implementing computer assisted control was made. The computing objectives specified in this first attempt were:

1. To provide speedy verification of company decision sheets.
2. To provide fast allocation of market sales and intercompany trading.
3. To produce accurate copies of decision sheets and accounts as an aid to later verification of manually produced accounts.
4. To provide a simulation model for examining the versatility of the Hogwash Ltd exercise.

The subsequent simulation model was written in strict ANSI FORTRAN and used to test the effect of relaxing the limits imposed on the major exercise parameters of price variation, publicity, recruitment of salesmen and investment in plant. The results obtained from the trial simulation runs confirmed that Hogwash Ltd would remain stable with increased limits i.e. would retain its education value without becoming an exercise in gamesmanship and consequently the limits were relaxed, allowing a greater variety of company decisions, in time for the first application of the simulation model in a live run of the Hogwash Ltd exercise.

The ANSI FORTRAN simulation model was eventually used in two live runs of Hogwash Ltd in 1975, once using a Modular I computer and on the second occasion using an ICL 1906A computer. On both occasions the computer had to be abandoned and the exercise completed under manual operation. In the first application slow interactive response extended the time required to verify decisions and allocate sales well beyond the 15 min provided and on the second occasion a maintenance break at the remote site removed the computer at a key time. The decision was consequently made to return to manual supervision of the exercise but a valuable lesson had been learned; when applying computers in education careful specification of both hardware and software requirements is essential.

In 1976 the computing objectives were respecified under the headings of hardware and software requirements and a second attempt was made at achieving the mechanistic conversion to computer assisted control. The respecified computing objectives were:

Hardware

1. Continuous availability of a highly reliable computing system (Hogwash Ltd required 3 days including evenings and weekends).
2. Speedy input and output of information. (This could mean sole or high priority use.)
3. Ease of programmability in an acceptable high level language (FORTRAN and BASIC were the main languages in use by staff).
4. Periodic dumping and restore facilities. (To prevent complete collapse with faults and to allow overnight breaks.)
5. Limited printing facilities. (For production of accounting and decision records.)

Software

1–4 Same as initial computing objectives.

In 1977 a WANG 2200 PCS4 single terminal computer, with in-built cassette drive and a forty column matrix printer was purchased with the specific hardware objectives in mind. With 32K of user area available for BASIC programs and data matrices, modular linked programs were constructed to create an elementary management information system around which the four software computing objectives could be satisfied. The resultant programs were to be used successfully for controlling the administration of Hogwash Ltd until 1979 when the period of objective academic and computing development was to start.

The first noticeable change with interactive computer assistance was a progressive reduction in the level of supervision required. For the two controllers less concentration on routine market calculations was needed and far more time was available for planning and implementing the full incident program. For company tutors the availability of accurate accounts allowed greater emphasis on the tutoring of academic objects including planning and control measures, thus introducing the fourth major academic objective.

With the availability of highly accurate accounts however an important question of principle arose concerning the use of the computer and that was the question of whether to allow each company direct access to the computerised accounts. After several experimental trials it was found that allowing direct access to the computerised accounts was working against the objective of providing self-teaching in accountancy practice. It is the dilemma of applying computers in education that the removal of direct personal practice and skill development may ultimately reduce the rate of acquiring knowledge. Over enthusiastic programming in which the exploitation of computer facilities available subordinated teaching objectives had to be resisted in the case of Hogwash Ltd and the computer had to remain as a device for background simulation of the exercise in parallel to each companies efforts, rather than to be used as a direct access teaching medium.

This phase of mechanistic conversion from manual to computer control had also relieved the time pressure within the 15 min sales allocation interval to the point where the number of companies was increased firstly to 6 and then to 8 companies. In increasing the number of companies however the decision was made to move away from standard BASIC and to take advantage of special features associated with the WANG system for information packing.

In assessing the success of simulation based control for the Hogwash Ltd exercise the final point of importance was the very high level of reliability and accessibility achieved during each run. In common with other machines in the new generation of small computer systems the WANG 2200 series did not require a regular maintenance interval that could interrupt the 3 day programme and component reliability was high enough to ensure no hardware fault during any of the 20 runs that occurred between 1977 and 1979. The accessibility of the small computer system, being available at any time and portable to a variety of locations with comparative ease whilst allowing priority use, was again ideal for real time teaching of management subjects.

Objective development of computer and exercise

With an on-line control of Hogwash Ltd fully functional, in 1979 the objective development of both exercise and computer together was started in order to achieve the best combination of the two, particularly with a view to exploiting the word-processing capabilities of the BASIC language. The improvement in exercise objectives suggested by word-processing were:

1. To allow an increase in the number of industrial incidents that could be included in each exercise run.
2. Increased participation in tutoring from released controllers.
3. Further relaxation of exercise limits.

To achieve this the additional computing objectives specified were:

Hardware

1. To provide printing facilities of a standard for basic word processing.
2. To provide higher rates of data storage and retrieval.

Software

1. To transfer timing and printing of incident programme memoranda to computer control.
2. To transfer the actual evaluation of incidents wherever possible.
3. To provide summary analysis for exercise controllers.

The hardware requirements were achieved by adding a 132 column matrix printer and a twin floppy disk drive to the existing WANG 2200 system and by late 1979 copies of 36 memoranda had been transferred to disk storage for automatic processing by computer.

With integrated word-processing arranging the timing and despatch to each company of memoranda the last source of potential major faults had been removed and a full incident program could be included with reduced effort, whilst still retaining full control by the game umpires.

At present the Hogwash Ltd exercise is being transferred to a new WANG 2200MVP system with 64K user memory with the advantage of background printing to speed up turnround time and this is envisaged as the final major joint objective development of computer and exercise together that would be worth instigating.

CONCLUSIONS

The experience of designing, implementing and using the computer model of the business simulation exercise described has identified the following points of note for those interested in undertaking similar projects.

1. The process of developing a business simulation exercise can be considered as firstly a mechanistic conversion of necessary calculations and secondly as the objective development of the best features of equipment and exercise.
2. Concentration on the mechanistic phase will provide the greatest gain in the short term and will provide the experience of use necessary for identifying opportunities for objective development.
3. Academic objectives should remain the priority consideration and should not be diminished by computer operation.
4. Guaranteed accessibility and high reliability are essential for the application of computers in the teaching environment and the new generation of small computers appear most suitable for this role.
5. The specification of equipment requirements is of major importance in computer aided learning, even in those applications that do not involve direct access by students.
6. Many applications of simulation in teaching industrial management represent a high investment in time and equipment. There should be adequate use of the subsequent work to justify the investment.

Acknowledgements—The author wishes to acknowledge the encouragement and assistance given throughout the work described in this paper by Dr N. Carpenter, Assistant Director of Industrial Studies, Liverpool University, who originally introduced the "Hogwash Ltd" business exercise and who jointly with the author carried through the expansion and computerisation of the exercise over the past 5 years.

Comput. & Educ. Vol. 6, pp. 133 to 140, 1982

Printed in Great Britain

0360-1315/82/010133-08$03.00/0

Pergamon Press Ltd

UNDERSTANDING PHASE DIAGRAMS

AN EXAMPLE OF THE INTEGRATION OF INTERACTIVE GRAPHICS INTO A CAL AUTHORING SYSTEM

A. Demaid, P. G. Butcher and J. Verrier

The Open University, Walton Hall, Milton Keynes MK2 6AA, England

Abstract—This paper describes the philosophy and execution of the first in what is intended to be a series of related computer assisted learning programs designed to teach particular technological skills. The skills with which we are concerned are those used to interpret diagrams which represent physical phenomena; e.g. phase diagrams, and Pourbaix diagrams. This form of representation traditionally poses major difficulties to students, requiring the physical interpretation of complex diagrams, in addition to an understanding of the concepts and a confident numerical ability within the theory. Interactive raster scan graphics provides a dynamic medium for manipulating diagrams that is unavailable in any other medium. This new approach links such a facility into a general purpose CAL system to provide a powerful and attractive tool for teaching the interpretation of such complex visual representations.

The first program which has been written deals with the teaching of phase equilibrium diagrams to students of the Open University course TS251, An Introduction to Materials. The students are taught the fundamentals of the subject through the correspondence text and are given a lecture at the start of their week's summer school. Thus the function of the program is not to teach the subject from first principles, but to allow the student to develop confidence and skill through practice. The interactive program does this through the normal methods of questioning, assessing and prompting the student on the various aspects of the diagram, with the student using both textual (through the keyboard) and positional (through the cursor) input when answering. In designing the program the analogy with a map has been adopted to enable us to recognise subsets of teaching techniques and to develop a consistent method of programming. Thus the identification of major topological features and, say, routes which involve calculation are seen to involve different structures.

The material has been developed using the STAF authoring system to present and control the dialogue, and graphics on a SIGMA 5670 series, raster graphics terminal. Technical details of the implementation are described.

PHASE DIAGRAMS

With regard to the wide variety and range of experience represented amongst the readership of an article on CAL, we make no apologies for starting this paper with a brief statement of what a phase diagram is, and what its importance is to technologists in general, and metallurgists in particular.

Figure 1 shows a nicely complicated, copper–tin phase equilibrium diagram, the copper–tin alloy being more commonly known as bronze. Fortunately the complicated form of such a diagram can be split into four basic subsets and it is one of these subsets which we have chosen as the basis for the first in a series of CAL programs.

The lead/tin or solder alloy shown in Fig. 2 wholly illustrates the eutectic reaction which is the subset of interest. The field of this diagram represents the phase changes which occur as a result of varying the composition and temperature of the alloy. Pliny refers to solder for joining copper and iron as containing two parts of tin to one of lead, the reverse proportions being favoured by plumbers for joining lead pipes. These two compositions are shown on Fig. 2 by the lines A and B. The first alloy freezes very rapidly at a lower temperature, whereas the second alloy has a pasty behaviour over a considerable range of temperatures. Therefore with this kind of diagram the constitutional behaviour of alloys can be seen at a glance and the inelegant recipes of the Romans are replaced. The understanding and interpretation of these diagrams is further complicated by the requirement that equilibrium cooling take place. This, by definition, takes an interminably long time and never occurs in practice, therefore the diagram is used as a guide with the cooling rate of the melt causing variations in the predicted properties.

Traditionally the teaching of phase equilibrium diagrams poses problems in conventional Universities and in this respect they may be part of a large group of diagramatic representations which test the abilities of teachers. Technology is particularly adept at using these diagrams to represent lists, recipes, or conditions. For example, Pourbaix diagrams show the variation of electrochemical potential with pH in corrosion problems; and bending moment diagrams represent beam loading in structures.

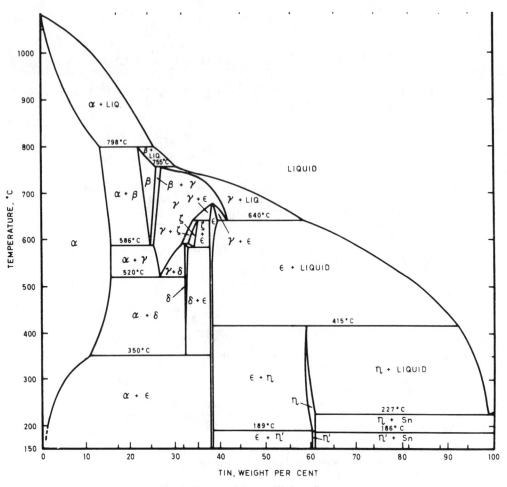

Fig. 1. Bronze phase equilibrium diagram.

CONTEXT

The Open University has not been immune from problems in teaching the understanding of phase diagrams to its students in the course TS251, An Introduction to Materials. This course has been running for 8 years, teaching some 500 students per year and consists of a front end containing the basic science and technology required by a materials engineer followed by a series of case studies showing applications to engineering problems. Case studies include: transformer cores, a milk bottle recycling study, porcelain, and car bodies. As part of their studies phase diagrams are taught in

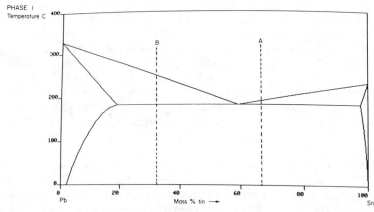

Fig. 2. Eutectic diagram.

conjunction with the use of a home experiment kit which involves preparing brass samples and examining their structure under a microscope. All students are required to attend 1 weeks summer school at Sussex University, the content of the summer school being designed around practical work which assumes an understanding of, and ability to interpret, phase diagrams. At an early stage in the life of the course it became apparent that the first requirement was a lecture/tutorial on phase diagrams and microstructure which, however good, was not entirely satisfactory as students did not have sufficient time to develop real proficiency before embarking on their practical work. This was the background to the decision to develop a CAL program to teach phase diagrams. Thus the program has been designed on the assumption that the student has already studied the subject by reading the basic concepts and definitions, and by going through worked examples. So the program will provide a skilled tutor approaching the "individualised instruction" claim by Hooper[1], basic teaching occurs in the program only as a direct result of student error.

APPROACH

The analogy which we have taken in developing the program is that of the map, with boundaries, topography, and routes. The properties of an alloy can vary markedly depending on which area of the diagram is pertinent and the route to a particular temperature and composition also defines the final properties of an alloy. Boundaries between different areas represent the positions beyond which it is thermodynamically favourable for a reaction to occur; whether that reaction occurs or not may however be governed by the kinetics. In essence then the equilibrium phase diagram is not mathematically "clean" and thus it cannot be dealt with in the way described by McKenzie[2] where the parameters in a formula can be varied and the result of the variation displayed graphically.

One consequence of this is that a necessarily sophisticated representation and display of the information which the student is being asked to interpret is required.

In order to illustrate one of many possible routes through the diagram consider the progressive cooling of an alloy of composition 30% tin/70% lead shown in Fig. 3. At point A the first solids nucleate from the liquid, these solids have a composition indicated by B on the diagram. The precipitation of α phase depletes the remaining liquid of lead, and on further cooling the composition of liquid will be given by the line AD, similarly the line BC describes the composition of the α phase on decreasing temperature. At point E the proportion of liquid is given by the ratio CE/CD and this liquid solidifies as an intimate mixture of α and β in proportions DF/CF and DC/CF. This then sets the, rather complicated, scene for the CAL system which was designed.

SYSTEM DESIGN

The selection of appropriate hardware and software to run the project was interdependent. The proposed application involved combinations of:

Textual and numerical output;
Graphical output with the ability to selectively highlight and erase lines and areas;
Textual and numerical input;
Positional input via the cursor;

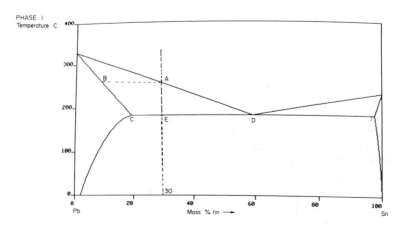

Fig. 3. Progressive cooling.

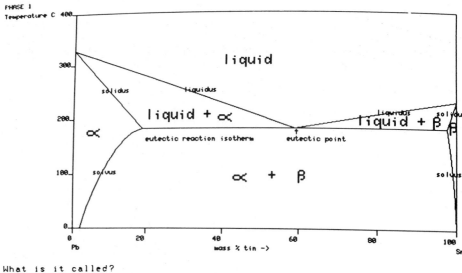

What is it called?
 Wrong
This has a special name — the eutectic reaction isotherm
[RETURN]

This is the complete labelling of the diagram showing the important features.
[RETURN]

Fig. 4. Screen arrangement.

In the STAF authoring system the University already had a software environment capable of handling the envisaged textual dialogues on scrolling terminals and wished to capitalise on its experience with this system and also extend it to graphical applications. The need for selective erasure of the graphics screen points to a raster scan graphics terminal and the nature of the application demanded relatively high resolution from such a device. Consequently a SIGMA 5670 series raster scan graphics terminal was purchased which provides not only high resolution graphics (768 by 512) but also a separately addressable "alpha" screen which can be made to scroll over only part of the screen. Figure 4 shows the screen as it is used, with the top 75% (approx.) used for displaying the graphical information and the dialogue between the program and the student scrolling over the bottom 25%.

The STAF system has been designed to allow the interaction between the student and the computer to be as natural as possible. Thus the language used by the student and the computer is as close to natural English as possible with allowances being made for spelling mistakes and trivial errors of nomenclature. Descriptions of dialogues enabled through STAF are well documented elsewhere[3–6]. This project extends this natural interaction between student and computer by adding a pictorial display which may be addressed by both the computer and the student. The aim of this project is to incorporate all of these features into a powerful dynamic teaching program.

The package allows interaction with the diagram in the sense that the student may point to lines, areas, and points and in that coordinate readings may be taken using the cursor; all of this is under control of the teaching program which can follow the student's attempts to perform set tasks, which include calculations. If the student is having difficulty the program will be able to recognise this and take the student through the principles of the calculation on the diagram. This is usually done by an animated calculation on an alternative diagram, which uses a simpler system (such as that shown in Fig. 5) to illustrate the major teaching points.

To identify a position on the screen, and relate it to the phase diagram showing, the teaching software has to describe the diagram using numerical methods as a sequence of lines (rather than a sequence of data points to be joined). This in turn enables areas to be similarly defined and the structure is established for both animating the diagrams and identifying areas, lines, or positions to which the student is pointing. The routines for handling the diagram have been written in FORTRAN and may be called from the STAF teaching program ("CALC" routines). When STAF programs "converse" with these routines parameters may be passed both ways. For example the STAF teaching program may call a routine to display the cursor and return co-ordinates when the student presses the "hit" button. These co-ordinates when returned may be evaluated and discussed with the student before progressing or regressing.

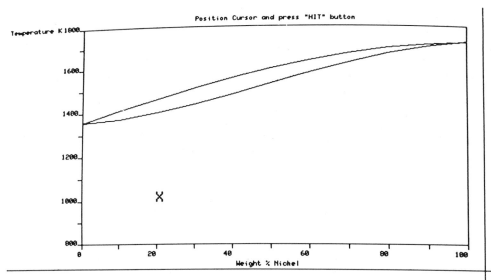

solid solubility.
The flashing area is a SINGLE PHASE SOLID SOLUTION
[RETURN]

Consider an alloy of composition X (see diagram). This would be
described as a solid solution of nickel in copper.
Use the cursor and point to a solid solution of COPPER IN NICKEL.

Fig. 5. Complete solid solubility.

The composition of the software suite is as follows:

The STAF teaching program is used to
present dialogue
accept and match textual and numerical responses
control the teaching dialogue
keep information on student responses and program performance
keep student records e.g. how far the student has progressed and the current performance rating
label the diagram (axes excepted)
FORTRAN routines are used to
describe the diagram (application specific)
provide general purpose graphics routines.

This relationship is shown diagramatically in Fig. 6. It is envisaged that in time general purpose functions will be added to the STAF system so that the graphics device may be controlled directly from within a STAF teaching programme.

DISCUSSION

The interactive nature of this program offers learning opportunities which are unique to this medium, this by virtue of the intimate association between the textual and graphical interaction. The programe has not, as yet, been used with out students on TS251, thus many of the lessons that will be learnt are about how students interact with the program and will reflect how students cope, or fail to cope, with the complexities of the diagram. The route tracing ability of STAF will be invaluable in determining what the real, as opposed to tutor imagined, problems of understanding and interpreting this type of diagram are.

The program has been written, with student enjoyment very much in mind, in a "game" format. The name of the game is WORKS METALLURGIST (Fig. 7) and students are accorded a rating, dependent on their performance, varying from OFFICE CLEANER (reserved for those who are testing the program) to WORKS METALLURGIST (for those whose performance is faultless).

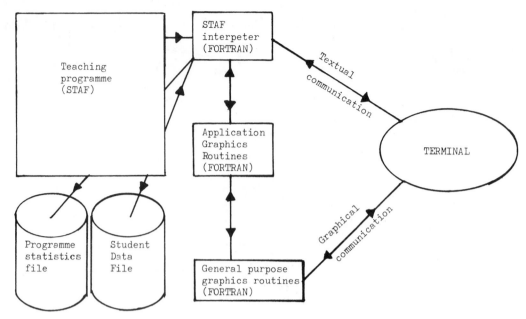

Fig. 6. Software organisation.

Errors in particular sections of the program cause more questions to be asked until proficiency at that level is established. Errors are dealt with by teaching in alternative subsets of the equilibrium diagram and then returning to the question which was failed. In the main it has been adopted as policy that two levels of prompting are employed before teaching on the main diagram takes place.

It was not assumed that students were familiar with the use of a terminal and the combination of text and graphics available on the screen was ideal for teaching the use of the terminal (Fig. 8).

The STAF teaching programs are inherently portable[7] from computer to computer and it is not envisaged that the FORTRAN routines provided to drive the SIGMA display will in any way inhibit this portability, but with the combination of graphics and scrolling text on one screen the application is currently very terminal dependent. Other raster scan devices that provide positional input, either through cross-hairs or a light pen, may however provide alternative solutions in the future.

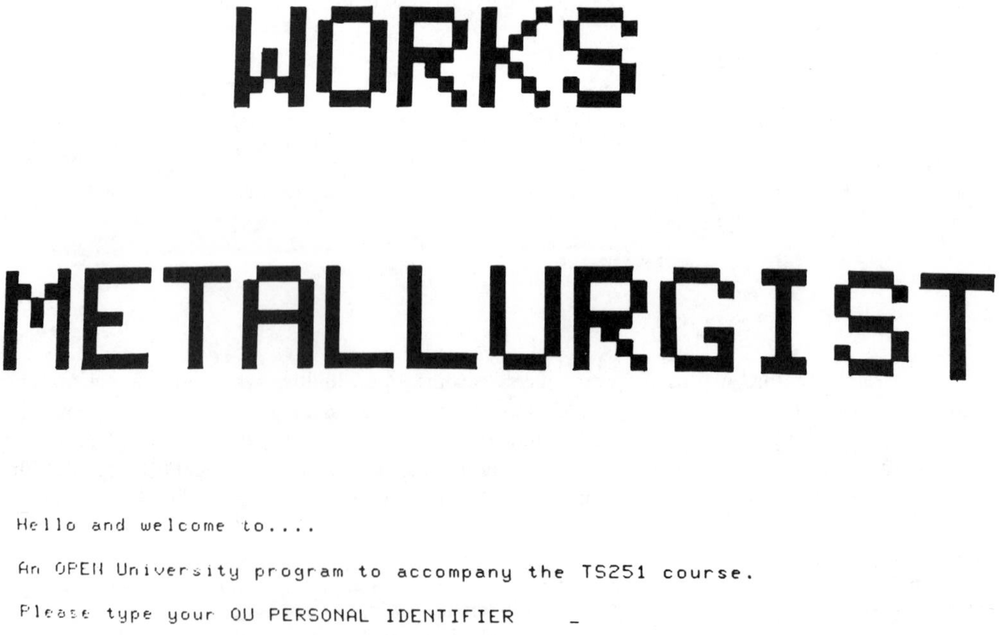

WORKS

METALLURGIST

Hello and welcome to....

An OPEN University program to accompany the TS251 course.

Please type your OU PERSONAL IDENTIFIER   _

Fig. 7. Programme title.

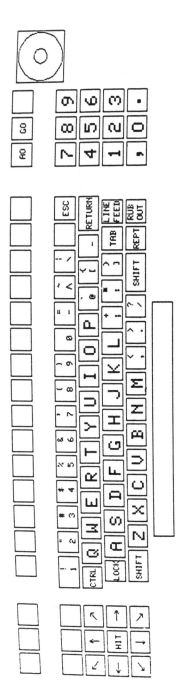

Fig. 8. Keyboard.

REFERENCES

1. Hooper R., *Int. J. Math. Educ. Sci. Technol.* **5,** 359 (1974).
2. McKenzie J., *Comput. Educ.* **2,** 25 (1978).
3. Tawney D. A., *Learning Through Computers*, pp. 1, 29–42, 212–213. Macmillan, London (1979).
4. Peterson J. W. M., Writing programmes in STAF CALCHEM. Department of Physics and Chemistry, Leeds University.
5. Ayscough P. B., STAF Author Guide, CALCHEM. Department of Physics and Chemistry, Leeds University.
6. Ayscough P. B., Morris H. and Wilson J. A., *Comput. Educ.* **3,** 81 (1979).
7. Peterson J. W. M. and Sessions A. E., *Comput. Educ.* **2,** 331 (1978).

Comput. & Educ. Vol. 6, pp. 141 to 144, 1982
Printed in Great Britain

0360-1315/82/010141-04$03.00/0
Pergamon Press Ltd

BIOLOGICAL SIMULATIONS IN DISTANCE LEARNING

P. J. Murphy

Biology Department, The Open University, Walton Hall, Milton Keynes MK7 6AA, England

Abstract—Interactive computer simulations can be very effective educationally, but, at the present time, are not easily provided as part of a distance learning system. The problems of introducing biological simulations into two Open University courses and the proposed solutions are discussed in relation to sound CAL practise.

INTRODUCTION

Much experience and expertise has now been acquired, with "live" classes at both secondary and tertiary level, in the use of computer simulations in the teaching of biology [1–3]. This culminated, as far as the present author is concerned, in the development of an entire undergraduate practical course in genetics based very extensively on computer assisted learning (CAL) [4].

In this course an approach was developed in which a key feature was the interaction of individuals or small groups of students with computer models of the systems they were studying. The idea was that students should attempt to answer increasingly more "open-ended" questions about the systems—questions which have been posed either by the tutor or, even better, the students themselves. Students arrived at answers by analysing output from programs, in each of which several parameters were left under user-control. It was important to leave as much initiative with the students as possible. This is in marked contrast to many laboratory-based exercises, in which all decisions relating to experimental design are taken in advance by the tutor because he/she dare not risk the time and/or expense of students adopting inappropriate or inefficient strategies. With computer simulation, "mistakes" can be made, detected and corrected within minutes. Answers quite often led to further questions and consequently several sessions at the computer terminal might be required to investigate a single simulation thoroughly. Finally, results and conclusions were presented in the form of a written, and sometimes also verbal, scientific report.

It was perhaps natural to attempt to translate as many features as possible of this approach, which had proved so successful with conventional university classes, to the rather different distance learning environment of The Open University, whose students study part-time for their degrees through the use of correspondance texts, television, radio, audio-visual aids, summer and day schools and limited contact with part-time tutors. Difficulties were encountered, the magnitude of which became apparent only as the work progressed. In overcoming these difficulties it was necessary to re-appraise the whole concept of using computer simulation in distance learning and to decide which features of the approach outlined above were essential, and which merely desirable. This paper discusses some of the difficulties and how they were overcome, taking as examples two Open University courses which had rather different reasons for wanting to use CAL.

The Open University has had quite extensive experience in the use of computers for educational purposes [5], particularly tutorial CAL in a true distance learning mode and simulation CAL at summer school. However, comparatively little use had been made of simulation CAL by students working from home without the presence of Open University staff.

EVOLUTION (S364)

This course [6] is being offered for the first time in 1981. It was the original intention of the course team that the practical side of this third level joint Biology–Earth Science course be fulfilled by a 1-week residential summer school at a suitable venue. However, permission to have a summer school was not granted and alternative provision had to be made at relatively short notice. After consideration of the options available, it was decided that each student should carry out one of a number of biologically-orientated projects and report their work in the form of a Tutor-marked Assignment (TMA). It was, however, no trivial task to devise and developmentally test projects on topics such as speciation and natural selection, appropriate for unsupervised students living anywhere within the United Kingdom and which require not more than 10–12 h study time. Not surprisingly, it was not known until shortly before the course was due to go out how wide the choice of projects would be during the first year of presentation.

One of the projects will be based on a computer simulation (EVOLVE) written specially for the course. EVOLVE models the genetic and evolutionary consequences of two populations of a single flowering plant species coming together after a period of genetic isolation. It is similar to a model developed for research purposes by Crosby [7]. Apart from the educational advantages which accrue from students interacting with simulations such as EVOLVE (which in fact highlights several important concepts in evolutionary theory), the course team was also influenced by the fact that development of this project could continue independent of biological seasons and that there was no danger of the relevant species being restricted to only certain regions of the United Kingdom, considerations which were imposing severe constraints on the development of other projects.

The author originally visualised an operation similar to that employed in the genetics course referred to above [4], with each student running EVOLVE on one of The Open University's computer terminals at a Study Centre. Each student would "discover" for himself/herself the basic attributes of the system modelled and would then go on to investigate a single aspect of particular interest. It was realised, from previous experience, that it was unrealistic to expect students to go through both of these stages in a single visit to the terminal. This was true even of students who had some familiarity with computing and the use of simulations for educational purposes. For most students, however, this would be a relatively novel experience. On the other hand, it was also both unrealistic and unfair to expect students to make several visits to the terminal since many would have considerable distances to travel and would have problems in booking the University's very heavily used computer terminals. A further problem was that students would have to decide between the various projects at quite an early stage during the course. How could the relatively unconventional simulation project be judged with only a printed description for guidance?

GENETICS (S299)

This course [8] came into existence in 1976 with a 1-week summer school as an integral component. At summer school students performed various experiments on microbial and quantitative genetics, all but one of which required relatively sophisticated laboratory facilities. The exception was an experiment in which the inheritance of a continuously varying character, height in wheat, was analysed biometrically. Students spent some time measuring previously grown samples of wheat representing the six relevant generations and then considerably longer going through the fairly elaborate statistical analysis required to interpret the data. Considerable assistance was usually required at this stage from the tutors and demonstrators.

Due to rearrangements necessitated by the introduction of several new biology courses, S299 will lose its summer school from 1981. In partial replacement, an additional 4 h of tutorial time is being provided. This time is being added to the existing 10 h, which is being rearranged to provide the equivalent of two half-day schools—one in June/July on population genetics and the other in September on biometrical genetics. The schools will take place at 2 venues in each of the University's 13 Regions and it is hoped that students will benefit considerably from assistance with what are generally reckoned to be the most demanding parts of a fairly demanding course. Although it was originally hoped to retain the "wheat experiment" for the biometrics school, it soon became clear that the cost of replicating the material for use in 26 widely dispersed venues almost simultaneously would be far too great. Moreover, given the amount of assistance students need with the statistical analysis, it would still be very difficult to do in the time available.

An obvious solution was to write a computer program (WHEAT) to model the inheritance of height in wheat and have small groups of students interacting with the program. There would be the added benefit that students would have to think about and specify the genetic crosses themselves, rather than be presented with previously grown plants.

However, appealing through it was, this proposed solution gave rise to a host of new problems. Few of the Open University's Study Centres have computer terminals in rooms suitable for the day schools as a whole. On the other hand, installing computer terminals and telephones in suitable rooms for half a day was much too costly to entertain. Microprocessors might seem to be the answer here—but for the fact that the University does not have sufficient suitable machines, which in any case would have to be transported to the venues. With one or two terminals or microprocessors per group of about 20 students there would have to be some sort of circus arrangement with other relevant activities. Yet, a single tutor would be running each day school and its is known that students need a lot of assistance with the statistical treatment of such biometrical data. Finally, the people employed to tutor the course generally, and the day schools in particular, are appointed on their ability to teach the subject matter of the course. It would have been wrong to insist upon, or assume, familiarity with CAL as an educational technique or with the working of terminals or microprocessors (although, as it happens, some are indeed expert). Given all these difficulties, a different approach was clearly required.

SOLUTIONS

The problem, in the case of S364, was that students could not be expected to make multiple visits to Study Centres to run the program and, in the case of S299, it was the difficulty of providing cost-effective interactive computing at remote sites for short periods of time. The solution, in each case, appeared to fly in the face of sound CAL practise and, until recently, would not have been advocated by the author.

Two versions of EVOLVE were produced. One is fully interactive and is to be accessed through Study Centre terminals, and the other is non-interactive, having been designed to be run in the batch stream of the University's DEC system-20 at Walton Hall.

The non-interactive version of EVOLVE is individually run for each student enrolled on the course for a standard 100 generations, with appropriate default settings for the various parameters. Because the program is stochastic, each run is unique. Nevertheless, the various, apparently quite different, outcomes can all be accounted for by the same evolutionary processes. Early in the academic year these printouts are mailed to the students, along with notes describing all the projects in detail. Students are therefore in a position to evaluate the various projects and to decide which one to do themselves. This decision has to be made as soon as possible, since several of the field investigations have to be underway by April. Thus, even students who opt not to do the simulation project will have had the chance to see, and think about the reasons for, the quite striking evolutionary changes apparent in the printout.

The simulation project is two staged—corresponding to the use of the mailed printout (Stage 1) and the interactive program (Stage 2). There are also two cycles of work for students who undertake the project.

In the first cycle of work, students are required to examine the printout, note the changes and, based on a synthesis of many concepts from S364 itself and the Science Foundation Course (S101), account for the changes in terms of natural selection theory (upon which the model is firmly based). They then prepare a *very* brief report of their conclusions and an outline of the investigation they propose to do using the interactive version of the program. This report is submitted to the tutors early in the summer. It is not assessed at this stage, but tutors advise students whether they are "on the right lines" in their interpretation of the Stage 1 printout and whether their proposed Stage 2 investigations are reasonable in terms of time, effort and intellectual content. These safeguards are very important because the project TMA, being non-substitutable, is effectively a compulsory element of the continuous assessment component of the course. If a student acquired a totally wrong idea about the Stage 1 printout, it is rather unlikely that useful Stage 2 work would result. It would be unfair to have part of the project wholly dependant on getting something else correct. The tutor who advises a particular student after the first cycle of work, will also mark that student's submitted TMA and so can allow for assistance or advice given. It is also important that the student is well prepared for the one visit to the computer terminal and that the proposed investigation is not hopelessly ambitious for the time available. Again, having to tell the tutor in advance what is intended helps to optimise the students' limited time. Nevertheless, both students and tutors are advised that students should allow some time during the one 1-h computer session in case unanticipated results need further investigation.

Students are permitted to use the interactive version of the program at Study Centres from 1st September onwards. This restriction was necessary because of the severe overloading of the computer facilities earlier in the academic year. However, it does serve the useful purpose of preventing students completing the TMA before studying the most relevant units in the course (Unit 10, *Evolution by Natural Selection* and Unit 11, *Evolutionary Ecology*). The full report on both Stage 1 and Stage 2 is then written up and submitted to tutors by the TMA cut-off data in late September. The tutors are asked to look for well summarised data and biologically sensible deductions from Stage 1 and evidence of a systematic approach in Stage 2, even if conclusions have to be tentative because of lack of time at the terminal. Students can submit only Stage 1 work if they desire, and still obtain a pass grade. However, good work in both stages is required for high grades. Because it should be quite possible to grade students on the basis of their submitted work, they are not discouraged from co-operating at the stage of interaction with the computer if they feel apprehensive about computers and computing.

It will not be known how many students have opted for the simulation project, rather than one of the others, until late 1981. Some monitoring of progress during the year will be possible through informal contact with part-time tutors, but most feedback will reach the course team at the time of the Examination Board meeting in November. Unless the exercise proves to be completely disastrous, the intention is that the project will be offered again in 1982 with such improvements as seem necessary. Meanwhile, other simulations will be developed which can be substituted in subsequent years.

For S299 an entirely non-interactive, but stochastic, version of WHEAT has been written. This program too is run in the batch stream at Walton Hall. Printout of sufficient runs is supplied to each biometrics day school tutor, who will distribute them, along with a specially written booklet, at the day school. The printouts come in two sections, each of which is identified with the same run number. The first sections, which are given to students, consist of data that might have been collected by measuring actual plants, although simple statistics (such as means and variances) are also given to save time. The second sections are retained by the tutors for use at the day school. Guided by the booklet and assisted, when necessary, by the tutor, students will process their own data sets with the ultimate object of calculating such parameters as broad and narrow sense heritabilities. The tutor is in an excellent position to help and to generally "trouble-shoot" because the second section of each printout has the detailed steps of each individual analysis set out for rapid consultation. It is anticipated that the tutors will run group introductory and concluding sessions, with students working on their own, or in small groups, in between. While attendance at the day school is not compulsory and the work done there not directly assessed, there will be a TMA assessing this part of the course. There can be little doubt that day school attendees will be at an advantage.

In overcoming serious logistical problems, the interactive element of CAL has been lost entirely. This is more than offset by the much improved tutorial support afforded by the adopted scheme. As well as having the second sheet to "crib" from, the tutor can also ensure that all the runs used at a day school illustrate points which he/she wants emphasised or that a range of different systems (for instance, from total additivity to complete genetic dominance) are represented.

DISCUSSION

It can be seen that, because of a variety of difficulties, it is not always possible to transfer an approach to using computer simulation from the local to the distance learning environment without considerable modification. The changes sometime seem quite contrary to demonstrably sound CAL practise, particularly when the essentiality of interaction is called into question. However, the important point is whether learning is aided overall or not.

If several visits to the computer terminal could reasonably have been expected of S364 students, it might have been better to have required them to use only the interactive version of EVOLVE and "discover" for themselves even the basic features of the system modelled. However, how many would have decided not to "risk" trying something relatively unknown and how many would have failed to see the fundamental point of the exercise without a tutor on hand to ask questions and proffer advice?

While the S364 solution might be regarded as tolerable compromise dictated by expediency, the S299 solution has resulted in an approach significantly better than would have been possible using interactive terminals (given the resources currently available to The Open University) and possibly an approach educationally superior to that of the original summer school exercise.

The moral seems to be that hard-won experience in certain contexts should not be allowed to prevent pragmatic new solutions in changing circumstances. This should be borne in mind as the time approaches when, as a "spin-off" from computer-based T.V. games, The Open University can assume that all homes are, or can easily be, equipped with computing power. Clearly this opens out a whole range of fresh possibilities for the use of simulations in distance learning.

Acknowledgements—The work reported here would not have been possible without the co-operation and advice of other members of the S364 and S299 course teams and of The Open University's Student Computing Service.

REFERENCES

1. Leveridge M. E., In *Computers in the Biology Curriculum* (Edited by M. E. Leveridge), pp. 1–15. Schools Council/Edward Arnold, London (1978).
2. Lal S., Wood A. W. and Cunningham P., In *Interactive Computer Graphics in Science Teaching* (Edited by J. McKenzie, L. R. B. Elton and R. Lewis), pp. 132–147. Ellis Horwood, Chichester (1978).
3. Wood A. W., In *Learning Through Computers* (Edited by D. A. Tawney), pp. 11–22. Macmillan, London (1979).
4. Garbutt K., Murphy P. J. and Vardy A., *Comput. Educ.* **3**, 353 (1979).
5. Bramer M., *Comput. Educ.* **4**, 293 (1980).
6. The Open University, *S364 Evolution*. The Open University Press, Milton Keynes (1981).
7. Crosby J. L., *Heredity* **25**, 253 (1970).
8. The Open University, *S299 Genetics*. The Open University Press, Milton Keynes (1976).

Comput. & Educ. Vol. 6, pp. 145 to 151, 1982
Printed in Great Britain

0360-1315/82/010145-07$03.00/0
Pergamon Press Ltd

COMPUTER AIDED MODEL BUILDING AND CAL

Joachim P. E. Wedekind

Institut fuer Erziehungswissenschaft II, Universitaet Tuebingen, D-7400 Tuebingen,
Federal Republic of Germany

Abstract—Model building has become an educational objective at the tertiary and the secondary level. There are reservations in regard to the suitability of computer simulations for integrating modelling into the education process. Interactive simulation systems can be designed to meet educational requirements, presenting a preprogrammed simulation environment which only has to be supplied with the model itself. The model can be supplied as a set of statements ("missing-link"- program) or as a block diagram representing the structure of the system. Examples are presented for both possibilities and their respective characteristics are discussed.

MODEL BUILDING AS AN EDUCATIONAL OBJECTIVE

Within Computer Assisted Learning (CAL), computer simulation is one of the most important modes of use. This importance corresponds to its growing relevance in many research areas. Computer simulation may be defined as follows:

> Simulation means working with the model of a specific system. In the case of *computer simulation* it is always a mathematical model, which is implemented as an executable program on a computer.

This definition of computer simulation stresses the intimate linkage between simulation, model building and the system theoretical approach. This makes it evident that there are two significant steps before really starting to simulate. The first is to define a certain system out of the total reality. The second is to transform the system into an adequate model containing all the relevant elements and interrelations concerning the problem in question.

A number of good reasons have often been stated for using computer simulations in educational contexts. These include their possible role as a substitute for laboratory experiments, the support of inductive forms of learning, and the visualization of complex phenomena. These are meaningful applications when the simulation is not misused to produce facts by magic, but where the students always realize that they are gaining hypothetical results with the aid of a hypothetical model. The growing relevance of computer simulation has to be interpreted as a growing relevance of mathematical models. Thus it appears that, in addition to the educational use of computer simulation, there is a need to integrate modelling as a fundamental topic into the science curriculum. Some authors speak of modelling in cases where the students work with different models concerning one problem, and where they then compare the different results with experimental data[1]. This can be realized if several different simulation programs are placed at the students' disposal or, if in one simulation program several switches are built in, allowing the consideration of additional factors or of alternative submodels[2]. Another method is to set up a simulation program as a black box. The students do not know the underlying model but they control the input parameters and they can observe and interpret the resulting outputs. In this way they are asked to determine the model by a process of induction[1]. Nevertheless, it is my own opinion that these few attempts to extend the scope of computer simulations to the undoubtedly important area of modelling have to be rated as provisional.

In research, modelling means in a much wider sense the choice, the modification or the creation of a model (model building), and the testing of the model[3]. In this process the computer simulation is nothing but a fast and easy way to get the necessary information about the model in the phase of model testing and again in the phase of model experiments. Model building includes the implementation of the model on a computer, that is, the choosing of suitable algorithms and programming in a suitable programming language. This procedure is the crucial point which mainly inhibits the introduction of modelling in instruction. But as modelling has become an educational objective at the tertiary and even at the secondary level, there is a considerable demand for software tools which allow the implementation of models without preliminary knowledge in EDP. In the next paragraph I want to discuss some software attributes of *simulation systems* which meet these requirements.

SOME CHARACTERISTICS OF SIMULATION SYSTEMS

Modelling is a special type of scientific practice, comparable to observation or experimentation, and it has a corresponding general importance in research. It is not surprising that we can find many attempts to develop programming aids in order to reduce some scientists' reservations against using computers for the development of models, primarily without their educational use in mind. But what in this instance is called "user-orientation" is a good basis for "learner-orientation" in the design of simulation systems.

The term simulation system will be used for entire computer programs or program packages which provide a comprehensive simulation environment. This statement has two implications. On the one hand, it is necessary to have different simulation systems available which are adapted to the characteristics and the nomenclature of a certain problem class. On the other hand, the single simulation system must be general enough to enable the treatment of as many models as possible within these limitations. That is, the simulation environment has to include, in a preprogrammed manner, everything except the model itself. This means the inclusion of the entire interaction between the user and the program in order to control the process of model building and simulation with special commands and a determined nomenclature. A simulation system thus may be considered as a sort of interpreter. Moreover, it means the inclusion of all necessary numerical routines. This is an essential factor because their implementation does not only require programming qualifications but also a deepened mathematical understanding of adequate numerical procedures. In addition most routines already exist in tested versions and need not be programmed again and again For educational use the choice of these routines forces a compromise between accuracy and computational speed. In some cases, the utilization of a sophisticated routine may lead to results of high precision but will need an unacceptable time whereas a simpler routine may lead to results with tolerable deviations but will maintain a real dialogue between student and program. The simulation environment has to include other modules to organize the output of the results. Various forms of output are possible, namely on a display or on a printer, in tabulated form or in graphical form. The simultaneous output of the results of different simulation runs is especially valuable in the phase of model testing. It implies the possibility of saving and storing results and of recalling them if required. The flexible design of the graphical output is another essential factor, because this normally requires good knowledge of the special graphics package used by the available computer configuration.

There are several ways of achieving the goal of an easy-to-use simulation system. I will now describe two ways in some detail. One is the use of an accomplished program package which needs only to be supplied with the desired model (what I call a "missing-link"-program). The section to be supplied consists of a number of statements containing the model equations, which are formulated in a high-level programming language. An alternative way is to construct simulation systems based on interactive computer graphics which take advantage of the possibilities of graphical inputs.

MISSING-LINK-PROGRAMS: ENZKIN AND DIFGLE

At the University of Tuebingen two program packages of the first type have been developed. ENZKIN is devoted to the manipulation of complex enzyme kinetic systems which can be described by a set of first order differential equations. Enzyme catalyzed reactions are of great importance in physiology and biochemistry. In contrast to ordinary chemical reactions they are characterized by very high velocity constants of some of the reactions and by large differences in the concentrations of the involved reactands (differing e.g. about 10^4 between substrate and enzyme). These extreme conditions require very efficient routines for the numerical integration of the resulting equations. We have used Gear's algorithm (DIFSUB), which showed good accuracy in the results and the necessary computational speed.

The missing link in the program is the set of model equations which must be supplied by the user. For this purpose an elaborate command-file guides the user to two locations; the first, where he has to define the correct dimensions, depending on the number of differential equations and the number of parameters (up to 20 equations and up to 50 parameters are allowed at maximum), and the second, where he has to insert the equations themselves. All further compiling, linking etc. is executed automatically. The user can pass immediately to model testing and simulation. In every model the user has defined, he can vary the initial concentrations of all reactands and all velocity constants. For the evaluation of the models several aids are supplied like Lineweaver–Burk plot, Dixon–Webb plot or Scatchard plot. These plots are especially useful for the investigation of different types of inhibition. In addition to the simulation mode, one has the option of putting in experimental data and evaluating them with the same instruments or of comparing direct experimental data and simulated results. The completed program consists of six modules and a supervisory program. The supervisor controls the execution of ENZKIN, coordinating the four modules and linked subprograms. Different menus are

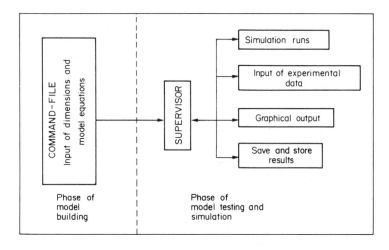

Fig. 1. ENZKIN: process of the implementation and the use of models.

offered to the user for selecting the desired options on the two levels, either the supervisor or one of the modules. The entire process of implementation and use of the models is illustrated in Fig. 1.

DIFGLE is a somewhat modified version of ENZKIN which permits the general treatment of sets of ordinary differential equations. It does not contain the special plot options of ENZKIN. On the contrary, it offers different integration routines and is extended by x–y plots. The interaction between the student and the program is comparable to that of ENZKIN and does not need a special consideration in this context. Both programs can be classified between special simulation programs and more general simulation languages for continuous dynamic systems, like CSMP, SIKOS or MARSYAS. The more general character of the latter and their dedicated determination for research purposes, which is manifest in a greater number of integration routines, plot options etc., make them very powerful but hardly suitable for educational purposes. The limitation of the missing-link-programs in that they deal only with a special class of problems proves to be their special advantage in the context of teaching.

INTERACTIVE COMPUTER GRAPHICS

The second form of simulation systems presented here is based on interactive computer graphics. I want to use this term in a more comprehensive manner than is usual. In most cases, interactive graphics means the graphical presentation of the quantitative aspects of a system, combined with the interactive input of data and control of the program by the student[4]. Specifically this consists of the graphical presentation of time-dependent developments of dynamic systems in time series, plots or phase planes (e.g. predator–prey systems, world models etc.), or of certain time-independent system-states (e.g. atomic orbitals etc.). We will extend this meaning to include the graphical presentation of the systems structure. Figure 2 shows an example of the description of a system in a causal loop diagram, containing the components of the system and their causal interdependence. Such diagrams

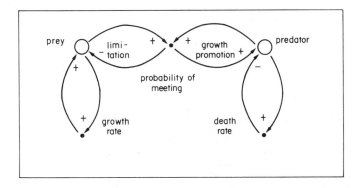

Fig. 2. Causal loop diagram of a predator–prey system.

can be used for computer simulations if they are constituted of clearly defined symbols which can be assembled in block diagrams, and if there is an isomorphism between the block diagram and the mathematical formalism describing the system.

There are diverse symbolisms originating in different scientific areas, whose applications have not been limited to their original fields. As a result the same system can now be symbolized in different but equivalent notations. Three classes of symbolisms can be classified:

1. symbolization of the structure
   (electric circuit diagrams)
2. symbolization of the flow
   (chemical reactions, System Dynamics)
3. symbolization of the mathematical relations
   (analog computer wiring diagram).

We can then take advantage of the fact, that on the one hand the same system can have several representations, and that on the other hand different systems can show the same behaviour. Both facts are based upon their identical mathematical equations. For example, the well-known Lotka–Volterra equations are used for the description of a predator–prey system in ecology and for the description of two coupled autocatalytic reactions in chemistry. The incorporation of the different symbolisms into their respective simulation system allows the student to work in a familiar notation and allows the phase of model building by making up block diagrams.

INTERACTIVE SIMULATION SYSTEMS: GRIPS AND DISIKOS

The group of potential users of simulation systems is getting larger with the growing relevance of mathematical modelling. Consequently these systems have to be more and more user-oriented and today we can state that the evolution of these instruments is nearly bridging the gap between scientific and educational requirements. In comparison to CAD (Computer Aided Design) we can speak of Computer Aided Model Building (CAMB). We can refer to a remarkable number of simulation systems, based on the principles mentioned above, which have been developed for scientific and technical applications. I will name two programs in particular. The one is SPICE (Simulation Program with Integrated Circuit Emphasis), developed at the Department of Electrical Engineering and Computer Sciences of the University of California, Berkeley, which serves to analyze electronic circuits. The other is CSMP-1130 (Continuous System Modeling Program) of IBM, to analyze sets of ordinary differential equations. The programs are named because they are examples of two alternative ways of achieving a running simulation program from the block diagram of a desired system. The important difference is that in SPICE the structure of the block diagrams has to be put in tabulated form, whereas in CSMP the block diagram can be constructed directly on the screen using graphical input. In the following I want to outline the concept of two programs: one for each possibility. In comparison to programs like SPICE they are reduced in size and have limited scopes, but they are sufficient to allow the students to engage in modelling in an active and autonomous manner.

The first program is the GRaphical Interactive Programming System (GRIPS). GRIPS is used to build, to modify, and to test continuous dynamic systems which can be described by a set of ordinary differential equations:

$$dx_1/dt = f_1(x_1,\ldots,x_n; u_1,\ldots,u_m; p_1,\ldots,p_1; t)$$

$$dx_n/dt = f_1(x_1,\ldots,x_n; u_1,\ldots,u_m; p_1,\ldots,p_1; t)$$

x_i are the state variables which can be measured, indicating the state of the system

f_i are the functions representing the structural interconnections

u_i are the exogenous variables; these are inputs to the system which are not system-dependent themselves

p_i are the system parameters

t is the independent variable time.

Many systems of this type can be represented by a block diagram using the symbols shown in Fig. 3. The block diagram itself can be constructed on the display by graphical input. The user has to choose the respective symbols from the menu given on the screen and to place them in a reserved area which is overlayed by an invisible coordinate system. This allows the exact location and connection of the symbols. Figure 4 shows the resulting diagram for the Lotka–Volterra equations. The diagram is

Symbol	Variable	Math. Description
◇	State Variable	$S = \int_0^t \sum_{i=1}^{3} e_i \, dt + S(\emptyset)$
⬡	Exogenous Variable	$E = F(t)$
▭	Function	$F = F(e_1, e_2, e_3)$
→	Path	$a = ce_i$
⌒	Feedback	$a = ce_i$
◯	Loop	$a = ce_i$

$$a = \text{output}$$
$$e_i = \text{input } i$$
$$c = \text{constant}$$

Fig. 3. Symbols used to build block diagrams with GRIPS.

drawn by the computer as a feedback to the inputs, to confirm to the user that the computer has converted the inputs correctly. The total interaction is divided into five different steps. After the entry of the block diagram, in a second step the appropriate functions have to be supplied. GRIPS offers 18 different functions (like adder, divider, sine, cosine etc.) and eight different exogeneous variables (like delta impulse, ramp, table functions etc.). In the next step the numerical characteristics of the system are required (initial values for the state variables, parameter values etc.). After the setting of the run time data (integration step size, output interval etc.) the computation of a simulation run follows. In a final step different outputs can be chosen.

The second program DISIKOS (DIgital SImulation of COntinuous Systems) is based on the same symbolism as GRIPS but it does not use graphical input. The procedure is first to develop the block diagram with paper and pencil. This will include the correct numbering of the elements and their interconnections (in GRIPS this is done automatically). Then these data have to be put in alphanumerical form. The result is a characteristic table for the system in question. Table 1 shows as an example the table derived from the block diagram in Fig. 4. In the actual version DISIKOS has less functions and exogeneous variables than GRIPS, but it can be easily extended if necessary.

Two other programs especially devoted to educational use, and also based on the extensive use of graphical input have to be mentioned here. Holtmann[5] has developed the concept for an introduction into the quantum mechanics of two-state-systems using an interactive simulation system named QUANT. It is based on Feynman's symbolism of idealized measuring instruments. With the program it is possible to transpose Dirac's calculus directly into a corresponding diagram by using elements, which are characterized by input/output relations corresponding to the operational definitions of the terms. Wood et al.[6] have presented an interactive graphics truss analysis program which requires the input of the shape, material properties, support conditions, and loading, and which outputs member forces and reactions.

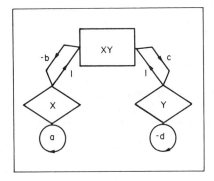

Fig. 4. Block diagram of the Lotka–Volterra equations with GRIPS symbols.

Table 1. Tabulated form of the Lotka–Volterra equations in DISIKOS

Block no.	Type	Constant	Input 1 parameter	Input 2 parameter	Input 3 parameter
1	1	—	$1,a$	$3, -b$	—
2	1	—	$4, -d$	$6,c$	—
3	3	—	$2,1$	$5,1$	—

CAMB AND CAL

Some years ago there was a discussion whether CAL is a form of CAD education[7] or, vice versa, whether using CAD in teaching is CAL[8]. Examples can be found to support both points of view, depending on the educational objectives and the organisational background. I want to add to this discussion the thesis that CAMB is CAL. Arguments to support this thesis can be found in the above description of diverse simulation systems. Above all, they meet the requirements of any CAL program. They are fully interactive, they are easy to handle, they check wrong inputs and logical errors and they are under total user-control. It is remarkable that they offer two intellectually different approaches for dealing with a problem. On the one hand, it is possible to start by setting up the mathematical equations and to continue by converting them into the diagram. Thus the user is able to run a simulation in a much shorter time than if he had to develop an entire new simulation program. On the other hand, it is possible to start with the phenomenon itself, to concentrate on the structural and functional relations and to postpone the mathematical formalism. The diagram reproduces these relations more clearly than the corresponding equations. The simulation system enables the user to remain in this mode of thinking.

Simulation systems in connection with "model banks", in which existing models can be saved and later recalled, support a method of learning in which the students has to pass through three different phases:

1. Aquisition of informations
   (carrying-out of simulation runs to get the characteristics of the system and to develop heuristics)
2. Systematization
   (carrying-out of a set of simulation runs relating to a special problem)
3. Problem solving
   (definition of problems, design of modification of models, implemention as a simulation program, test of the model).

When using common simulation programs the student need not know the model in its exact mathematical formulation. He can use it as a black box and analyse its behavior (phases 1 and 2). In a simulation system he always knows the structure of the model or the mathematical equations. This knowledge enables him to decide what to modify in case of necessity (phase 3). Thus simulation systems are adequate instruments to integrate modelling into education.

At the University of Tuebingen we have used ENZKIN, GRIPS and QUANT in various courses in biology and physics. Modelling was integrated as a new topic in the normal scheme of these courses. ENZKIN and DIFGLE have turned out to be an interesting tool for the teachers too, enabling them to implement a particular model in a very short time. Furthermore we have developed the concept of an introductory course on modelling and computer simulation. In this interdisciplinary course the students had the chance to gain practical experience in model building with GRIPS. Within a short time the students were able to work autonomously and to concentrate on their problems. It can be stated, that the majority of them succeeded in formulating their own ideas, in implementing the modifications, and in testing them. Our expectations that the interactive simulation systems would reduce reservations against using computers and achieve the educational objective of "model building" were verified. Indeed we have learned that it is only realistic to aspire to the achievement of this objective if the students have already a good theoretical and empirical knowledge of the phenomenon in question. In consequence, model building always requires careful preparation; but simulation systems are adequate instruments to bring together research and teaching in academic training.

HARD- AND SOFTWARE

All programs with the exception of DISIKOS were developed for execution on a PDP 11/40 running under the RSX11M operating system, and using TEKTRONIX 4012 as graphical displays.

The programs are written in FORTRAN IV, using the TCS PLOT 10 package and a subset of this package, called PLOT 9, which is written in Assembler. DISIKOS is written in BASIC and runs on an Apple II PLUS.

REFERENCES

1. Hinton T., *Comput. Educ.* **2,** 71–88 (1978).
2. Wedekind J. and Wöhrmann K., *EDV Med. Biol.* **8,** 44–47 (1977).
3. Tawney D. A. *Simulation and Modelling in Science Computer Assisted Learning.* CET, London (1976).
4. McKenzie J., Elton L. and Lewis R. (Eds), *Interactive Computer Graphics in Science Teaching.* Ellis Horwood, Chichester (1978).
5. Holtmann W., Quantenmechanik von Zweizustandssystemen: Simulationssystem QUANT. *Computersimulation und Modellbildung im Unterricht* (Edited by H. Simon), pp. 143–172. Oldenbourg, München-Wein (1980).
6. Wood R. D., Barker B. E. and Townsend P., The development and transfer of interactive graphics programs for teaching structural appreciation. Paper presented at a Workshop on "Computer Simulation in University Teaching", Paderborn (1980).
7. Smith P. R., *Proc. CAD ED* 104–109 (1978).
8. Boardman D., *Comput. Educ.* **3,** 381–389 (1979).

Comput. & Educ. Vol. 6, pp. 153 to 158, 1982
Printed in Great Britain

0360-1315/82/010153-06$03.00/0
Pergamon Press Ltd

COMPUTER SIMULATION PROGRAMS IN PROBLEM-ORIENTED MEDICAL LEARNING AT THE UNIVERSITY OF LIMBURG

R. Min, H. van Kan and H. Struyker Boudier

Department of Pharmacology, University of Limburg, P.O. Box 616,
6200 MD Maastricht, The Netherlands

Abstract—An important aim in problem-oriented learning at the medical school of the University of Limburg is that a student should be able to test his knowledge in relevant problem situations. This implies that learning resources such as text books and lecture notes are not sufficient. The curriculum of the school confronts the students as early as possible with real-patient encounters as well as a skills laboratory where they practice medical skills. However, many basic biomedical problems cannot be studied on this basis. Computer simulation programs based on mathematical models can give the opportunity to investigate fundamental concepts underlying complex biological systems. In fact modelling and computer simulations have over the last few years become important tools in the analysis of the normal and abnormal behaviour of such systems. Parameters involved can be easily and reproducibly manipulated to show effects on hemodynamic variables, drug levels or chemical reactions correctly and at once. An advantage of such simulations is that students can investigate problems by themselves without patients or experimental animals. Moreover, students learn to formulate hypotheses and to test them quantitatively. We describe here two of the programs developed and used at our medical school in the field of cardiovascular control.

METHODS AND PROCEDURES

The simulation programs are written in FORTRAN IV for a MINC 11 system of DEC. The operating system is RT 11 V03. The students work at a refresh terminal (VT105) with cursor manipulation at fixed frames, while graphic results are displayed on another terminal (Tektronix 4012). Students have the opportunity to make hard copies of the graphic screen using a hard copy unit (Tektronix 4631), allowing them to discuss and compare the results later away from the computer facilities. During the plotting time they also have the opportunity to interrupt the simulation in order to change model parameters for therapeutic interventions or to change recorded variables. With each interruption all simulation data are stored on a data file, allowing students to go back one step to the last interruption time to correct their data handling. The simulation programs work interactively in the Dutch language on the basis of fixed frames on the screen. English versions of the programs are available. In these fixed frames the students can always choose to (1) start (restart) the model; (2) continue the computer analysis; (3) change one or more parameters; (4) inspect the variables. This basic principle of the simulation programs is accomplished by four separate programs (Fig. 1). The simulation software system developed at the University of Limburg is made up of four automatically

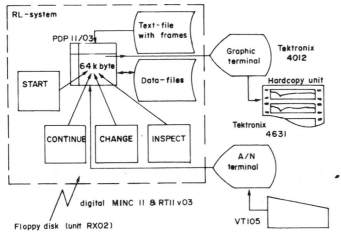

Fig. 1. MINC 11 minicomputer with floppy disks and two terminals.

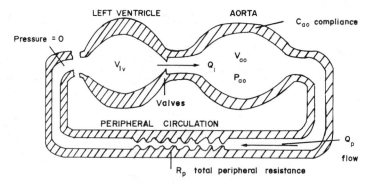

Fig. 2. The physiological model of the circulation in the simulation program AORTA: The left ventricle as an active pressure element pumps the blood through the aorta and the peripheral circulation. The aortic pressure is given by Pao and the volume of blood by Vao. The blood flow Qp flows through the peripheral circulation. The mean of the peripheral flow Qp is equal to the mean of the aortic input flow Qi.

chaining computer programs: CONTINUE, CHANGE, INSPECT and START. Each of these commands allows an interaction with the model. The output of the model is displayed graphically with a maximum of 8 variables against time. Upon the "inspect" command a tabular display of the value of each variable at that moment is given. The separate four basic programs work in common with a temporary random access data file and an editable sequential text file. The data file facilitates the interaction between the four chaining programs. The text file, on the other hand, gives the guarantee of a good lay-out of text frames on the screen, and flexibility by using a special text editor, particularly for creating and updating text frames. The use of these two files, for text and data, minimizes the size of the simulation program. Therefore we have the ability to analyse relatively large models. In this simulation project we have developed a library of subroutines for I/O handling, text handling, graphical output, cursor manipulation and drawing and reproducing pictures. In order to develop new computer simulation programs one needs only to adapt small parts of the source of the four basic programs and the text file. In this way we completed two programs AORTA and CARDIO, pertaining to the cardiovascular system, and we are developing programs on enzyme kinetics, pharmacokinetics and immunological processes.

THE SIMULATION PROGRAM AORTA

The computer simulation program AORTA simulates basic hemodynamics in the human aorta. The model on which this program is based was developed first with the simulation language THTSIM (University of Twente, The Netherlands). It is the classical "windkessel" model of the aorta (Fig. 2) in which the relation between the aortic pressure (Pao), the total peripheral resistance (Rp), the aortic compliance (Cao) and the left ventricular pressure (Plv) is as follows[3]:

$$Pao = \frac{1}{Cao} \int_{t_1}^{t_2} \left[Qao(Plv, Pao) - \frac{Pao}{Rp} \right] dt + \frac{Vao(0)}{Cao}.$$

Two physical concepts are important for students. The first is the relationship between aortic pressure, aortic blood volume and aortic compliance (Pao = Vao/Cao) and the second the relation between peripheral blood flow, aortic pressure and total peripheral resistance (Qp = Pao/Rp). The relevance of the first relation is clear from changes occurring in atherosclerosis in which a decrease in Cao causes a lower diastolic aorta pressure (Pao is lowered to 120/40 mm Hg from a normal value of 120/75 mm Hg if Cao is reduced by 50%). Increasing Rp, in the second relation, causes an increase in both systolic and diastolic pressure as occurs in hypertension (Pao > 120/80 mm Hg, see Fig. 3).

The student uses this program to investigate basic hemodynamics in a 6 week course on atherosclerosis in the first year of the curriculum. In a computer simulation session, students usually start with programmed instruction on modelling and computer simulation. This program starts with the aim of the program and with a picture on the screen of the three parts of this aorta model (Fig. 2). Then the physical concepts of resistance and compliance with an estimation of values of compliance, total peripheral resistance and the maximum ventricular pressure are displayed. The students are then presented a computer output with an abnormally low diastolic pressure and are asked to find a solution to normalize hemodynamics through simulation. The only solution to normalize the blood pressure is to increase the aortic compliance. Manipulation of other parameters does not lead to the

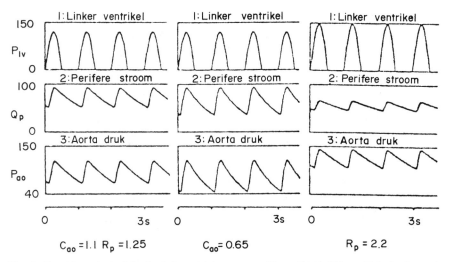

Fig. 3. Graphic output of 1: the left ventricle pressure Plv = $f(t)$ (0–150 mm Hg); 2: the peripheral flow Qp = f(Rp, Pao) (0–100 ml/sec) and 3: the aorta pressure Pao = f(Vao, Cao, Qi, Qp) (40–150 mm Hg). On the left the normal pattern with Cao = 1.1 (ml/mm Hg) and Rp = 1.25 (mm Hg s/ml). In the middle the pattern with Cao = 0.65 (ml/mm Hg). On the right the pattern if Rp is increased to 2.2 (mm Hg s/ml) and Vlv max = 150 (mm Hg) to prevent a decrease of Qp.

normal pattern. After this program's case the student is free to undertake other investigations with this model.

In Fig. 3 several cases are simulated: the normal aortic pressure, the effects of decreased compliance as in atherosclerosis and the increased resistance of the peripheral circulation as in hypertension. Left ventricular pressure, peripheral blood flow and aortic pressure are displayed on the screen simultaneously, giving the students enough information to make their conclusions.

THE SIMULATION PROGRAM CARDIO

The simulation program CARDIO allows the analysis of overall control of the circulation on the basis of a model of the cardiovascular system and its control mechanisms. The model was developed originally by Coleman of the University of Mississippi[1]. The program itself has been further developed at the University of Limburg.

The model consists of the heart, vasculature, kidney, fluid compartments and nervous reflexes (Fig. 4). With this model and this simulation program it is possible to study the behaviour of relevant cardiovascular parameters under normal and pathological conditions. There are two kinds of intervention:

(A) Changing of a constant (normally effective: 100%):
   1. Renal artery resistance;
   2. Renal mass;
   3. Protein intake;
   4. Water intake;
   5. Selective venous constriction;
   6. Selective arterial constriction;
   7. Heart strength;
   8. Metabolic demand.
(B) "Therapeutic" interventions (normally not effective: 0; effective = 1):
   9. Systemic vasodilator (dilates systemic arteries);
   10. Vasoconstrictor (norepinephrine/α-adrenergic agent);
   11. A. V. fistula;
   12. Diuretic;
   13. Cardiac glycosides (digitalis);
   14. Sympathetic nervous activity;
   15. Blood loss.

Figures 5 and 6 show several studies with CARDIO. The student has the opportunity to measure and register maximally 8 hemodynamic parameters of the model. The 5 clinically most important

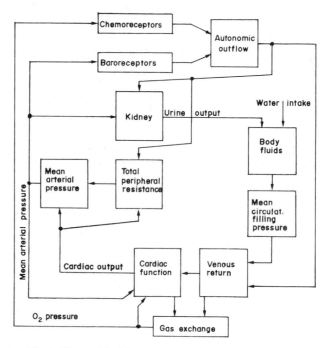

Fig. 4. The model of the overall control of the circulation[1].

variables are normally displayed on the screen, e.g. mean arterial pressure (AP, 100 mm Hg normal value), cardiac output (CO, 5000 ml/min), total peripheral resistance (TPR, 0.02 mm Hg min/ml), urine output (UO, 1 ml/min) and heart rate (HR, 70 beats/min).

The model can simulate pathologies such as renal artery stenosis, cardiac failure, blood loss, dehydration and increased metabolic demand. Moreover, it allows pharmacotherapeutical manipulation such as diuretics, vasodilators, sympathicolytics and digitalis. In one of the courses in their third year students are asked to simulate cardiac failure by changing the heart strength to 70% (light failure) and to 30% (strong failure) of the normal value (100%). In the case of HSB = 70% of normal all hemodynamic variables on the screen return to normal values within 14 days after the simulated cardiac failure, which is compensated for by renal retention of fluid. The extra-cellular fluid volume is increased (from 15000 to 17000 ml) and likewise the blood volume (from 5000 to 5400 ml) and the right atrial pressure are increased. Although the heart fails as a pump, the systemic filling pressure causes a higher arterial pressure and a normal value of the cardiac output. By examining the values of

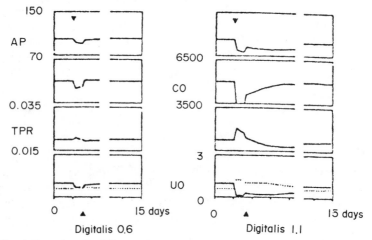

Fig. 5. Simulations of cardiac failure and its therapy. Graphic output of 1: mean arterial pressure (AP, 70–150 mm Hg); 2: cardiac output (CO, 3500–6500 ml/min); 3: total peripheral resistance (TPR, 0.015–0.035 mm Hg min/ml) and 4: urine output (UO, 0–3 ml/min). Also dashed is drawn 4a: heart rate (HR, 50–150 beats/min). Time scale is 1 day and the maximum plotting time is 15 days. Left: heart strength is decreased to 70% of normal and digitalis is given after a half day (0.6 units). Right: heart strength is decreased to 30% of normal and digitalis is given (1.1 units).

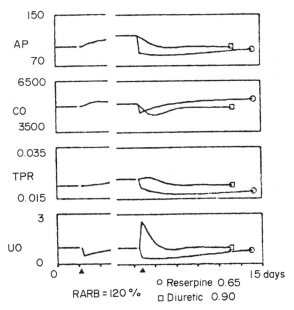

Fig. 6. Simulation of hypertension and its therapy. Graphic output as in Fig. 5, but now the intervention is an increased renal arterial resistance RARB to 120% (normal is 100%). The arterial pressure is increased from 100 to 125 mm Hg, Two therapies are given: reserpine (0.65 units) and a diuretic (0.9 units).

these parameters the students find out why a minor cardiac failure can be compensated for. At any moment the student can inspect all the variables and compare their values with those at other moments.

In the same study the student can interrupt the model half a day after cardiac failure and give an amount of digitalis (0.6 units). After 14 days he notices an important difference between the data of the untreated and the digitalis treated patient. There is no increased systemic filling pressure and increased right atrial pressure, whereas arterial pressure and cardiac output are normal (Fig. 5, left). If the cardiac failure is more serious (HSB = 30%) compensation is impossible. The patient dies on the first day because of acute pulmonary edema. Only with a digitalis therapy (1.1 units) the patient is still alive after 14 days (Fig. 5, right).

In this study students also can try diuretic and vasodilator therapies in cardiac failure.

Figure 6 shows a simulation in the therapy in a case of hypertension, caused by an increased renal artery resistance. After steady state (9 days), the student has given reserpine (0.65 units) only and in a second experiment a diuretic only. On the screen both results are drawn in order to be able to compare the difference in the effects. The diuretic therapy gives an increased urine output and a normal arterial pressure in one day. The fall in blood pressure is parallelled primarily by a fall in cardiac output and a secondary fall in total peripheral resistance. Reserpine therapy gives an immediate fall in blood pressure and total peripheral resistance. Some fluid retention occurs during reserpine therapy.

PERSPECTIVES

From the literature a number of models have been collected by our group in the areas of the cardiovascular system, respiration, pharmacokinetics, enzyme kinetics, immunology, endocrinology and the ATP system. These models look very promising for CAL applications on the basis of simulation. The cardiovascular simulation programs AORTA and CARDIO have been used by over 250 students now in their curriculum. We regard simulation of basic biomedical systems as an interesting new and valuable asset to the medical curriculum, stimulating students in problem-oriented learning of basic medical sciences.

Acknowledgement—The authors gratefully acknowledge the contribution of Dr T. G. Coleman, University of Mississippi, U.S.A. to the program CARDIO.

REFERENCES

1. Coleman T. G. Computer analysis of overall control of the circulation. Internal paper; University of Mississippi (1977).
2. Guyton A. C., Coleman T. G. and Granger H. J., *A. Rev. Physiol.* **34,** 13–46 (1972).
3. Iriuchijima J., *Cardiovascular Physiology,* Igaku Shoin Ltd, Tokyo (1972).
4. Min R. and Struyker Boudier H., *Proceedings of the International Simulation and Gaming Association Conference,* pp. 186–196. Leeuwarden III (1979).
5. Struyker Boudier H. and Min R., *Proceedings of the International Simulation and Gaming Association Conference,* pp. 321–338. Leeuwarden I (1979).
6. Coleman T. G., *Proc. Joint Automatic Control Conf.* **4,** 77 (1978).

Comput. & Educ. Vol. 6, pp. 159 to 164, 1982
Printed in Great Britain

0360-1315/82/010159-06$03.00/0
Pergamon Press Ltd

A CAI SERVICE GROUP CONSIDERS COMPUTER MANAGED INSTRUCTION AND THE INTERACTIVE INSTRUCTIONAL SYSTEM

M. D. LEIBLUM

University of Nijmegen, IOWO-CAI Group, Bisschop Hamerhuis, Verlengde Groenestraat 75,
6525 EJ Nijmegen, The Netherlands

Abstract—This article deals with the design considerations and plans for a computer managed instruction (CMI) medical terminology course soon to be offered at the University of Nijmegen. Prior to initiating this project, the CAI agency assisting in implementation of the course determined what general functions could be performed in CMI. Twelve functions are described. A review of three large systems capable of supporting CMI functions to various degrees was made: Interactive Instructional System (IIS), PLATO Learning Management (PLM) and Programming Language for Interactive Instruction (PLANIT). This paper only includes a review of IIS's CMI function support capabilities since it was the system eventually chosen.

ORIENTATION

The Computer Assisted Instruction (CAI) Group at the University of Nijmegen, Netherlands, associated with the Centre for Research and Development in Higher Education (IOWO), is a permanently established university service group responsible for advising and assisting in the development and coordination of CAI activities. It is one of the few permanent CAI agencies in the country and consists of three full-time personnel; two educational technologists and one system programmer.

The University itself has an enrollment of close to 15,000 students and offers curricula in a wide range of academic disciplines, e.g. Medicine, Dentistry, Law, Science, Mathematics, Psychology, Humanities, etc. A large central computer centre housing IBM 370/158, 4341's as well as other smaller computers in time-shared and batch oriented environments, services most faculty needs. However there is an abundance of smaller dedicated computers found in various sub-faculties and departments. For CAI purposes, two major CAI systems are available; PLANIT (Programming Language for Interactive Teaching), and IIS (Interactive Instructional System), while additional languages are sometimes used for CAI purposes, e.g. APL, BASIC, FORTRAN.

Since its inception, the CAI Group has occupied itself primarily with CAI as opposed to CMI activities. Although never purposely avoiding CMI, until recently there has been little internal interest in this area of computer supported learning. The only exception was an application (not supported by our group) within the Dental Faculty, making linked use of a CMI system in Eindhoven. A fair number of CAI projects have been implemented, cautiously, with ground level support from various faculty members. The basic "CAI philosophy" in this traditionally conservative environment has been to select applications that help resolve specific instructional problems; to keep operating expenses at a minimum (by making use of existing facilities); and generally to keep a low profile. In many faculties there is still a hesitancy to use the computer for direct instructional purposes.

In late 1980 a request from the Medical Registration Department of the university hospital led us to investigate the possibility of initiating a CMI-type project. This article deals with the design considerations and plans for this project. It also presents a CMI function description list and indicates how it was used to assist in the evaluation of various CMI systems. A full report dealing with CMI at our university is expected later this year.

THE CMI PLAN

A catalyst for investigating CMI came from informal discussions with a physician associated with the hospital who was responsible for recommending innovative instructional practices. A course dealing with medical terminology for para-medical and medical support personnel (nurses, technicians, medical secretaries, etc.) was currently in use and was offered four times yearly. Enrollments averaged about 120 yearly but the user population could be expanded eventually to include first year medical students. Students were required to study a programmed-instruction (PI) text, to complete self-study tests, and to listen to cassette recordings of medical terms. Average study time was about 30 h. Also required was attendance at 12 weekly lectures. Due to conflicting work schedules students

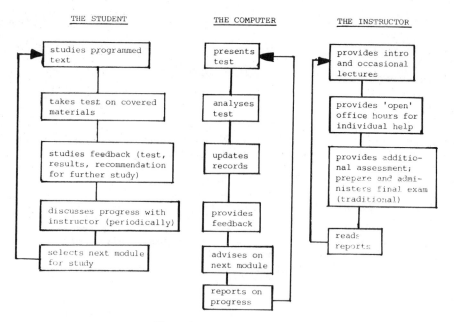

Fig. 1. CMI approach general.

were often forced to miss lectures and sometimes fell behind in their study schedule. Catching up was difficult due to the fixed course schedule. Instructors were forced to work within tight schedules and were often faced with the repetitive and uninteresting task of assisting students in a more or less rote learning activity. The basic problems to be resolved were: to reduce staff teaching time, to offer a more flexibly scheduled course while maintaining a "mastery" level of performance, and to increase the course completion rate.

The educational advisor initially suggested that the PI text be converted to a CAI format (approx. 1500 frames). Our reaction to this suggestion was negative since such a transfer violates the basic rule of not using CAI as a page turner. It would also prevent the flexibility of allowing students to study at home or in spare working hours using the well written PI text.

The suggested solution was the development of a series of computer administered subtests. Students would continue using the text and report to a test centre at regular intervals. After succesfully completing a subtest they would progressively continue this self study-subtest procedure. If a mastery level was not reached then immediate diagnosis would be performed, additional study prescribed or visits to the course instructor recommended, and the test could be retaken. Automatically produced computer progress reports would be generated for distribution to administrator and students. No regularly scheduled lecturers would be required except for an orientation session. Open office hours would be established so that students with special learning difficulties could be personally assisted. The frequent testing would also encourage students to keep up a regular study schedule but would be flexible enough to allow for occasional lapses and catch-up periods. Staff time spent in lecturing would be radically reduced, as well as many administrative chores. This common CMI design plan, similar to Rushby's[1], is presented in Fig. 1.

Further study indicated that the CMI system we selected would have to minimally supply 6 "functions":

1. item banking;
2. test construction and presentation;
3. test assessment;
4. assignment;
5. complete performance recording;
6. report generation.

CMI ELEMENTS AND THE SELECTED SYSTEM

Having established a basic plan for a medical terminology course, the next step was to determine which CMI system could satisfy the design requirements. A review of the literature helped us to produce Chart 1, which lists and briefly defines 12 possible components of a CMI system (derived from van Hees[2]). The functions expected to be fulfilled by the CMI system for medical terminology were previously indicated. Using the chart as a basis for comparison, several available systems could be studied to see how well, and with what effort and cost, each function could be supported. Naturally we also considered what additional functions could be useful for future applications. Three systems were evaluated; IIS, PLANIT, and PLATO (PLM). Full details of this study will be contained in a later report but a decision has been made to use an IBM product (IIS).

According to Baker[3], "Well-designed CMI systems place the courseware items (i.e., curricular plans, prescriptions, tests) in the data base and not in the software".

IIS does not qualify as a "well-designed" system if rated on this basis. In IIS most CMI functions must be performed within the instructional software and not via requests to a data base (separate accessible files). Still, the system appeared to provide the facilities we needed. It was recently installed by the computer centre and could be used at low cost. Our report indicated that the PLATO Learning Management (PLM) system provided considerably better CMI facilities, but given the current economic turbulence in Dutch higher education, we were not able to insist that PLM should be used. The CAI system currently in use (PLANIT) appeared to have some serious deficiencies in its ability to support CMI functions. The CMI system used by the Dental Faculty was designed to be used in a batch, not an interactive mode and thus was discounted for our purposes. In any case gaining practical experience with IIS also played an important role in the decision to use the product (it will be in regular use by the computer centre for DP courses).

The next section indicates how IIS supports the 12 CMI functions listed in Chart 1. (Due to space limitations, the review of PLM and PLANIT have not been included, but those wishing to obtain a copy of the full report should contact the author.)

CHART 1

*Computer Managed Instruction Elements**

1. Objective Banking
   The collection and maintenance of a structured set of objectives related to a lesson, a task, a course, a discipline or curriculum.

2. Learning Resources Banking and Library Information Retrieval
   The collection and maintenance of structured *lists* of educational facilities/resources/packages and/or a library information retrieval system (just books or printed materials).

3. Learning Material Banking
   The collection and maintenance of instructional *materials* (a learning resource center) limited to those types which can be stored in computer hardware/software or peripheral units.

4. Item Banking
   a. Collection of a structured set of items.
   b. On-line editing of items.
   c. Maintenance of item statistics.
   d. Maintenance of bank usage statistics.

5. Item Generation
   a. Generation of items via a framework or macro facility, e.g. random number generator.
   b. Generation of items through randomly selecting/substituting existing parts of the item (stem or answer choices).
   c. Generation of items based on a model/grammer representing the structure of the learning materials.

6. Test Generation
   a. Allocating items for individual study quizzes.
   b. Generating parallel forms of a specific quiz.
   c. Generating standardized final examinations from an item bank.

7. Assessment
   a. Scoring of individual quizzes.
   b. Scoring of final examinations.

8. Reporting
   a. Reporting (usually in printed form) of individual study results (tests) and lists of test results for a group.
   b. Reporting of individual and group study progress.

9. Evaluation
   a. Providing test analysis.
   b. Providing educational product analysis (formative evaluation).
   c. Providing educational process analysis, e.g. information about study time, intervals between attempts, number of attempts, questionnaire processing etc.

10. Assignment
    Assigning tasks (e.g. homework) based on objectives or study results.

11. Counseling
    Providing individual advice relating to study or career goals.

12. Scheduling
    Creating and maintaining schedules of educational facilities, i.e. of manpower or physical/instructional resources.

   * Derived from van Hees[2].

IIS REVIEW

The review plan is to list each of the 12 CMI functions. Without going into too great deteil (e.g. naming the exact command or key) the general method and means for performing each function in IIS will be described. A system may not be able to perform a function, or may do so in a very poor or inefficient manner, therefore the degree to which the function is performed automatically is indicated. The following code is used:

Automatic (A) = built-in routines to perform function, few if any additional user written programs/routines are required.

Semi-Automatic (SA) = some built-in logic or facility exists to perform the function but the user must supplement this with additional instructional software or logic written in the base language.

Manual (M) = theoretically possible to perform the function but considerable programming in the base language is required.

Not Possible (NP) = given the difficulty of performing the function, one should not use the system for this purpose.

Various routines and special functions (macros) are often written by user agencies to supplement a basic system, and they sometimes can be shared with other users. For this review only the basic manufacturer delivered system is considered. In specifying limits (e.g. maximum number of items in a "bank" or test size) the author used figures taken from released IBM documents. In many cases these figures are installation dependent, that is they can be varied based on user needs, thus figures given should be considered representative rather than absolute.

The exact system evaluated was the Interactive Instructional System, Rel. 6.1. marketed by IBM for all operating systems (IMS, TSO, VTAM, CMS) using the IBM Virtual Machine Facility/370 and the Course Structuring Facility (CSF) with Coursewriter III (1977). It should be noted that shortly after this review took place (late 1980), IBM announced a revised system wherein IIS is replaced by 2 sub-systems: the Interactive Instructional Authoring and Presentation Systems (IIAS, IIPS). It appears that this new release will not radically alter previous IIS facilities but may provide some additional features not mentioned in this report.

IIS–CMI FUNCTION REVIEW

CMI Function 1. Objective Banking   *Degree: M*

IIS (CSF) documentation hardly mentions performance or behavioural/objectives but rather refers to courses, sessions, and topics. The author may present objectives within those general units. CSF is a set of macros that assist authors in generating a course. Within a course description section, the author can list objectives (as normal text). Students, using a menu facility or "go to" instruction, can review the list of objectives. There are no pre-formatted data files for objective banking, no special routines to facilitate storage or retrieval or objectives. All access to objective lists are from within the built-in lesson logic. There is no provision for automatically generating tests based on objective banking.

CMI Function 2. Learning Resource Banking/Library Information Retrieval   *Degree:* SA

A list of courses (CAI) as a resource is easily obtainable. A resource list within the course/session/topic framework can be entered via a text display macro, quiz framework macro, or worksheet. A built-in macro links resources to test questions rather than to objectives but this occurs in a test review mode. There is no file structure to independently store learning resource lists. The author can create a "session" entry which contains a resource list but there is no prompting mechanism to help generate one (except within the quiz review section).

Degree: NP

The ISS system operation under TSO, VTAM, or CMS does not include library information retrieval system facilities. If the user is running under IMS however, it is possible to exit IIS and enter a sophisticated data base retrieval system (STAIRS) in which bibliographic storage and retrieval is possible. Reentrance to IIS is then permitted.

CMI Function 3. Learning Material Banking   *Degree:* A

Complete facilities are available for CAI learning material banking. There is no separate CMI sub-system thus no need to transfer back and fourth between CAI and CMI components. A computer graphics package is separately purchaseable but not standard with IIS, thus learning material resource storage is limited to text presentable materials. It is possible to link usage of various AV and audio devices to the system.

CMI Function 4. Item Banking   *Degree:* SA

There are no automatic facilities to generate or to access an item bank but items may be stored (and created) within a pre-structured quiz framework. Fifty test questions (items) for a "final" quiz (per course) can be stored in a file. The user may change this limit by making a minor change to the macro generating quiz labels. In addition each session (lesson) has a structure permitting a pre and post session quiz containing 20 items each. There is a 20 session maximum per course, thus using the standard CSF facilities, 850 items can be handled. One ISS system can contain a maximum of 50 files each housing 42 courses, thus the theoretical item storage facility is great. Unfortunately items are stored within the course design framework and are not independently accessible. Macros exist to assist authors in writing MC, TF, ranking matching, and open-ended questions. There is no framework for identifying items by subject, content, author, date, etc. but usage data is collected in separate student performance records (discussed later). Items are not automatically linked to objectives.

CMI Function 5. Item Generation   *Degree:* M

Using Coursewriter III, some macros provided by CSF and individual initiative, the user is able to generate variations of a single problem type. Earlier complaints about the limited calculation facilities of CW III have been partially overcome but the system still cannot be classified as having strong calculation facilities (important for mathematical problem generation). All numerical variables must be stored in registers/counters/buffers directly and the user must keep a record of their usage. The item generation process needs to be performed within the lesson structure. CSF does not specially provide features for rearranging items, i.e. allowing permutation of the stem of a question or the random selection of alternative MC answer choices, but the author may create a macro to do this.

Generating items (using CSF, CWIII) based on a model or semantic analysis representing the structure of learning materials (artificial intelligence) would be extremely difficult in IIS.

CMI Function 6 Test Generation   *Degree:* SA

Test items must be stored within the course/session/topic structure. As indicated earlier, CSF provides a pre, post, and quiz framework in which test items can be placed. The test maker cannot however just specify the type of test desired and expect the system to generate it. The author may randomly select items for presentation but does so using a random number generator and self created test design logic. The system cannot easily be used to generate parallel forms of the same test using known difficulty indices or to generate a test by selecting items with known characteristics or linked past performance. Hard-copy print-outs of a test can be requested from the system administrator but some special formatting routines would have to be prepared.

A quiz framework macro exists which: generates "labels" for a quiz (the standard size is 50 but this is expandable), links review material to each question, eventually presents items and process responses, and provides a quiz summary (see under reporting). Using this macro, the author may specify how many questions are to be presented but this is done sequentially and would result in identical tests for every student. The author may also specify the "mastery level" required.

CMI Function 7. Assessment   *Degree:* A

Scoring of tests is done automatically by the system. Students may see test results (if allowed) of the last test taken. Prior test performance is stored but additional programming is required to supply a "test history" printout. The quiz framework macro allows for some automatic generation of commentary relating to score, review materials, need to repeat, etc. Counters are automatically updated containing: total number of responses, number of correct/incorrect/unexpected answers, number of requests for hints, time etc. Test results per student or group can be obtained by the instructor but this normally requires the services of a specially trained "administrator". Statistics automatically provided include the average (mean) of the previously identified counters.

CMI Function 8. Reporting *Degree:* A

Recorded performance and usage data can be used to prepare a number of pre-formatted reports: Course Activity (per student), Course Activity Summary (per group), Student Response (showing all responses made to questions), Course Utilization (time data), Completion Statistics.

Students/instructors can also send messages to each other and a report of this usage is available. Report preparation is normally handled by a trained administrator, largely due to the complexity of the system and as a precaution against misusage. IIS saves voluminous data relating to usage thus requests for reports must be very specific. In many cases the built-in reporting formats are not easily read because special codes are used. An Administrative Guide (193 pages) listing about 60 commands must be studied. The instructor can however, using a "show" command, review the status of selected students while seated at a terminal. The other reports are normally produced off-line.

CMI Function 9. Evaluation *Degree:* M

No true test analysis is performed; just summative data is available. To perform a product or process analysis, the raw data can be retrieved and submitted to appropriate statistical analysis packages. An item by item response summary is available which can be used for item analysis purposes. There are no built-in statistical routines other than those calculating means or totals, and an occasional "ratio".

CMI Function 10. Assignment *Degree:* M

Assignments may be presented within the session/topic/quiz structure as normal text. There are no special assignment files nor is the author prompted to specify them. Introductory comments initiating a course can contain assignments or references. Students cannot independently access an assignment file unless the author defined a separate lesson or created feedback messages containing such materials.

CMI Function 11. Counselling *Degree:* M

A counselling dialogue can be written within the session structure, using CSF or CWIII, but there are no prompting mechanisms to help generate such a dialogue. All dialogue code and logic would have to be author created.

CMI Function 12 Scheduling *Degree:* M

There are no automatic facilities to handle non-CAI class scheduling, or scheduling of other resources. No optimilization logic is provided.

CONCLUSION

It is clear that IIS cannot be considered an "ideal" CMI system; nor, in fact, can the much publicized PLATO Learning Management System supply all automatic facilities to neatly handle the 12 CMI functions mentioned in this paper. While PLM provides many more standard CMI related features, its cost presents a barrier to many potential Dutch university users. Thus a compromise was made. Although IIS does not fulfill all our needs in an elegant manner, it can partially be made to act like a CMI system. This will require additional programming effort on our part. An important question can be raised however. Is it appropriate to ask that CMI functions be performed via a single large combined CAI/CMI system as opposed to a collection of smaller, separate CMI packages (even operating on different computers)?

The CAI Group at Nijmegen is currently reviewing this problem. It appears that in this rapidly changing era of computing technology it is unwise to make a long term committment to a single system.

REFERENCES

1. Rushby N. J., *An Introduction to Educational Computing*. Croom Helm, London (1979).
2. Van Hees E. J. W. M., *Computer Managed Instruction: een breder perspectief en een implementatie*. Katholieke Hogeschool, Tilburg, The Netherlands (1979).
3. Baker F. B., *Computer Managed Instruction: Theory and Practice*. Educational Technology Publications, Englewood Cliffs, NJ (1978).

Comput. & Educ. Vol. 6, pp. 165 to 174, 1982
Printed in Great Britain

0360-1315/82/010165-10$03.00/0
Pergamon Press Ltd

CAL SOFTWARE DESIGN FOR TRANSFERABILITY

C. BLANDFORD

Engineering Science (CAL) Program Exchange, Computer Assisted Teaching Unit,
Queen Mary College, Mile End Road, London E1 4NS, England

Abstract—The successful transfer of CAL software is often thwarted by differences between the computer system on which the software was developed and that on which it is required to be implemented. Facilities which CAL programs may exploit are usually those most vulnerable to change between different computer systems.

Drawing upon experience gained in the design, programming, and subsequent transfer of CAL programs in engineering, examples are given of features which may cause problems during implementation and alternatives or improvements are suggested. FORTRAN and GINO-F are proposed as machine and device independent standards, for implementation language and graphics subroutine library, respectively.

Good programming practices are described with a view to obtaining readable and easily maintained programs of a sound quality. Importance is placed on modularity in design as the key to writing transportable programs. The idea that every module should conceal some design decisions from all other modules is described with reference to modules that have proved to be particularly useful or advisable. This technique enables a design to be produced in which machine dependencies and difficult design decisions may be confined to a handful of routines. This makes the program more adaptable and gives the teacher and programmer greater freedom to change the implementation, allowing the program to move to any computer system where similar functions can be implemented.

INTRODUCTION

Production of any computer software these days is an expensive and time-consuming matter. CAL software in particular often calls for the use of special hardware and software, and very rarely do teachers find that they have a pool of computer experts from which to draw in the design, development and refinement of their ideas. Quite often work is shelved, half-completed or meted out in diluted form as topics for student projects.

Not surprisingly, the last few years have seen a growth in the demand for ready-made CAL software which is obtained through program libraries, interest groups, and exchanges. Most material is available for what amounts to a token price when compared with the original development costs that were entailed.

Once the software has been acquired, two problems face the user: the material may not meet the desired teaching requirements and thus needs tailoring for individual use; and secondly the user may discover that successful transfer of the material is thwarted by differences between the computer on which the software was developed and the computer on which it is now being implemented.

If it is assumed that the content of the material is matched to the user's needs then only the implementation "differences" remain to be resolved. This paper draws upon experience gained in the design, programming, and subsequent transfer of CAL programs in order to offer practical solutions to avoid some of the implementation problems that might otherwise be encountered. The ideas explained would be applicable, in general, to program design in most high-level programming languages.

The programs discussed in this paper are simulations of engineering systems. By means of an interactive computing environment the user can investigate the properties and responses of a mathematical model of the engineering system. Terminal dialogues are computer-initiated and other methods of interaction include selection by item number from a list of options presented on a screen, tabular data entry, and the use of cursors to define and modify structures, waveforms and networks. Output takes the form of graphs and diagrams presented on the screen which can be reproduced on a plotter or hard copy device, and also accompanying numerical data which may be printed at a teletype paired with the graphical display screen, or centrally by the computer system lineprinter at a later stage[4].

FACILITIES OF CAL PROGRAMS

In writing a program, the programmer usually has a good idea of the computing environment in which it will be used, that is: the host computer and software available on it, the type of terminal and desired method of interaction, and also the likely degree of training or skill of the user. Facilities available are usually fully exploited, but in the interest of transferability, it is advisable to exercise a good deal of restraint because features may prove to be dependent upon a particular computer or operating system or a certain type of graphics terminal. It is unlikely that teachers will be aware of the uniqueness of some features. In this event the experience of programming staff must be called upon, and programmers must be made aware of any constraints to be placed on facilities used.

This may appear to be unduly restrictive for programmers and contrary to recommended practice in "software psychology", but one must consider the extra work involved in transferring the program to another computer which does not have the facilities formerly available.

Ideally a program should be portable over a range of different computers without alterations so that it compiles and runs satisfactorily. In transferring a program between computers, some changes are usually necessary before a satisfactory run is obtained. A program is transportable if the modifications that are needed to achieve a satisfactory run on each computer are easy to effect and are such that the resulting program is recognisably similar to the original[3].

Generally, it is better to aim at producing a program that can be transferred easily while consideration of efficient use of computer resources comes second. Indeed, response times of the better multi-user minicomputers and some of the more expensive microcomputers remove to some extent the need to code efficiently. Where degradation of the performance of a running program is noticed, it may be beneficial to concentrate on refining the routines that are used most frequently, or by using some other strategy to reassure the user that the program is running successfully.

The individual tasks performed by hardware and software on computer systems become increasingly more difficult to classify as more software functions are carried out by faster hardware components. This is particularly evident in the microcomputer field with the use of read-only memory in order to emulate computer instruction sets, to interpret instructions and languages, and to plot graphs and diagrams.

Typical facilities that CAL programs may exploit are usually the facilities most vulnerable to change between different computer systems. For example, successful interaction demands that the program should react sensibly to any data input from the requesting terminal. This usually calls for some validation of the input data to take place, which may be combined with a provision for free-format data entry. Yet languages for scientific programming offer little in the way of validation before the erroneous data has reached the program, possibly causing it to fail. To avoid this, use may be made of computer manufacturer's enhancements to standard language input–output statements which allow control to be transferred to a special routine on the detection of an error. A more general character handling routine which replaces the conventional, or enhanced, input statement can provide the necessary validation and free-format entry and also offer better prospects for transfer.

Graphical display may be used to present attractive forms of input to the user and the availability of a thumbwheel cursor or light-pen will affect the design of the interaction. Alternatives such as table filling may provide the advantage of easy transfer in addition to attracting the user's eyes to the presence of missing or extra values. [Fig. 1(a) and (b)].

On output, the type and size of the display area will affect the amount of information which can be displayed and also the structure of the program. For example, a calculation may have to be repeated in order to redraw a diagram on a storage tube after some data has been displayed, whereas selective erasure would be possible on a refresh screen. Use of a pen-plotter to provide diagrams sometimes involves the co-operation of the local operating system. A program is more likely to communicate with its operating system when external data files containing results of previous calculations are used to provide comparisons between graphs, or when this data is to be sent to the fast printer. The way in which a program communicates with its local operating system is a major problem in moving programs from one environment to another.

LANGUAGES AND GRAPHICS FOR CAL SOFTWARE

One of the problems associated with writing transferable software is in choosing a suitable language. Programs should be written in a defined language subset so that no problems of language dialects are met on transfer. This should also apply to any graphics software that is used, although it is most likely that this will not itself be transferred because of copyright restrictions, and in such cases a graphics package which is generally available should be used.

The development of one's own graphics package with a view to transfer with CAL software is a process fraught with problems. Such graphics software is usually tailored for individual requirements and is inevitably dependent upon a particular hardware and software combination, sometimes relying

CROSS HAIRS CONTROLLED BY THUMBWHEELS. SYMBOLS INPUT ON THIS KEYBOARD.

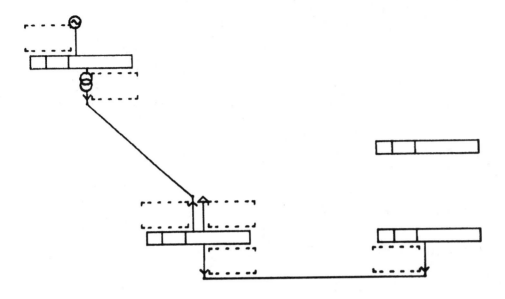

CROSS HAIRS CONTROLLED BY THUMBWHEELS. SYMBOLS INPUT ON THIS KEYBOARD.

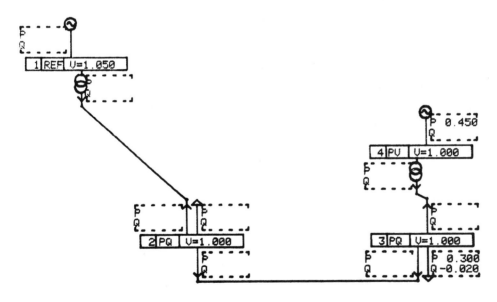

Fig. 1(a)

Fig. 1. (a) Stages in the specification of the positions, connections and parameters associated with elements in a power network. Thumbwheel cursors are moved manually to the desired position, and particular characters (which do not appear on the screen) are typed on the keyboard in order to give context to the point of intersection of the cursors. This method of interaction is dependent upon the graphics terminal possessing some means by which the user can identify specific parts of the screen.

MEMBER CONNECTION TABLE

MEMBER NUMBER	FIRST END JOINT NUMBER	SECOND END JOINT NUMBER
1	1	2
2	2	3
3	2	5
4	1	5
5	5	3
6	1	4
7	4	3
8	5	4

CHANGE A LINE OF DATA BY RETYPING
THE LINE

TYPE   F   IF INPUT FINISHED

TYPE   E   TO EXIT TO OPTION LIST

JOINT COORDINATE TABLE

JOINT NUMBER	X-COORDINATE	Y-COORDINATE
1	-1.000	0.000
2	0.000	1.000
3	1.000	0.000
4	0.000	-1.000
5	0.000	0.000

CHANGE A LINE OF DATA BY RETYPING
THE LINE

TYPE   F   IF INPUT FINISHED

TYPE   E   TO EXIT TO OPTION LIST

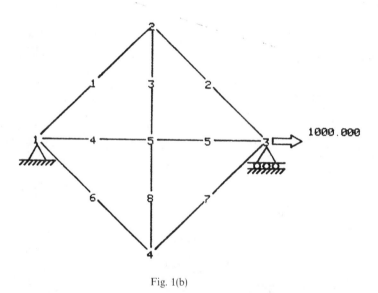

Fig. 1(b)

(b) Specification of the connections and positions of elements in a pin-jointed truss. A sequence of tables, which are presented on the screen to the user, enable the structure to be fully defined and easily modified. The diagram allows a check that the structure has been correctly entered. This method removes the need for the user to point explicitly at the screen, thus allowing successful transfer of the program to installations possessing a variety of different graphics terminals.

on very primitive or low-level features of system software which are not easy to modify or simply not available on other computers, such as terminal drivers and multiplexers.

The Computer Assisted Teaching Unit at Queen Mary College has selected FORTRAN to the 1966 standard (ANSI X3.9-1966) as the chief programming language because of its wide availability; it is well supported and runs on almost all computers, even today's better microcomputers. The language is sufficiently well standardised that programs can be written to run on a variety of systems. In a real sense, FORTRAN is close to being a universal language; it is certainly not dead despite its idiosyncrasies.

For graphics, routines compatible with the GINO-F graphics package that is marketed by the Cambridge Computer Aided Design Centre are used. GINO-F, written in FORTRAN, is widely available in the U.K. and remains device-independent by providing nomination routines for each different device available on an installation.

The quality of CAL software can be very variable, even when programs are obtained from the same source, and often leaves something to be desired. Too frequently huge monolithic programs are produced with subroutines in evidence only when the programmer realises that there is some repeated code to deal with. Such programs are difficult to maintain and modify as one simple change has the effect of rippling disastrously through the remainder of the code.

The code is often very contorted; languages such as **BASIC** and **FORTRAN** with the free use of "GOTO" can lead to hard-to-follow constructs where the programmer becomes so confused and frustrated that at best it is not known why or even whether a program works. Both languages have a deficiency in control statements and appearance and it can help if the missing language structures which are so natural to use are simulated (Fig. 2).

Figure 2 illustrates an effective utilisation of comments and indentation in order to clarify what each statement controls. The confined use of "GOTO" helps to remove ambiguity from the IF-ELSE statement, particularly when these are "nested". A "statement" as shown in the figure, could be one or more FORTRAN statements that are to be executed. Good programming practice would exclude the use of "GOTO" to branch out of these statements and into the middle of another structure. Notice that the "GOTO"s meet at a focal point instead of diverging throughout the code; this serves to close the structure properly.

It is true that the structures of Fig. 2 are typically used as the building blocks for well-structured programs. By coding with a restricted set of control flow structures a more coherent, readable, and less error-prone program is obtained. Readability is a good test of program quality; an easy-to-read program is probably a sound program. Emphasis must be placed on writing neat, comprehensible code, saving efficiency considerations for the end. The code should be checked and tested while it is being written. Extra effort given to design and coding will minimise the much more expensive and tedious correction of errors[2].

DESIGN TECHNIQUES

There are quite a few terms being used these days to describe ways of improving the programming process; the list includes structured design, top-down design, structured programming, and successive or step-wise refinement. These are important concepts that are intended for humans and not for computers and so they concern themselves with program correctness and ensuring that programs are readable and easy-to-change. Each of these disciplines can improve programmer productivity and the quality of code produced. However, the blind application of any particular technique in the belief that it will lead automatically to good programs is dangerous.

The tool of structured programming is a useful technique for writing correct and easy-to-follow programs but it does not help to divide the programming task into manageable pieces. The skill of decomposing a program into modules is the key to writing transportable programs. The ideas of modular design and transferability are complementary; the one helps to achieve the other.

Modularity allows the replacement and reassembly of individual modules without the reassembly of the whole program and allows one module to be written with little or no knowledge of the code of other modules. A module may be considered to be a subroutine or a collection of subroutines that are interdependent, so that the sequence of instructions that is necessary to call a given routine and the routine itself are part of the same module[1].

Conventionally the criterion that we use for decomposition is that each major step in the processing should be a module ("functional modularity"). This is rather too general to be of use in writing transportable programs, since to some programmers the "major step" could mean the graphics output stage in the program, whereas others may feel it necessary to divide this up into the separate functions: axis drawing, line drawing, and title writing. A better criterion is to decompose with respect to "difficult" design decisions or decisions which are likely to change or be machine dependent, and then to construct each module to conceal this decision from the other modules.

For example, a program may require that several sets of results be retained for comparison. These are held as data files on some secondary storage device such as a disc. The routines that define, assign, and access these files almost invariably have different names and parameters on different computer

Control statement   FORTRAN equivalent

```
IF  (condition)                         IF  (.NOT. condition) GOTO 10
    statement 1                             statement 1
ELSE                                        GOTO 20
    statement 2                     C   ELSE
                                    10      statement 2
                                            GOTO 20
                                    20 ...



WHILE (condition)               10 IF (.NOT. condition) GOTO 20
    statement                           statement 1
                                        GOTO 10
                                    20 ...




FOR (initialise; condition;
    reinitialise
    statement
                                        initialise
or                                  10 IF (.NOT. condition) GOTO 20
initialise                                  statement
WHILE (condition )                          reinitialise
    statement                               GOTO 10
    reinitialise                    20 ...




REPEAT                          10 statement
    statement                       IF (.NOT. condition) GOTO 10
    UNTIL (condition)
CASE i                              IF (I .LT. 1 .OR. I .GT. N)GOTO 99
IN                                  GOTO (10, 20, 30, ..), I
    statement 1,                10      statement 1
    statement 2,                        GOTO 100
    statement 3,                20      statement 2
         .                              GOTO 100
         .                      30      statement 3
    statement N                         GOTO 100
DEFAULT
    statement D                             .
                                            .
ENDCASE                         99      statement D
                                        GOTO 100

                                100 ...
```

```
CASE c                                  IF (C .NE. PLUS) GOTO 10
  IN                                          statement 1
      '+' : statement 1,                      GOTO 100
      '-' : statement 2,            10 IF (C .NE. MINUS) GOTO 20
      ' ' : statement 3,                      statement 2
         :     :                              GOTO 100
      'E' : statement N             20 ...         :
  DEFAULT
      statement D                         IF (C .NE. LETE) GOTO 99
  ENDCASE                                       statement N
                                               GOTO 100
                                    C DEFAULT
                                    99          statement D
                                               GOTO 100
                                    100 ...
                              where   DATA PLUS / 1H+ / ,MINUS / 1H- /,..
                                      LETE / 1HE /
```

Fig. 2. Examples of simulation of control flow structures missing from FORTRAN X3.9-1966.

systems. If the code needed is isolated in a module, then it will be only this module that will require modification on transfer to a different computer. Indeed, another implementation may not need to use external data files at all, and may have the ability to store all results in primary memory. The difficult design decision that this example illustrates is that of whether stored result data sets should be saved internally or externally by the program. Such a decision may arise when it is not certain how much space the results will occupy, and thus the principle is not solely of concern to programs written for transfer.

This "information hiding" criterion means that every module is characterised by its knowledge of a design decision which it hides from all other modules. The module "interface" or definition is chosen to reveal as little as possible about its inner workings.

Some further examples

Consider the use of a graph plotter in a program. Another computer installation may not possess such a device and the program will have to be modified so as to avoid its use. This may prove to be as simple as reassigning externally an input-output unit that corresponds to the plotter, and having the "plot" appear elsewhere (on a display screen for instance), but modification is rarely as simple and straightforward as this. It would be easier if the entire plotting routines and option lists were encapsulated in a module which could be replaced by a "stub" or dummy routine returning control to the calling module, and thus effectively denying the existence of the plotter. Where the code concerned is used by different devices within the same program, such as to obtain a hard copy from a display screen by using a plotter, then using the procedure name as an actual argument in a subroutine call, is a convenient method enabling the same graphic output to be directed to different devices (Fig. 3).

The characteristics of various display devices influence the design of the program. It is advisable to conceal in a module the machine characteristics of both hardware and software such as device dimensions, input–output unit numbers, maximum and minimum achievable numbers, smallest real number that the computer can distinguish from zero, character codes and other dimensions—to name but a few examples. By using this decomposition, designs become more general; no longer are screen sizes referred to in screen "points" or millimetres, but as variables which make the actual dimensions more abstract, and thus reduce the program's dependence on them.

An area of difficulty when writing transportable programs is that of arithmetical precision and associated numerical characteristics which arise from the different hardware and software in use. For example, a number that is quite acceptable on one computer may cause overflow on another, a real number may be truncated beyond a certain precision on one and be rounded on another. With numerical algorithms arithmetical accuracy is usually vital and there is no easy solution to this problem[3].

```
      EXTERNAL DRAW1, DRAW2, DRAW3
      REAL A, B, C,
      :
      CALL OUTPUT ( DRAW1, A, B, C)
      CALL OUTPUT ( DRAW2, A, B, C)
      CALL OUTPUT ( DRAW3, A, B, C)
      :
C  OUTPUT - Displays diagram drawn by SUBRTN on graphics screen
            and plotter if required

      SUBROUTINE OUTPUT ( SUBRTN, A, B, C)
      EXTERNAL SUBRTN
      REAL A, B, C
      INTEGER IQUERY, IKEYIN
C  CHARACTER KEYIN, LETY, C, GETCH
      INTEGER KEYIN, LETY, C, GETCH


      COMMON /CHANNL/ IQUERY,IKEYIN
      DATA LETY /1HY/
C
      WRITE ( IQUERY, 10)
10 FORMAT ( 44H DO YOU WANT TO DISPLAY THE DIAGRAM?  (Y/N) )
      KEYIN = GETCH ( IKEYIN, C)
C  GETCH is a function returning the next character from
            channel IKEYIN
      IF ( KEYIN .NE. LETY ) RETURN
C  ELSE Display on graphics terminal
            CALL SUBRTN (A, B, C)
C            OUTPUT TO PLOTTER ?
            CALL PLOTTR ( SUBRTN, A, B, C)
      RETURN
      END
C  PLOTTR - Prompt and produce plotter diagram using SUBRTN
C
      SUBROUTINE PLOTTR ( SUBRTN, A, B, C)
      REAL A, B, C
      INTEGER IQUERY, IKEYIN
C  CHARACTER KEYIN, LETY, C, GETCH
      INTEGER KEYIN, LETY, C, GETCH
C
      COMMON / CHANNL / IQUERY, IKEYIN
      DATA LETY /1HY/
C
      WRITE ( IQUERY, 10 )
10 FORMAT ( 40H DO YOU WANT A COPY ON THE PLOTTER ? (Y/N) )
      KEYIN = GETCH ( IKEYIN, C)
      IF ( KEYIN .NE. LETY ) RETURN
C  ELSE
            CALL T4662
            CALL SUBRTN ( A, B, C)
            CALL DEVEND
```

```
          C          T4662 and DEVEND nominate and relinquish the
                          plotter as plotting device
               RETURN
               END
or
          C  PLOTTR - Stub routine as no plotter exists on this
                          installation
          C
               SUBROUTINE PLOTTR ( SUBRTN, A, B, C )
               REAL A, B, C
               RETURN
               END
```

Fig. 3. Extracts from a FORTRAN program that illustrate the use of the "EXTERNAL" statement to allow the names of drawing routines (DRAW1, DRAW2, DRAW3) to be passed as actual parameters in place of the dummy parameter SUBRTN. The drawings usually appear on a graphical screen, and the PLOTTER routine is being used to reproduce the drawings on a pen-plotter. Notice that the second version of the PLOTTER routine completely conceals the existence of a plotter.

Sometimes the selected mathematical method may have an absolute bound on the precision of result it can compute and so it is impossible to extend the precision to achieve a greater accuracy. In this case other algorithms must be found, and the particular module replaced by the new algorithm. Concealing the precision of constants by using variables in parts of the program that are susceptible to problems of accuracy, accompanied by clear documentation describing suitable values, allows the constants to be expressed to the required accuracy on the installer's machine.

In FORTRAN a variable can be implicitly introduced by the first use of a new name, but in almost all other languages new variables must be introduced by means of declaration statements. This practice can be simulated in FORTRAN by using type statements such as: INTEGER DIGITS (10), REAL MAXNUM (see Fig. 3). Although this does not protect against mis-spelling, it does allow the rules for determining type from the initial letter of the name to be overridden, enabling more meaningful, and less terse, variable names to be used. More important, it is possible to reduce the massive undertaking involved in changing the precision of the program; for example, variables introduced as type REAL may be lengthened to DOUBLE PRECISION by a simple change to the source program. This allows more time to be spent identifying critical parts of the program, instead of wasting time finding the occurrence of each variable used implicitly in the program. Clearly it does not matter if some calculations are performed to a higher accuracy than is strictly necessary provided that the additional space and time required is not excessive.

Associated with the hardware and software characteristics of a particular computer is character handling. Although the 1977 FORTRAN standard includes the type CHARACTER; the 1966 standard merely states that characters may be placed in variables of any type. The number of characters contained in one "storage unit", and the number of bits used to store each character varies from computer to computer. A useful parameter is the number of characters that can be stored in a computer word, since this can be used to provide a powerful portable input-output method of character handling. Generally, it is advisable to store one character per word.

Reluctance to exploit special facilities of the hardware, extra features of the compilers or services of the operating system, if they are non-standard, all lead to an inevitable sacrifice in performance. In general, the ease of implementation and reliability of a piece of software is traded for some loss in efficiency. Where high performance is essential, loss in efficiency can usually by recovered by employing superior algorithms or by "fine tuning", once the program has been adapted, so as to reflect the new system or modifications made to the implementer's software. Modular design allows inferior modules to be replaced with the minimum of disturbance to the remainder of the program.

CONCLUSIONS

In order to make the benefits of CAL software available to a greater number of users in different educational locations, careful attention must be paid to ensure that programs are transportable.

After taking into account the requirements of, and facilities available to, potential users, a suitable choice of programming language and graphics package may be made.

The production of transportable software can be aided by simple principles of program design, good programming practices, and the deliberate exclusion of some attractive, but not widely available, programming language features.

The use of an "information hiding" technique by which to decompose the complete programming task into modular functional units has the advantage of producing a design which confines machine dependencies and difficult design decisions to a handful of routines. This gives the teacher and programmer a greater freedom to change the implementation, and allows the program to migrate to any computer system where similar functions can be implemented.

REFERENCES

1. Parnas D. L., On the criteria to be used to decompose systems into modules. *Commun. ACM* **15** (1972).
2. Kernighan B. W. and Plauger P. J., *Software Tools*. Addison–Wesley, New York (1976).
3. *Software Portability* (Edited by P. J. Brown). Cambridge Computer Science Texts, (1977).
4. Smith P. R. and Blandford C, Graphical design of teaching simulations. Paper presented to the Annual Conference of the British Educational Research Association (1980).

Comput. & Educ. Vol. 6, pp. 175 to 177, 1982
Printed in Great Britain

0360-1315/82/010175-03$03.00/0
Pergamon Press Ltd

INTEGRATIVE CAL
MULTI COMPUTER AND MULTI MEDIA

Jesús Vázquez-Abad*, Laura R. Winer and P. David Mitchell

Department of Educational Technology, Concordia University, Montreal, Quebec,
Canada H3G IMB

Abstract—This paper describes an instructional system that incorporates several kinds of instructional material and media intended to teach a complex set of concepts and procedures to students who lack most or all of the usually expected prerequisites. It illustrates a systems approach to instructional design whereby media and methods are selected on the basis of capability.

The arrival of microcomputers has been widely heralded as the dawning of a new age for education. One major advantage of a micro is that it is more cost-effective than many large systems. A disadvantage however is its limited processing capacity. In the preparation of a self-instructional module on a topic like the one we were faced with, there are unquestionably benefits in utilizing a microcomputer with colour graphics capability (such as the Apple-II 48 K). Using colour graphics enables the concepts involved in the particular subject dealt with to be more clearly demarcated so that the user can see at a glance what is being presented and accomplished. However, there may be more complex levels for which the micro is inadequate. And for some instruction it is still more cost-effective to use the printed page. All these are facts that instructional designers seem to overlook, perhaps blinded by the glitter of appealing apparatus.

THE PARADIGM OF COMPUTER SCIENCE

The history of numerical analysis, which is also the history of the development of algorithms, can provide us with an example full of insight and with direct implications for instructional design. In many ways, this history has been the history of the development of three areas: mathematical knowledge, real world problematics and computing instruments. The algorithms developed, say, to find the value of an integral at a time when machines could do little more than add and multiply were definitely intended to minimise the work of the people who would use them. Nowadays, available computing devices show a variety of characteristics; consequently, an efficient algorithm developed to be implemented on a large computer cannot be the same as the one sought when the use of only a hand-held calculator (with a very limited storage capacity) or a micro-computer (with limitations in program length, memory requirements, and complexity; e.g. "nesting" of subroutines, but where execution time is not a constraint as in the case of large computers) is envisaged. Because of this, computer scientists are not merely applicators of algorithms. Rather, they frequently have to develop algorithms, using available knowledge and considering the computing device that will be used.

In short, one can conclude that Computer Science, the Science of Algorithms (following Knuth[1]) takes into account not only the task to be undertaken but also what could be called the "cognitive style" of the machine to be used for that task. Can we say the same of instructional technology?

It is our contention that instructional designers must take into account the requirements of both the target learner population and the capacities of the instructional media to be used when developing instructional materials. In this sense, we feel that computers in general, and micro-computers specifically, have to be used for what they do best. No computer is cost-effective when it is used as a mere "page-turner", or even a "teaching machine" in the sense of a provider of programmed instruction. Computers are, on the contrary, irreplaceable devices for performing simulations, i.e. computer based experiments aimed at exploring the behavior of a system, or some components thereof, under a variety of different conditions which would be very difficult to study without its aid[2]. Also, the particular characteristics that are peculiar to large (or macro) computers, as opposed to microcom-

* Under a scholarship from Universidad Nacional Autómona de México, Mexico City. Present address: Department de Technolgie Educationnelle, Université de Montréal, Montreal, Quebec, Canada.

puters, have to be exploited if really cost-effective Computer Aided Learning is to be developed. It was under these principles that we developed the instructional module explained below.

THE PROBLEM

The Graduate Programme in Educational Technology at Concordia University is organised around the application of the Systems Approach to educational problems. One course directly connected with this is Educational Systems Analysis (ESA). A main topic in this course is Linear Programming (LP) and its applications to educational problems. Briefly, LP is a mathematical programming technique that enables one to allocate scarce resources to maximise intended benefits—or conversely to find an optimal allocation which minimises costs[3]. The concepts and procedures that make up the structure of knowledge needed to understand LP (as well as other Operational Research methods present in the ESA syllabus) include some that normally assume significant mathematical background. Post-graduate students of educational technology, however, may come from any kind of undergraduate background; most have studied little mathematics since secondary school and seldom have any studied linear algebra. This situation creates a difficult position for the instructor, as the ESA course is not the place to teach these prerequisites that are, however, necessary in order to be able to understand a methodology whose applications to educational problems are as varied as they are valuable[4].

Notwithstanding these difficulties, in special cases it is possible to present the major concepts of LP graphically; an example of this approach within an educational context which has been successfully used in previous ESA courses can be found in Mitchell[5]. Often students are asked to plot a variety of graphs to solve simple LP problems with only two or three variables. This entails the applications of much simpler notions from Analytic Geometry, and ideally the concepts acquired in this process will generalize to multi-variable problems. Thus, LP is a good candidate for CAL when the computer is used to help the student explore a variety of situations which would otherwise require a tremendous effort in repeating somewhat mechanical operations that would not represent a challenge but would discourage the student.

THE SOLUTION

The self-instructional module on LP that we developed is made up of several components with a certain amount of overlap and redundancy built in. In this module, instruction is presented via a printed booklet, reference books, a Apple-II 48 K microcomputer, and the University's CDC Cyber 172 time-sharing system. These four components in combination exploit the unique capabilities of each medium, thereby optimising the cost-effectiveness of the entire package. The built-in redundancy and overlap serve the instructional aim of offering students different paths to the same end; it is intended, therefore, to serve those who choose to skip one or another of the component lessons as well as to reinforce learning for those who study all topics.

Simple prose material is presented mainly by printed material although remedial information in print form is provided by both computer programs. Simple examples of LP problems (limited to two variables and six constraints) are presented on the Apple's colour graphic screen. However, the Apple allows for more than presentation of examples. It is programmed to accept student-provided data for 2-activity and 6-constraint problems. This capability is linked to exercises presented on paper as well as being open to student-generated problems. For each constraint entered, the region defined is displayed visually using different colours; the overlapping area is identified as the feasible region and the value of the objective function is calculated for each of the feasible corner points. The visual display of feasible and optimal solutions is accompanied by a printed output for each feasible point and the identification of the optimal solution. Such illustrations are intended to reinforce the conceptual understanding of the student as well as to provide solutions to simple problems. Although the Apple graphics program handles only limited applications, it allows the student to manipulate constraints, trying a variety of alternatives and literally seeing the results immediately. It is, in effect, a simulator. Thus the concepts of LP are reinforced symbolically and visually.

The Apple is limited in the complexity of problems it can handle so students then shift to the University's system where an interactive program, Simplex, allows them to use up to 60 variables and 30 constraints. It also provides brief introductory notes and references if needed. When the Simplex program was used alone before other materials were prepared, students could not understand what was happening when the printer produced reams of data. Now with the microcomputer graphics program they understand what is occurring and can handle the more advanced LP procedure with ease. Printed booklets provide additional examples to be used with Simplex and students are encouraged to experiment with their own problems or those from reference books.

CONCLUSION

In sum we describe a multi-media system which provides students with a much greater understanding of LP than could be achieved with any of the component media alone. The unique capabilities of each medium are exploited to provide the richness of experience which, we believe, ought to be normal procedure for CAL. Computer *Aided* Learning does not limit the instructional design to any particular machine or even to computers alone.

REFERENCES

1. Knuth D. E., *Fundamental Algorithms*. Addison–Wesley, Reading, MA (1972).
2. Naylor T. H., Balintfy J. L., Burdick D. S. and Chu K., *Computer Simulation Techniques*. Wiley, New York (1968).
3. Mitchell P. D., Educational systems analysis, course notes No. 5: Are OR models applicable to educational research? Unpublished manuscript, Concordia University, Department of Education (1974).
4. For a review of the applications of OR techniques (and in particular of LP) in educational planning, see Vázquez-Abad J., Mathematical models in educational planning. Unpublished manuscript, Concordia University, Department of Education (1980).
5. Mitchell P. D., A method for allocating scarce resources to meet multiple policy objectives. Paper presented to the Canadian Educational Researchers Association, Fredericton, NB (1977).

INDEX